Tilting the Tower

Tilting the Tower

edited by **Linda Garber**

X **lesbians**

X **teaching**

X **queer subjects**

ROUTLEDGE New York • London

Published in 1994 by

Routledge
29 West 35 Street
New York, NY 10001

Published in Great Britain by

Routledge
11 New Fetter Lane
London EC4P 4EE

Library of Congress Cataloging-in-Publication Data available.
British Library Cataloguing-in-Publication Data also available.

ISBN 0-415-90840-X (HB)
ISBN 0-415-90841-8 (PB)

Contents

Classrooms: High School

Institutions

Introduction
Linda Garber

When I began working on this anthology in 1988, there seemed to be an emerging need to collect the feminist and lesbian voices that were speaking about lesbian studies, at a time when gay and lesbian studies was first being talked about seriously on the institutional level. Six years had passed since Margaret Cruikshank's anthology *Lesbian Studies: Present and Future* defined the multidisciplinary field of lesbian studies which had grown out of a decade of women's studies scholarship and feminist activism.[1] In 1993, the need is no longer emergent, but urgent. Despite budget cutbacks and right-wing backlash against progressive politics in the humanities, lesbian and gay studies (or as it is also known, "queer studies") is a minor growth industry, one of the very few new fields to emerge in a shrinking academic job market. In that context, it is important to remember the specific political and institutional history of lesbian studies. Lesbian studies grew out of women's studies and feminist activism, and it appears in danger, now, of being subsumed under the banner of queer studies.

The enthusiasm for this anthology voiced by contributors and others indicates the importance of an extended conversation about the institutionalization of lesbian and gay studies and the need for a forum in which teachers can share their pedagogies and strategies for professional survival and success. In order to encourage a productive, varied dialogue, this small book includes many short essays rather than a few lengthy ones. Contributors range from graduate students to tenured program directors, high school teachers to community college and four-year university professors. They offer perspectives on doing lesbian work in a variety of fields, and based in a diversity of US cultures. They include commentators well known for their work in lesbian and women's studies as well as newcomers with fresh perspectives, often formed by the spirit and content of the contemporary politics that calls itself "queer."

The complex problem of terminology posed by doing lesbian studies in the queer '90s is explicitly addressed by many contributors, whether they come from backgrounds in women's studies or the street activism of Queer Nation or Lesbian Avengers. Although Queer Nation has come and gone in San Francisco where I live, the activist group has left behind a powerful label representing the attempt at (if the not the achievement of) a coalition of lesbians, gay men, and bisexual and transgendered people. Some contributors take the inclusiveness of queerness for granted, while others contest the term on grounds that it elides the presence of lesbians (much as the false-generic term "gay" does). Clearly, "queer" means different things to different people; nevertheless, many opt for its use as a sort of shorthand for all or part of "les/bi/gay/transgender," or the even longer "lesbian, gay, bisexual, and transgender"—and this doesn't approach the issue of how to order the terms.[2] It should be noted that few contributors explicitly include transgender in their discussion of queer or lesbigay studies; however, most include bisexuality. Still, the formal name of the field seems to be "lesbian and gay studies," if one is to go by the couple of books recently published on the topic—Abelove, Barale, and Halperin's *The Lesbian and Gay Studies Reader* and Minton's *Gay and Lesbian Studies*.[3] Abelove, Barale, and Halperin indicate their own preference for the term "queer studies" but note "the force of current usage" (xvii).

Some of the lesbian, bisexual, and straight contributors to *Tilting the Tower* describe themselves as queer subjects; others comment on their inquiry into queer subjects in the classroom. (Any introduction is, of course, an oversimplification; some contributors discuss "queer subjects" in both senses.) Among the most hopeful things about this collection, I think, are the number of straight women taking seriously the challenge to learn and teach about lesbian and other queer topics, and the number of white lesbians taking up the challenge of multiculturalism, an imperative with at least two clear directions. First, there is a recognition of the need to pursue a lesbian studies that takes seriously all lesbians, not just white ones, to base pedagogies and strategies on the writings of women of color rather than merely tokenizing their work. (Audre Lorde is a powerful presence in this collection, for example.) Concurrent with this is the willingness of many of us who are white lesbian scholars and teachers to acknowledge our own race/ethnicity (in my case, as an Ashkenazi Jew), in an attempt to defuse the power of those categories to stigmatize people of color exclusively. Second is the argument, made most explicitly here by Polly Pagenhart, that notions of multiculturalism are in need of a "queering," that lesbigay studies must be properly seen as part of the larger movement toward cultural diversity in the classroom.

I hasten to add, however, that the multicultural work of white lesbians and the lesbian work of straight women in no way justify the exclusion of lesbians of color and white lesbians, respectively, from anthologies, faculties, and course syllabi. While it may be argued that the authority of experience is a dubious claim to expertise, erasing the actual voices of lesbians/women of color is neither theoretically nor politically justifiable. Essays by contributors who are women of color make clear that white lesbians (among others) have a lot to learn about the realities of institutionalized oppression. (I am thinking, especially, of essays by Donna Keiko Ozawa, Merle Woo, Sharon Holland, Anneliese Truame, and doris davenport.)

This point is especially germane to the third section of *Tilting the Tower*, titled "Institutions." There, essays address the importance of learning from an institutional history (of ethnic studies and women's studies) which should teach us that lesbian and gay studies must be multi-issue in order to survive, as Merle Woo writes, and to do so "with integrity." Alisa Klinger and Nancy Stoller provide concrete suggestions for setting up successful lesbigay studies programs; Evelyn Torton Beck, Sarah Chinn, Toni A. H. McNaron, and Jacquelyn Zita discuss different aspects of surviving thoughtfully, and with one's politics intact.

The "Institutions" section deals with the broader institutional context for the issues tackled in the "Classrooms" section, which focuses the anthology on issues of self-presentation and the presentation of lesbian material. Essays explain how to, why to, even when to come out to students. Most contributors relate stories of the alternately exhilarating and terrifying queer subject position of the lesbian teacher; Wendy Chapkis and Michèle Aina Barale break the tense silence about the force of the erotic in the classroom, especially as it plays out in the queer classroom. Some contributors describe courses focused on lesbians, while others discuss integrating lesbian material into women's studies or other classes. Three essays focus on straight teachers teaching queer subjects (Sally Kitch, AnnLouise Keating, and Allison Berg et al.). The section on high school classrooms poses and begins to answer Janet Pollak's pointed question "Lesbian/Gay Role Models in the Classroom: Where Are They When You Need Them?"

The intent of this introduction is to provide a glimpse of the main ideas on offer here—to entice, not to schematize. I invite readers to browse, moving back and forth among the essays, to enter into the conversation begun here by educators deeply engaged in lesbian and other queer pedagogies and politics.

The scope of this collection is determined, first, by my own limitations as a white literary scholar; second, by the fact that certain disciplines have been more accepting than others of lesbigay scholarship and teaching (of progressive work in general); and finally, overwhelmingly, by the institutionalized racism and classism of academia.

Special thanks are due to three extraordinary women: Barbara Blinick, my partner in life, whose commitment to being out in the classroom brought us together; my dear friend Ann Pellegrini, who endured my editing and got her chance to turn the tables in the end; and Peg Cruikshank, to whom I dedicate this volume.

Notes

1. Margaret Cruikshank, ed., *Lesbian Studies: Present and Future* (New York: Feminist Press, 1982).

2. See Teresa de Lauretis, "Queer Theory: Lesbian and Gay Sexualities/An Introduction," *differences* 3:2 (Summer 1991).

3. Henry Abelove, Michèle Aina Barale, and David M. Halperin, eds., *The Lesbian and Gay Studies Reader* (New York: Routledge, 1993); Henry L. Minton, ed., *Gay and Lesbian Studies* (New York and London: Haworth Press, 1992).

Classrooms:
College/University

1

On Being a Change Agent:
Teacher as Text, Homophobia as Context
Mary L. Mittler and Amy Blumenthal

> Disneyworld? No, I've not been there, at least not yet. We are taking
> the kids there in June.
>
> Sorry I had to miss class Wednesday. My car wouldn't start and
> Pat had already left for work.
>
> I know what you mean. I still remember how nervous I was at the
> thought of my first real date . . . what to say, how to act, what to
> wear.

Innocent enough remarks. College teachers say such things to students all the time, in and out of class. And while recognizing that some
limits must be observed, most teachers would agree that such remarks
are not necessarily inappropriate, not in and of themselves distracting
to the teaching/learning process. Students also find such comments
acceptable, and from these bits of information fashion their image of
who we are, really, beyond the classroom walls.

But what if the context changes? What if the teacher is gay or
lesbian? What if there are children, but no husband/wife? What if Pat
is a lover? What if that first date that occasioned those nervous feelings
was boy/boy, or girl/girl?

Professorial self-disclosure occurs most often in the context of seemingly mundane remarks. So mundane, in fact, that few realize the
importance of what is actually being said. But gay and lesbian teachers
know. Even if their colleagues are aware of their orientation, at what
point may they, can they, should they make themselves known to their
students? And is there a point at which they must?

In preparing a paper on ethical issues in higher education, Mary

Mittler, assistant vice president/dean at Oakton Community College, sent a memo to several faculty members requesting comments on ethical dilemmas they experience in their work. Amy Blumenthal, assistant professor of English/ESL specialist, responded. During the following semester, the two engaged in a written dialogue within which they explored the questions posed above. What follows is an edited version of that dialogue.

AB: As a faculty member, one of my more persistent dilemmas involves coming out, letting others know that I am a lesbian. As an educator, I want to be a positive role model for all my students and a special support for lesbian and gay students. I am sure that the great majority of my students assume that I am heterosexual, especially if they learn I have a child. To let this false assumption stand feels dishonest. I also believe that one of my professional obligations is to be a change agent, especially when that change leads to greater understanding. And while I strive for honesty in all other areas of my life, at this college I have never come out in the classroom. This creates a split in me that I think is not good for me or my teaching.

MM: You raise issues any thoughtful educator faces: role modeling, personal honesty, forming vs. informing students, risk taking, limit setting. And while there may not be any official policies prohibiting coming out to your students, we both know policies don't have to be official to be real. In light of this, let's start with your need to be a role model to gay and lesbian students. Whether covert or overt, in the classroom or out, I think self-disclosure goes on all the time. Everything you bring into the classroom—dress, attitude, behavior— will be read by students probably more eagerly than your formal class materials. You, as teacher, are another kind of text, and I think your students will each take from you personally what they see, according to what they need. Ellen Hart argues that "gays are not as invisible to themselves as they are to others."[1] If this is so, and I think it is, don't gay and lesbian students see you as they need to without a formal declaration?

AB: Maybe, but aren't they seeing yet another "professional in the closet"? Doesn't this set up silence and invisibility as a model for what "good" lesbian and gay professionals do? Of equal importance is what constant self-censorship does to someone, to me. I teach best when I am *whole,* when I don't have to *think* about censoring myself.

MM: But don't we all censor our behavior at one time or another? Role playing, as well as role modeling, is a fact of life. We're all nicer to some people than we'd really like to be, act differently around friends than around strangers. So here you stop short of the outright confession; aren't we all entitled to "pick our spots" for disclosure?

AB: Look at that word—"confession." It implies wrongdoing, guilt. However, in coming out, I am saying that there is no confession of wrongdoing. There is honesty, yes, but not confession. This is not a question of what I do, but of who I am. And yes, we should all be able to pick our spot for disclosure. Why can't that spot be in the classroom? Self-disclosure can be directly related to content. In English as a Second Language classes, controversial issues are included in many texts as a way of stimulating discussion and writing, teaching US culture and history, and teaching appropriate conversation strategies. Most ESL reading texts, for example, contain articles on racism, sexism, ageism; but heterosexism and homophobia haven't yet made it there. What are the effects of this omission? For one, I think it denies both straight and lesbian/gay students the opportunities to learn about and develop a better understanding of this part of our culture, to develop and practice the language and social skills they need to discuss or write about these topics. If it is a given that learning about the civil rights and women's liberation movements is important for ESL students, then how can we justify not including the lesbian/gay rights movement?

MM: You're right about the general lack of textbook material that is other than heterosexual. This is hardly unique to ESL classes, and there is no justification for it. But the matter of using specifically gay and lesbian materials is still separate from the issue of self-disclosure in the classroom. Students come into your class with a set of expectations, almost all rooted in course content, not the content that is you. Consequently, if your coming out creates a "hostile environment," one that infringes upon a student's right to learn, the institution must deal with the always horrible tension of conflicting rights. That's hard. Each student has an unwritten contract with the institution which requires it to provide—among other things—competent instructors who will teach the content specified in the catalog and course descriptions. What if the student claims that this term of the contract has been broken— that the instructor actually prevents learning by introducing distracting material that the student believes is inappropriate and personally offensive? As much as I might want to say, "Hey, maybe you need to hear this stuff. College is a place to learn about difference, so grow up and go back to class, or take a hike," neither I nor any other administrator automatically can or will.

AB: But there are two issues here. The first is whether the teacher's homosexuality has become the focus of the course. I agree that I am not the text for my courses. Then the second issue is institutional responsibility. What if a white student has a black instructor, and complains to the dean that she cannot learn because the instructor is black and slants the course in a way the student finds objectionable? Or the instructor is Jewish, and the student Palestinian?

MM: No question that the college would need to investigate no matter whether the complaint was based upon race, gender, sexual orientation, or cultural politics. I think, however, that most administrators would feel more comfortable with racial or political controversies; such have been around longer, been discussed and experienced more than sexual/gender-based complaints. Few administrators would be willing (publicly, at least) to let their own prejudices in these areas blind them to the extent that their ability to adjudicate the case was seriously impaired. And even if it were, peer/collegial/legal pressure would present a countervailing force. Unfortunately, I believe homophobia is so widely spread in our society, indeed within our own institution, that a student's claim that gender or sexual orientation issues were being raised inappropriately by a self-proclaimed lesbian, and that these interfered with her ability to learn, might be met with more sympathy than a complaint based on race, for instance. Hence my caution: coming out must be clearly tied to content. If it is, the student may claim that the content prevents her from learning, but this is a claim not likely to win any more points than a student claiming that fractions interfere with her ability to learn math.

AB: But my role is not simply to give information to my students. I think my role is to guide learning and to model learning, to be a learned learner. To me, this means not only should I be a support for gay and lesbian students, but I should challenge all students to examine their attitudes and behaviors, especially when these are oppressive to a large group of people. The *New York Times*, in an article published on June 25, 1989, noted, "In a nationwide survey of 1481 adults in the spring of 1988, the National Opinion Research Center found that 57 percent said homosexuals should be allowed to teach in a college or university." The amazing thing is that this statistic was used as an example of Americans seeming *more* tolerant of homosexuals. What about the other 43 percent who feel that homosexuals should not be allowed to teach at the college level? I don't think this attitude will change unless more people begin to see—and get to know—teachers, doctors, lawyers, secretaries, librarians, marketing reps, carpenters, accountants who are gay. That's what I mean by modeling: letting students, faculty, administrators, and the community at large know that I am a hard-working, conscientious educator who is good at her job, caring of her students and current in her field, and some of that may be even because and not in spite of the fact that I am a lesbian.

MM: "Because . . . "?

AB: Well, to the extent that I have faced both overt and subtle discrimination, and as a member of a minority group that's had to struggle with issues that involve being seen as "other," I can bring an important perspective to bear on class discussions. I think I am especially sensitive to the need to encourage students faced with issues that involve race, sex, ethnicity, religion, politics, or sexual orientation, and at the same time to lead others to examine their own biases. Just as I believe that I must be a professional, female educator, so too do I believe that I must be a professional, female/lesbian educator. Each word there expands upon my role and enriches it. Some heterosexual teachers choose personal neutrality in the classroom, just as you made a choice in this dialogue to be neutral. Whether I come out to students or not is of far less importance than that I too have the freedom to choose.

I know that one of the consequences of coming out is the tendency students in general will have to gossip. Remember, this is an issue that is rooted in sexuality, and gossip about anything sexual flies fast. But since I am out in all other areas of my life, it is quite probable that I will be known as a lesbian without having ever self-disclosed in the classroom. And this too is all right. As students get to know and appreciate me and my skills as a teacher, those same speculations that may begin as not so idle gossip may serve to bring change and growth in both students' attitudes and their actions. I have seen this happen time and time again when I have been the guest speaker for classes and community groups discussing homosexuality.

MM: But in such a setting, you have been asked specifically to discuss homosexuality, and the listeners are there for that purpose. To view the classroom in the same way as community meetings is unfair. In those meetings, you were the equal of those whom you were challenging. In a classroom, the challenge is different. The power issues are different. So to view the classroom in the same way as any other group where roles are balanced, as is power, is patently unfair.

AB: I agree, but I do not believe that personalizing what may have been an abstract issue has to be done in a way that abuses a teacher's power. Having students read and write about heterosexism and homophobia does not mean that the needs of all of us in the classroom—

teacher/students, homosexual/heterosexual—are not being met if it is done in a way that draws on the connections between people and issues while still recognizing, celebrating, and learning from difference. By definition, this means that any one group must not be silenced. And while this is separate from issues of self-disclosure, and should be seen as important by heterosexual teachers also, you know as well as I that it is those of us who are gay/lesbian who must take the lead. But are there risks? Of course. Job security, for one. The other day I iccame across an account of a gay teacher's experiences following the publication of his article on gay/lesbian young adult fiction. Although he never referred to his own sexual orientation in the original piece, he received threatening letters and was denied employment.[2] I doubt that there were any official policies that were violated, but as you said earlier, policies don't have to be official to be real. I might not have to worry about job security in the same way were I tenured, but I'm not.

MM: No question about that. But tenured or not, the real issue of job security is whether or not you're doing your job ... teaching students the content of your course. There is danger that, should someone complain, the "real issue" will become not competence but deviance. I can teach Henry James or Virginia Woolf quite easily without dealing with questions of their sexual orientation. It's been done for years. But if I choose to broaden the spectrum and include such an issue, is this proper and necessary? I think so, but there's the risk that others who hold more power may not. On the other hand, outside the classroom the need to educate faculty, administrators, and staff is also great. Challenging a colleague's suggestion at a meeting that seating be "boy-girl-boy-girl," or displaying/reading from works such as this article at the English department annual "brag party," or volunteering to sponsor a student gay/lesbian club are also ways of promoting awareness and change, and don't leave you as vulnerable to job action by those who may feel threatened.

AB: But here too there are risks. I am not so naive as not to be very much aware of how threatened people are by questions of sexuality. Perhaps many, if not most, teachers, administrators, and/or students have a great stake in working in a space that is "safe" from these issues, or at least where there is the illusion of such safety.

MM: Yes, but while exploding the college-as-haven myth is risky, exploding the classroom-as-haven myth may be even more so. The notion of energizing the classroom is an old one; the notion that a considerable part of that energy is sexual is simply not discussed as openly or as often as it should be. Given that, and given that *all* instructors need to establish boundaries in the classroom, won't these boundaries for the lesbian or gay teacher be more strongly or more openly challenged? Should the boundaries, then, be even more strict, even more clear?

AB: I don't think there can be any set formula for determining appropriate boundaries. What is appropriate for one instructor in one setting may not be appropriate for another in a different (or similar) setting. But your point is important. I think many lesbian and gay teachers do establish boundaries that are very rigid and very distant. I sometimes wonder if, in not coming out, my own are too rigid or that I am too distant because I fear my students will find me out. Energy that could be focused on my teaching and on my students' learning may be too focused on maintaining my boundaries. Why should I need to be afraid that I am somehow being unprofessional by being who I am in my classroom?

MM: In talking about being afraid, aren't you really talking about institutional climate? As an administrator, I work with faculty and other administrators, as well as students. There are gays and lesbians in each of these groups. Some I know. Some I don't. Some choose to be invisible. Others are closeted because they are afraid. I don't think anyone can do her best work when she is afraid. Because some of this fear may be related to the college environment, and because part of my job is to see that the environment is conducive to teaching and learning, I and every other administrator must be concerned about all of this. And yet, before now, I've not really talked with my colleagues about it. In some ways, then, what is most insidious may be how many educators are unaware a problem even exists.

AB: Yes. And many heterosexual educators don't realize that they come to their roles from a position of privilege. The casual mention of a wife or husband in or out of class, insurance benefits for heterosexual spouses, the ability to leave work without penalty to attend the funeral of a loved one—these are privileged acts that are not at this time rights for all of us. If self-disclosure leads to more dialogues of this kind, perhaps the risks we discussed earlier will lose some of their power. Maybe this is the real meaning of academic freedom.

In 1958 Eleanor Roosevelt wrote, "Where after all, do universal human rights begin? In small places, close to home . . . the world of the individual person; the neighborhood he [sic] lives in; the school or college he attends. . . . Such are the places where every man, woman and child seeks equal justice, equal opportunity, equal dignity without discrimination. Unless these rights have meaning there, they have little meaning anywhere."[3]

During the course of this dialogue, each of us came to understand that some of our assumptions about ourselves, about others, about our institution were not altogether valid. Self-disclosure, coming out, creating and respecting boundaries: these are all complex and important issues, each involving questions of rights and responsibilities, both personal and institutional. Yet rarely do faculty members and/ or administrators discuss them. We believe this must change, and now is the time.

Notes

A slightly different version of this essay was published in the *Journal of the American Association of Women in Community and Junior Colleges* (1990).

1. Ellen Hart quoted in M. B. Barrett, *Invisible Lives: The Truth about Millions of Women-Loving Women* (New York: Morrow, 1989), dedication.

2. E. L. Hart, "Literacy and the Lesbian/Gay Learner," in Sarah Hope Parmeter and Irene Reti, eds., *The Lesbian in Front of the Classroom* (Santa Cruz, CA: HerBooks, 1988), 27.

3. Eleanor Roosevelt quoted in R. D. Mohr, "Gay Studies in the Big Ten: A Survivor's Manual," *Teaching Philosophy* 7:2 (April 1984): 98.

2

Explicit Instruction:
Talking Sex in the Classroom

Wendy Chapkis

In 1990, I had the extraordinary opportunity to teach the only regularly scheduled lesbian and gay course at the University of California at Santa Cruz: Politics 80A, Sexual Politics: Lesbian and Gay Liberation Movements (recently retitled Queer Politics). The course is offered every spring; it is the result of courageous and visionary works by politics professor David Thomas, who for many years was one of the only out gay faculty members at UCSC. David ordinarily teaches the class, but that year he was unable to do so, and I was given the opportunity—or to be more honest, I seized the opportunity—to teach the class in his stead.

It was a particularly good time to teach that class, too. Vito Russo had been a visiting professor at UCSC the quarter before, teaching his wonderful film class, The Celluloid Closet, to hundreds of eager students, and also a smaller seminar, called Documenting Lesbian and Gay Social Activism, a sort of how-to-be-a-queer-militant course.

By the end of winter quarter, students were applying what they were learning in Vito's classes, taking it to the streets. A powerful "queer and colored" coalition developed on the campus among undergraduates, with lesbian and gay students (both white and of color) and students of color (both straight and gay) forming an alliance demanding more university support for ethnic studies and lesbian, gay, and bisexual studies. They occupied university buildings, held forums, and generally raised hell.

And a lot of them—about a hundred and fifty of them—appeared in my queer politics class during spring quarter. This was indeed an environment that encouraged my already powerful predisposition to being outrageous. Not only did I have fabulously interested and aware

11

students and a subject matter about which I was passionate, I was also newly unleashed. This was the first time I would design and teach my own course. I was thrilled it was lesbian and gay politics; I couldn't think of a more auspicious way to enter the profession.

I committed myself to taking as many risks as possible with that course. Ignoring conventional wisdom, which suggests risks are better left to post-tenure years, I decided to plunge right in. I feared starting out timid, afraid that I would become only more careful over the years as I developed concerns about tenure, as I became more fully identified with academia. So I organized the course around points of conflict and division in the "queer community," moving from debates about identity to differences of sexual practices and the polarized theorizing they have generated. I devoted about half of the quarter to an examination of some of the most controversial issues in contemporary queer politics. My four concluding lectures were on increasingly explosive topics, starting with attacks from within the Gay community on "promiscuity" in the age of AIDS (counterposing Kramer and Shilts with safe-sex radicals defending the bathhouses and anonymous sex); moving to pornography in the context of the feminist sex debates (particularly looking at arguments over lesbian pornography seen as an avenue of liberation rather than as further evidence of internalized patriarchal oppression); followed by a discussion of lesbian and gay sadomasochism (exploring the meanings and menace of leather sex); and ending with a lecture on the politics of intergenerational sex.

Needless to say, it was a wild quarter. It certainly taught me that explicit instruction is a complicated dance, for both teacher and student. I believe I was at least partially successful in encouraging students to think critically about sexual desires—to be self-conscious about their socially constructed passions—while also being respectful of those desires. In other words, I tried to make them aware of the unnaturalness of desire without demanding that they attempt to discipline theirs to the dictates of a political line. For instance, after several weeks of discussing diversity within our community, and talking about making political alliances across our many differences, I wanted to challenge the class to think about how social divisions are echoed in the construction of desire. If, as we had seen, our community is racially diverse and extends across class divisions, is there any place for sexual desire that stems from those differences, or must our sexual practices be color- and class-blind? Or even, following the lead of some bisexuals, gender-blind?

The tool I used to focus thoughts on these issues was a class assignment to write and run a personal ad. I asked students to try to envision what it was that they wanted sexually, and to think about how to ask for it; to notice when their desires seemed to conflict with their political ideals; for example, when they wanted lovers of a certain race, sex, body type, age, or perversion. Where did principle and pleasure intersect? Where were they at odds? It was my hope that further theorizing about desire would be rooted in a sense of the unruliness of our passions. What we want isn't always what we think we should want. And the enactment or satisfaction of fantasy isn't always what we thought it would be. This was particularly useful when we turned to subjects like pornography, s/m, and intergenerational sex.

In the classroom, we shared sexual anecdotes, argued sexual politics, debated sexual theory. The content of the course and my style of teaching highlighted the erotically charged environment of the queer classroom. In fact, one of the most effective moments for me in the class occurred during my last lecture, when I was able to draw on the sexual dynamics of the classroom while talking about intergenerational sex. I started the lecture by acknowledging the seriousness of childhood sexual abuse, but also by challenging the stereotype of the lecherous old queer preying on the innocence of children. Most intergenerational gay sex, I reminded my students, is sex between people of my age (around 40) and people of your age (late teens). When you hear "intergenerational sex," I advised, think of sex between people like you and people like me. Their knowing laughter suggested that the comparison was both effective and provocative.

I always tried in my lectures to foreground what was at stake for me in the debates—politically, personally, sexually—and to ask students to do the same. This was partly about intellectual honesty, partly about self-consciously and explicitly drawing links between theory and political practice, and partly about breaking some of the rules of traditional scholarship—about locating ourselves in the debates rather than claiming a place of scholarly neutrality someplace outside of them.

It increasingly seems to me that our work in lesbian and gay studies is transgressive. Among feminist and queer academics there exists a valuable suspicion of many academic conventions. We tend to question authority, to criticize established methods of research, and to see our work and our lives as explicitly political. We also are often at the forefront of rethinking pedagogy—how we teach and the relationship between students and teachers. We attempt and sometimes succeed in creating a classroom environment that is collegial, that is, where students are colleagues in the political and intellectual endeavor.

Because of the content of feminist and gay/lesbian courses, those of us teaching them often find ourselves dealing with material once thought to be unspeakable. Breaking silence creates its own tensions and intimacies. Anyone who has ever taught a women's studies course, an ethnic studies course, or an explicitly gay/lesbian course, knows about the complicated intertwining of "theory" and "experience," the fear and emotion that accompany discussions of violence, desire, oppression, self-naming, liberation. These conversations often entail a level of vulnerability and exposure uncharacteristic of more traditional course work. In all these ways the conventional boundaries between the public and the private, the academic and the intimate, are blurred. Is it possible that in such a context sexual intimacy between those differently positioned in the academy also comes to seem like just one more politically progressive violation of the norm?

In teaching Sexual Politics, I was always aware of the ways in which I presented myself as an object of desire to the class. I dressed in my very best dyke drag for each lecture, complete with leather and rhinestones. The costuming was partially protection: giving a lecture to over a hundred people was clearly performance, and the outfits were effective props. But it was more than that. My costuming was also an attempt to perform gay culture as well as to teach it. My appearance was intended to serve as a model of the pleasures of gender transgression (bright red lipstick under a full blonde moustache) and of a shameless lesbian sexual presence.

But how to combine that unabashed sexuality with the necessary distance between student and teacher? The queer classroom complicates our discussions of sexual harassment in interesting and fruitful ways. I have witnessed lesbian desire across both sides of the student/teacher divide, and despite my flamboyant style—or better yet, because of it—I appreciate the prohibitions against sexual intimacy between the ranks in the context of gross institutional inequality. These prohibitions provide protection for people like me, who insist on bringing sex into the classroom but have no intention of taking it home with them.

Lesbian and gay faculty already share with lesbian and gay students a profound sense of commonality. We are not simply divided by differences in institutional power; we are also joined by our minority status in society. We share cultural and social space in the communities in which we live. For this reason, maintaining boundaries outside the classroom is both difficult and precious. Ever since I started teaching, I have been tremendously nervous about cruising in the local gay bars. This is a college town, after all. Chances are that the woman flirting me up on the dance floor, or the woman I'm sizing up across the room, is a UCSC student. The sexual complexity of the academic relationship does not simply disappear off campus or after hours. At their best, sexual-conduct guidelines can serve as a useful tool in maintaining boundaries between professional and personal life.

Still, as they now stand, sexual harassment policies tend to have a distinctly heterosexual bias. I have found myself involved in complicated arguments with colleagues, both lesbian and straight, on where to draw the line on bringing queer sexuality to the university. For instance, is it appropriate to have sexual gay imagery tacked to our office doors or on our office walls? Is such material when displayed by a lesbian or gay faculty member an appropriate assertion of her or his political identity, or is it rather an aggressive intrusion of lesbian/ gay sexuality into colleagues' and students' professional lives? In other words, is such a display comparable to militant ethnic markers on the door of an African-American professor, or is it more like a girlie calendar hanging on the walls of a heterosexual male professor's office, which sexual harassment guidelines suggest inappropriately sexualizes the work space?

These difficult questions are unavoidable in an institution committed to diversity, sexual and otherwise. Unfortunately, just as women and ethnic minorities have been accused of politicizing the classroom, queers will be accused of sexualizing it. But politics, including sexual politics, are always already there. The difference is that, rather than bowing to a naked emperor, we call him a nude and proceed to investigate the problems and pleasures of exhibitionism.

3

The Romance of Class and Queers: Academic Erotic Zones

Michèle Aina Barale

As gay academics, our dual identities as instructors and queers mean that ideas and readings previously not part of the traditional academic curriculum are given voice within our classrooms and among our colleagues. In the classroom we might well find that we are met by shocked as well as eager responses; some of our students will be pleased with our discussions, but many others will be embarrassed, angry, even openly hostile toward us and our subject matter. In departmental interactions, unless we are teaching in a women's or gender or gay studies curriculum or have been invited by a department to teach queer courses, we can expect little support or advice from the majority of our colleagues. In fact, many of their responses to our subject matter will match those of our least happy students. The public articulation of our queerness and its presence in our class lectures will only intensify those colleagues' dismay, if not their distrust. Their feeling is that we have transgressed instructional boundaries by bringing our private sexual lives into the forum of the classroom. At best, they will judge such transgression to be juvenile, a form of adolescent show-and-tell. At worst, however, they might consider us as unethical as they consider our material unacademic, deeming such self-revelation a not very covert attempt to seduce students to our modes of thought and even behavior.

The irony, of course, is that it is far more likely to be the teacher who feels seduced by a liberal rhetoric of academic freedom and intellectual diversity, only to be abandoned in the face of a familiar homophobia. The environment is, therefore, ideal for alienating those of us who are queer from our colleagues as well as from a great many of our students. It's not unusual to find ourselves so marginalized that our academic and pedagogical roles are distinctly affected. Unable to take advantage of the hallways and xerox room as sites where teacherly miseries and successes can be aired, we must somehow make the classroom itself provide what's needed. Ignored or dismissed by colleagues, we often get much of our intellectual stimulus from our students. However, using a classroom already fraught with its students' emotional responses to queer material to fulfill its instructor's needs for an intellectual community can instigate a dynamic that feels better than it teaches. In this environment it can become all too tempting to enter not only our students' intellectual lives but also their beds.

Thus, while the factors that might put us in those beds are external ones—the result of a systemic homophobia—it is, ultimately, our own needs that make us erotically susceptible to such placement. Intensely engaged by what we do, we necessarily become intensely engaged with those who do it with us. This is true of all good teachers, of course, whatever their sexuality or subject. But the queer professor's alienation is more likely to make encounters with students the most vital site for shared intellectual pleasures. I do not imagine that there will soon be a change in the existing system: previously ill-at-ease colleagues will not come rushing down the hall next week, eager to press us into discussions of queerness and pedagogy. Therefore, if we are to resist the comfort of students, it seems useful to consider the ways that the queer studies classroom becomes an erotic site and its professor a pedagogic object of desire. My concern here is not to inveigh against teacher-student consensual relations. Although I do not think we should ever sleep with our students—even when both parties, sober, thoughtful, and still clothed, find it a pretty nifty idea—my interests are in the factors that make queer pedagogical endeavors into academic erotic zones whose boundaries are unusually vulnerable to transgression.

I first began teaching in the women's studies classroom. There I found that my sense of boundaries was constantly challenged. Students seemed to think that any attempt to renegotiate some of the usual hierarchies of power meant I had, instead, instituted the teacher-as-buddy system. That misperception, combined with notions of the personal as political, allowed students to feel that personal narratives—the more intimate the better—were the preferred material of the classroom. Struggling to redirect discussion to the day's reading could result in resentful silence. At the same time, however, both I and my students were utterly caught up in the excitement of the material, much of it new, raw, still rough-edged and unmediated by academic niceties.

Emotions ran high, whether inspired by readings or by personal narratives, and the learning process that took place in those classes bore no resemblance to anything I had experienced in graduate school or in the more traditional courses I taught. It was clear that, whatever the subject matter might be in women's studies courses, students were seeking and finding some reflection of their own lives. It was equally clear that my own life, intellectual and personal, was more fully part of my instructional role than it had ever been before.

I don't think that I am quite the same teacher now that I was then; ten years, several thousand students' essays, hundreds of classroom hours, and countless repetitions—the pattern rather than anomaly—of student discomfort and/or pleasures in dealing with gender and sexuality as analytical systems have made me crabbier than I used to be. The intellectual thrills and fascination with the material remain, and so does my excitement with teaching. But I exert conscious control in my classroom in ways I didn't used to, and I am less willing to teach myself into the ground than I was then. I'm a better teacher because I am no longer than evangelist of old. I'm savvier, sneakier, more capable of the usefully ignoble, cajoling, demanding, and infuriating. Yet, none of this makes the erotic disappear from the classroom. Easier to deal with, yes. But because the material itself is so very provocative, it isn't enough that we are not.

The experience of a class focused so directly upon issues with personal relevance is a heady one, for teacher and student. Jane Gurko has suggested that all intellectual exchange, particularly when it occurs in a power imbalance, is sexually stimulating, no matter what the subject matter or the sexes involved, and can trigger romantic fantasies on both sides of the desk.[1] But the presence of a queer instructor serves to further eroticize the classroom exchange. Not only is the sexual energy of intellectual dialogue focused upon the material at hand, but sexual interest is easily focused on us as instructors as well, if for no other reason than that our coming out is often perceived as an act of intimate self-disclosure by both lesbian and nonlesbian students. While heterosexual instructors are certainly known as such, and although their husbands/wives/lovers and families may be the subjects of classroom anecdote, their sexuality tends to fade into the background because it is the norm.[2] It is not at all difficult for the gay instructor, particularly in a lesbian- or gay-focused course, to feed rather than quell students' infatuations.

For all our students—men and women, straight and gay—any queer teacher can become the perfect symbol for a variety of meanings.

We may represent all the possibilities of rebellious sexuality—a very appealing thing for many young students; we can become sites for the expression of both their liberalism and their bigotry, their fascination and their horror; certainly we are the dramatis personae of private dramas enacting the fears and thrills of sexual identity; and god knows that we play out parental roles we can't begin to fathom, were we even to want to. What all those representations have in common, however, is their casting of us in oracular roles: we are thought to have knowledge and insight about things they are most eager to know about themselves. Sometimes their curiosity is apparent; other times, because it is cloaked as something else, it is nearly incoherent, instigating questions equally easy and impossible to answer. Behind many students' spoken queries are the unspoken ones: Am I gay? Can you tell? Does it show in some way? Should I worry about my relationship with my best friend? How come I'm so interested in all this stuff? What are the first five signs of indisputable queerness?

Such questions come as frequently from straight students as from those who are gay. While the queer students may not be so curious about the particulars of sexual behavior, they are terribly curious about the particulars of romantic relationships. Searching for difficult-to-find models, they look to us for practical paradigms.[3] This role can be more than a little disconcerting to the instructor. All of us are more than eager to share with students the particulars of our intellectual history, are pleased to thrill them, at length and in detail, with the story of how we arrived at our present state of theoretical brilliance. However, we might be a little less enthused by requests to elucidate how we find time for a sex life in the midst of a busy academic life or to expatiate on how we have integrated theory into our own sexual practices. While I can sometimes feel intruded upon by my students' curiosity, and am even a bit embarrassed by their more personal questions, I am also quite moved by the urgency of their desire to know some still elusive part of themselves. It's the stuff of youthfulness, of that soon to be lost moment when one believes that a single piece of important information will make everything fall in place forever. And so my discomfort is matched by a desire to give them all that I can, evading the most personal aspects, redirecting their questions' intimacy. But if an instructor feels intellectually alienated from her or his department or isolated from its more genial social interactions, even the most personal of questions might be welcome and met with relief if it offers an opportunity for friendship, acceptance, even comfort.

The difficulty of negotiating between the private and the articulated is always further complicated when there is a shared sexuality and, therefore, a shared community. The teacher who meets a student at every social turn may feel invaded. We can't be just another patron drinking beer when we go to the local gay bar, just another dancing, softball-playing, or placard-carrying queer at dances, concerts, or ACT UP demonstrations. Our companion or lack of one, whether we touch, flirt, or look tenderly upon another, are not only noted but reported to classmates who weren't there. We are, quite simply, under scrutiny, and our activities are not at all unlikely to be mentioned to us—either in joking or in all seriousness. We may discover that even our more private activities are known. Somehow, in complex and usually benign ways, bits and pieces of one's history become public, if whispered, knowledge. Student X knows Y who knows Z who was the ex-lover of W who was the instructor's lover three years ago. Or student L knows M who cleans for O who is the instructor's best friend. If I am irritated by my lack of privacy within social settings, I can be made completely paranoid by the possibilities of my private life being made the subject of public narratives.

For gay students, private information about their teacher, even if it is misinformation, often serves to further eroticize that teacher's presence in the classroom. Some students will seek to establish a peer relationship with us. They have been known to offer advice, to suggest double dates or even suitable partners, on the one hand, and to propose themselves as such, on the other. The gaining or actual possession of insider knowledge about an instructor offers the student who has it a degree of status among her or his peers, and creates a kind of aura of intimacy between student and teacher when that knowledge is evoked publicly (as in—and I am not making these up—the case where a student loudly complimented an instructor on her new, wildly patterned sheets; or the situation in which a student made numerous references to her instructor's recent dinner party, naming who was there, what was eaten, and who stayed late.) Just like alienated instructors, students who feel ill-used and unappreciated by the academy can find solace in little pieces of covert information that seem to offer the chance of being cozy with the powerful.

While gay teachers and students share in the queer community, we share a sense of exclusion from the dominant culture also. That sense of exclusion is as potent a factor in our interrelations within a classroom as is our shared inclusion in the gay community. Both teacher and students can experience problems similar in kind if not necessarily in intensity, ones which provide a kind of glue that bonds us in ways that queer instructors probably don't feel with heterosexual students or even with heterosexual colleagues. The shared experiences of self-repression and discomfort that result from academic homophobia certainly enable the queer teacher to help her queer students focus their anger properly rather than internalize it into guilt or self-devaluation, and as such are a powerful instructional adjunct. But these shared experiences also mean that as instructors we might nonetheless expect and even seek greater comfort and understanding from our students than from our peers.

For instance, when we find ourselves discussing departmental politics and classroom dynamics with students in a manner that has more to do with accusation and insider knowledge than it does with furthering students' understanding of academic power relations, we are in difficult waters. No doubt about it, it feels good. And students are wonderfully willing to see things our way, to make murmurs of sympathy and shake their heads in woeful realization of our embattled state. Students are hungry for every piece of ammunition they can muster in the knowledge-equals-power game. They are therefore charmingly capable of helping us make such discussions into ones that can, effortlessly, become opportunities to divulge the idiosyncracies of colleagues' private and academic lives as well as occasions when their fellow students' intellectual failings can be affirmed by the instructor. It's a seductive moment for teacher and students alike precisely because the power roles are inverted: the teacher gets to be the confiding child and the student the soothing adult. Those students who are cast as confessors know their privileged position, and so does the rest of the class. They are usually the brightest, the best writers, the most articulate. They're perceptive and mature beyond their years. And best of all, they love us and value us and want to be just like us. This is pretty exhilarating. Our colleagues may not want us but some of the smartest students in the entire school do. And if we weren't jocks or cheerleaders in our past, we're cult objects now.

I do not believe infatuations can be completely prevented; I am not even convinced that they are necessarily bad or harmful in themselves.[4] The distinctions between being a role model and being the subject of a crush seem more hazy than categorical. Perhaps it's the case that role models, like good scout leaders, are desired for their ability to move, surefooted, through the thickets of academe smiling tough-love encouragement over their shoulders at the root-stumbling neophyte who hurries to catch up. The infatuated, on the other hand, may be more interested in hanging around the campfire than in undergoing the rigorous pleasures involved in getting there. In either case, whether trailblazing or marshmallow toasting, the situation can only be beneficially managed if the forces that created it are recognized, and if we keep in mind the primary boundary that cannot be breached: the sexual. In its strictest sense, this means that teachers don't have sexual relations with even their most willing students. But more broadly, I think it also means that we don't conduct our classes as proving grounds from which will emerge likely objects of desire with whom we will grace our summer as soon as grades are turned in. Nor, I think, does it mean that we manage to convey to our classes the teasing suggestion that we might do this were there world enough and time.

Since neither the material of the classroom nor pedagogy itself ever can or should be made off-limits for erotic pleasure, the students must be. The boundary that separates our sexual desire from that of our students has to be intentionally established to allow no negotiation, no flexion. If we are not clear to ourselves about our goals in being out in the classroom, we are going to find it very difficult to manage infatuations—our students' and our own—because it will be only too easy to use the classroom as a way to feel good about ourselves. Crushes will satisfy our needs, and we will find we are trying to deny and discourage the very things we also crave: attention and adoration. As long as we are unconscious of this internal conflict, it is not difficult to manipulate the continuance of an infatuation even while giving it the lip service of denial. In addition, when a teacher is looking to her students for affirmation, it is very easy to become infatuated with a student who offers it.

It is, alas, our incredibly onerous duty to establish workable boundaries with our students. Students can't be expected to carry out this job—in a sense, their job is to test those boundaries in as many ways as possible. Furthermore, there needs to be some consistency in our boundaries. Our ways of interacting with our students should not vary radically from student to student, or they will begin to interpret differences in our behavior as evidence of favoritism or even infatuation. Still more important, we need to feel comfortable with the boundaries we establish and the interactions that they do permit. While they offer both teacher and student protection from the inappropriate or abusive, their primary reason for existence is one of usefulness rather than deterrence. Boundaries are a positive feature in teaching, not negative. We all get weary of demanding that a specific student not overstep boundaries, and we get irritable when boundaries are persistently tested. But if we believe that boundaries have positive value, there's not much temptation to let down the rules and stretch those boundaries. When boundaries are felt to exist only to deter, if rules exist only to deny, and if all limitations have been experienced as serving only to prevent, then an instructor will have a hard time seeing the need for limits or rules of consistent behavior. In order to envision boundaries as a way of saying yes—as establishing what students can have and expect from teachers—an instructor will need to analyze what she perceives rules and limitations as denying her, and, therefore, as denying her students. This holds equally true, obviously, for the straight teacher as for the gay one. But since it is queer teachers who are most likely to be teaching provocative material that itself tests all kinds of boundaries—gay/straight, private/public, natural/constructed, nonsexual/erotic—we have, I think, a greater need for utter consciousness in constructing and then keeping in place our own.

I am aware that I could be heard to be advocating a kind of superlative chastity or launching a moral purity campaign to end desire itself: cold shower before class and hair shirts immediately after. I am not advocating the suppression of all reminders that we are sexual beings. I am not saying, "no red cowboy boots or muscle Ts or leather miniskirts or tight jeans; let's make the world safe for tweed again." That's not what I mean or what I want. Desire can't be policed; everyone is entitled to his or her fantasies about whomever. Besides, it doesn't much matter what we wear or how we look. No matter what, we symbolize sexuality and transgression; that's sufficient to make us far more appealing than anything our mirrors might suggest.

And that's not all that makes our jobs as queer teachers troublesome. I think that both our students and our colleagues are more likely to find us difficult to have around. And I think that we do—can't help but—make demands of them that they are not used to, that we ask them to stretch themselves and reevaluate all kinds of things in order to enter into useful pedagogical relationships with us. We're not the easiest folk to have around, and I don't expect that we'll get any more affable as we age. My point is that it is precisely our sensitivity to the discomforts we cause and, as a result, also experience that can make classroom erotics a tempting solution to academic alienation. None of us can transform the whole academy or modify all the various factors that sexualize our material and our presence in the classroom. We do have some effect upon existing homophobia, but it will often seem minor and ephemeral since students heartlessly graduate and go away just as soon as they've gotten smart enough to make us happy. New students arrive, and we start all over again. If we can be clear to ourselves about what we need as individuals and what we expect as teachers, it will be easier to give our students some of the things they need and many of the things we want them to have.

Notes

This article was originally published in a different format, in the *Journal of Women & Therapy* Vol. 8 (1/2) pages 183–194 by the The Haworth Press Inc. For information, please call 1-800-342-9678. An earlier version was reprinted in *Loving Boldly: Issues Facing Lesbians,* Esther D. Rothblum and Ellen Cole, eds. (New York and London: Harrington Parks Press, 1989). Grateful thanks are due Judy Frank, who has offered numerous useful suggestions for the revision of this essay.

1. Jane Gurko, "Sexual Energy in the Classroom" in *Lesbian Studies,* Margaret Cruikshank, ed. (New York: The Feminist Press, 1982): 25–31.

2. This is not to deny that heterosexual teachers become the subjects of their students' erotic imaginings. But, because the heterosexual teacher is so much the norm, his/her presence does not eroticize the classroom as does the queer's.

3. Women, in particular I think, are likely to feel that we have to be open books for our female students, and that we have to provide the answers for questions that feel too close to the bone, too personal, that ask us to bare our breasts more than feels comfortable. Twenty years' belief in the political nature of the personal makes us hesitant about establishing firm boundaries between what we share and what we don't.

4. For a discussion of the pedagogical uses of infatuation in an earlier period of history, see Martha Vicinus, "Distance and Desire: English Boarding-School Friendships," in *The Lesbian Issue: Essays from Signs,* Estelle B. Freedman, Barbara C. Gelpi, Susan L. Johnson, and Kathleen M. Weston, eds. (Chicago: University of Chicago Press, 1982).

4

Classroom Coming Out Stories: Practical Strategies for Productive Self-Disclosure

Kate Adams and Kim Emery

It was Kim's idea to write this essay, but it wasn't hard to talk Kate into coauthoring with her. The two of us mulled it over at the hammered-brass bar of an Austin, Texas, tavern. On the Sunday before Memorial Day, while well-dressed couples and families doing dinner out began to fill the tables around us, we worked on our initial outline. We had finished our coffees and moved on to beers before we were interrupted by the only other patron sitting at the bar: Joe. He was polite, in a befuddled kind of way, but finally obtrusive; he couldn't help overhearing us, he said: What in God's name were we talking about?

We looked at each other. "We're talking about being lesbian college teachers," Kim told him.

"We're writing a paper about coming out to students," Kate added.

"Huh?" Joe said. "How would that ever come up?"

Joe's question was one we'd heard before. It stems from the assumption that one's sexuality is a private affair which wouldn't ever be relevant to a classroom discussion. Kate asked him to think about the best teachers he'd had in his life, the ones that had made some connection with him over the body of knowledge that was the course's subject. Did those teachers ever talk about themselves in the classroom? Tell stories from their childhoods to illuminate a point? Make analogies to their family lives? Draw examples from their personal experiences with college, love, tragedy, pet ownership, or car repair?

"That," Kim said, "is how being a lesbian is relevant in the classroom. When lesbian and gay men feel they must suppress something so central to their identity as sexuality, something that constructs their social relationships as well as their sense of community, then they teach out of a context of anxiety. They speak encircled by silence, and both they and their students are cheated out of the full use of an important teaching tool."

"Yeah," Kate added. "When you can't make an analogy between systems theory and feeding the cats because you're afraid you might slip and use a revealing pronoun, you're teaching with one hand tied behind your back. Plus, people in the business of increasing knowledge shouldn't participate in hiding the fact that there are lesbians in the world."

"Huh," Joe said.

The three of us chatted a little longer while the bartender made occasional nervous checks of our side of the bar—were we okay? Were these two (lesbian) ladies being hassled by this slightly inebriated neighborhood regular? Joe did a lot of the talking. He gave us his opinion of teachers coming out in the classroom (most students wouldn't be able to handle it) and of the military ban (not going to go away anytime soon). In his questions and in his comments, in the way he looked us over, he also revealed his opinion of us: we were an oddity, two lesbians talking about classrooms in the middle of his neighborhood bar on a Sunday afternoon.

Joe's reaction to the two of us, and the bartender's slight nervousness about all three of us, reaffirmed our belief in the importance of coming out. The straight public just doesn't come across lesbians often enough in the mundane process of negotiating everyday life. Our initial uncertainty in responding to Joe's interest, the bartender's protective glances while we talked—these are signs of the risk we take when we take our lesbian selves into the public world. But the risk of coming out is also, always, an opportunity. Were we the first lesbians Joe had ever met? Will Joe remember us the next time he sees Jesse Helms frothing at the mouth on C-Span? We don't know; the point, which each of us felt and acknowledged in different ways, is that lesbian existence doesn't very often walk in and casually ask for a table in mainstream USA. Being a lesbian in public contexts is more often and too often a problem, an embarrassment (for somebody), equivalent to a diner's singing out, "Waiter, there's a fly in my soup!" Yet for us, for Joe, students, bartenders, Sunday diners at the Hyde Park Bar & Grill, a whole passel of opportunities opens up when lesbian and gay teachers, waiters, bartenders, and public-house philosophers dare to engage the world with the whole of their lives.

There are differences between barstools and lecterns, but what we said to Joe is what we believe about coming out, and why we do it in our classrooms. Nevertheless, we recognize that coming out in a classroom is much more difficult than falling off a barstool (or even pushing Joe off one). Determining the appropriate moment and manner in which to actually say "I am a lesbian" to a captive audience gathered to hear a lecture on dependent clauses or bell curves or the American Revolution—or anything other than what they might understandably think of as their instructor's "sex" life—is something else again. What follows are some of the strategies and concerns that have marked our own coming-out experiences.

How Do You Do It? Some Strategies and Anecdotes

Be yourself. What kind of teacherly manner do you adopt in the classroom? If you're a by-the-book, "That's *Doctor* Smith, to you" kind of teacher, suddenly switching gears and chatting about your love life could disconcert your students. On the other hand, if your classroom persona is relaxed and accessible, try not to turn all formal and uptight when you mention lesbianism—this could definitely give students the wrong idea.

Make the information relevant. Even if the question of whether to come out is long since decided, continually questioning the why of the matter should make choosing your method easier. Presumably, there is some reason that you want to come out to your classes. Whether it's about honesty, integrity, providing a role model for gay students (or straight ones), busting stereotypes, promoting cultural awareness, or any of the endless other positive objectives that responsible self-disclosure can help a teacher achieve, your motivation for coming out should inform your method of doing so. Think about it, and be guided by your best intentions.

Choose an appropriate occasion. Any day on which your class is discussing cultural values, community norms, gay or lesbian historical figures, civil rights issues, gender roles, or stereotypes is also a good day to come out. In any case, it's important to introduce the information in such a way that it enriches discussion rather than shutting it down—and in such a way that students feel respected rather than reprimanded. Tell them before, not after, soliciting comments about a lesbian writer's perspective on sexism, for instance.

National Coming Out Day (October 11) is always a good one, too. That's how one colleague of ours came out to her undergraduates. Her class had been reading selections from Abraham Cahan's novel *Yekl,* the story of an early twentieth-century Jewish immigrant to New York. When Jake goes to Ellis Island to meet his newly arrived wife, he is embarrassed by her old-country clothes, her "greenhorn" ways, and her general inability to blend in, to assimilate as he has done. Our colleague's students were disturbed by Jake's embarrassment, and the discussion that ensued focused on the differences between accultura-tion and assimilation, the social and psychological consequences of maintaining an ethnic or out-group identity in the face of mainstream distrust or disapproval, and the simplifications inherent in the myth of the melting pot. Near the hour's end, our colleague came out to her students. She told them about National Coming-Out Day, suggesting it celebrated the same spirit of diversity whose absence in Jake had troubled them.

Alternatively, rather than choosing an appropriate occasion in ad-vance, you can let an occasion choose you. We all know that great class discussions are often unplanned miracles: spontaneously asked (or answered) questions lead to brilliant-but-unscripted connections. Coming out can be the result of a similar instance of unanticipated, although not necessarily unearned, grace.

Come out before you come out.   Create a context. This isn't as difficult as it sounds. If you are dedicated to the idea that bringing all of yourself to the classroom is pedagogically productive, then you've taken on the responsibility of making the classroom a safe place for all of your students to be equally open—and of helping your students to question the ways in which the classroom and its curriculum frame, prioritize, and efface different parts of their complex identities and of knowledge itself. If you teach from this perspective, you are already building a context for your own and your students' productive self-disclosure, and it is likely that your first classroom reference to lesbian existence has already occurred and did not include your girlfriend's name.

A colleague of ours, teaching a course on immigrant women's litera-ture, made sexuality and gender the focus of questions/commentary as often as she made race and ethnicity the focus. She found herself coming out during discussion of a straight Korean woman's autobiog-raphy. When some students contested author Mary Paik Lee's claim that white women are more racist than white men, another student sided with the author, offering an analogy as a kind of evidence: straight men, she said, are more homophobic than straight women. Because our colleague had built a classroom in which the writings of women of color were central to, not isolated from, a larger critique of American history's failure to allow for difference, her student's analogy to another marginal group carried a lot of weight—certainly more than it could bear. Consequently, our colleague came out as a lesbian and was then able to create a productively complicated discussion from what might have lapsed into a series of simplifying stereotypes. She asked what would be gained by her either confirming or negating the student's assertion. The class was asked to think about the assumptions they were making about gendered and sexual identities. They were also asked to consider why a lesbian teacher's announcement would loom so large for them. Why are certain encounters with difference particularly marking and formative for us, while others pass almost unnoticed? This colleague's coming out was thus only a part of her nuanced complication of the class discussion. The whole exchange could happen only because the instructor had already created an open classroom, one where students were encouraged to see their own and others' identities as complex constructions.

Don't anticipate disaster.   Our gut feeling is that most of us expect to catch a lot more flak than we actually do for being openly ourselves in the classroom. The culture we live in—and that lives in us—encourages our anxiety and its consequent silence. In the most sensational of mass media narratives, not to mention in our own informal communication networks, the out teacher's supporting cast includes the Outraged Alumnus, the Homophobic Parent, the Neo-Nazi Student, and the Unsupportive Chair. Of course we recognize that for all of us—especially the untenured, underemployed, or otherwise easily expendable and essentially unprotected—the benefits of coming out must be balanced against actual risks, and nightmare scenarios do occasionally unfold. No one wishes gay and lesbian teachers to court personal disaster as a consequence of coming out. But generally speaking, we recognize that the intensity of our fear is simply evidence that the world has done its work on us.

Try one of these openers.   You're prepared; you've examined your intentions and your teaching style, created a context, identified an appropriate occasion, and considered the risks. Still, you're faced with that moment—on the first day or long after the midterm—when it's time to segue from quantum theory to queerness. Whether you're outing yourself or outing the subject, discussing homosexuality for the first time in the classroom is, for many of us, daunting. How about using one of these tried and true (well, true if not all tried) openers?

—In Intro to Linguistics, use examples of the slang specific to your lesbian softball league to illustrate the concept of community norms and sociolinguistic variation.

—In the mathematical theory seminar, after cracking your students' heads against Alan Turing's codes, reassure the class that it wasn't higher mathematics that led him to swallow cyanide in 1954; rather, it was the physically and emotionally destructive course of treatment he was forced to undergo after widespread public censure of his homosexuality.

—In the media law course, organize the section on censorship around examination of the precedent-setting US obscenity trial of Radclyffe Hall's *The Well of Loneliness*.

—During your discussion of connotative and denotative language in the English composition class, write the words "fag," "queer," "gay," "lesbian," and "dyke" on the board. Expore the ways those words have resonated for you at different points in your life. Talk about how, as a lesbian speaking in a lesbian context, you use the word "dyke" to mean something much more positive and courageous than what the gay-basher has in mind when he throws the word at you from the open window of a revving Chevy as you walk down the street with a group of gay friends.

—In the large lecture section of Music Appreciation 101, after playing that passage from *The 1812 Overture,* muse aloud about the influence of other composers—including Vladimir Shilovsky, his one-time lover—on Tchaikovsky's work.

—In the philosophy of science class, illustrate Kuhn's theory of scientific revolutions by providing a brief history of sexology and the changing scientific certainties about lesbian identity.

Finally, remember that coming out is simply a moment. Saying "I am a lesbian" in your classroom is finally merely a statement used to set a scene or create a context, not unlike "I am a farmboy" might introduce the autobiographical flourishes around the edges of your animal husbandry lecture, or "I am a Catholic" might be the natural, necessary preface to your story about the unique spin Sister Mary Ignatius put on the theory of original sin. You say it so that you can say something else. You say it because doing so allows you to say so many other things.

Was It As Good for You As It Was for Me?
Teachers and Students after the Fact

Nine out of ten lesbian teachers agree: coming out in the classroom feels good. The rush of energy we get from teaching well, the brisk step that a good class gives us as we leave our offices at the end of the day with all the reasons we chose this profession flooding back to us—that same exhilaration comes with coming out. When we allow the energy of our authentic selves, hard fought for and deep in us, to inform our teaching, our students rise to the challenge. Often, we are inspired by their willingness to follow us into the unexplored terrain where they have exiled their deep concerns about sexuality, gender, and difference. Your students will collaborate with you in exploring the complex of issues that coming out can raise. Still, some students may respond with types of resistance that will require pedagogical adjustments on your part.

The "native informant" problem. In a graduate seminar recently, a Korean-American friend was treated to a fellow student's use of the word "Jap" in an oral report. Each time the speaker used the word, the rest of the students and the teacher, all white, turned their eyes to our friend, waiting, we suspect, for her to object to his use of the word, as if the responsibility of objecting were uniquely hers. In another course, fellow students similarly deferred to her during class discussions of Maxine Hong Kingston. In both instances, she was experiencing the native informant problem, and one based on mistaken identity at that.

The only way that college classrooms are regularly and explicitly integrated is in terms of gender. For the teacher who is accustomed to meeting classes in which a single African American or Chinese American or Arab American sits among two dozen white students, the native informant problem is a familiar one. As teachers we work to keep students of color from becoming our class's native informant, from being asked to turn their individual racial or ethnic identities into a monolithic trope for the convenience of classmates. At the same time, we work to avoid effacing the particulars of their racial or ethnic experience by ignoring it, by turning to the easy conflation of equality with sameness that our culture's uneasiness about diversity makes readily available to us all, students and teachers alike. Still, while the native informant problem may be familiar to us, those among us who are white teachers may have little experience with being the native informant ourselves, especially if we are not yet out.

If you come out in your classroom, you will become a native informant. For some of your students you will be "the" lesbian professor, and every student's preconception, every gay-related issue in the media, every stereotype and misconception, will get stapled to you. If you're not careful, your desire to correct misconceptions, to address gay-related issues, may lead to your own uncomplicated acceptance of the native informant role.

Kate's failure to complicate for her students the issues surrounding her own native informant role became spectacularly clear to her several semesters ago, during a guest lecture by another lesbian teacher. This guest lecturer, who taught at a smaller university nearby, gave a brilliant presentation of the work of several lesbian poets. During the discussion section, she came out, but with a twist: "I am a lesbian and I teach at so-and-so university," she said. "But if you came up to me on my campus and said, 'Oh, I know you, you're the lesbian who read poems to us,' I would deny it to your face. I am not out on my campus because I cannot be." The lecturer's frank articulation of her own contradictory relation to her subject position as "lesbian teacher" helped keep the students in that classroom from making Kate the monolithic native informant after that.

The "I'm not gay so I wouldn't know" excuse.   Closely connected to the native informant problem is the opportunity it presents for students (especially straight students) to disavow their own intellectual responsibility for grappling with gay-related issues. For students eager to avoid hard thinking, a teacher's coming out can be considered either to completely compromise her authority on gay-related topics (obviously, a lesbian teacher must be unnaturally biased) or to increase it exponentially (she's the teacher and an actual lesbian—how could a straight student presume to contribute?). Either way, gay issues get pushed beyond the pale of intellectual analysis. Too personal, too foreign, or simply too controversial, they are considered by some students as unavailable to productive discussion. Our advice is to prove otherwise by presenting potentially problematic material and assignments as the reasonable, interesting, and integral aspects of the course that they are. If you engage those students who are willing to play, the others will come around.

The "I'm not hearing this" response. There are those who get it wrong, and then there are those who just don't get it. A couple of years ago, one of Kim's freshman composition students asked her what else she was teaching that semester. When she told him "a class on lesbian literature," he responded, "Man! How'd you get stuck with *that?*" Only after she explained that she had designed the course herself, inspired by her own interest in and familiarity with the subject, was this student able to entertain the possibility that his own English teacher might be a dyke.

We're not always so lucky. Kim, in fact, learned this lesson the hard way. In her first semester teaching, she did everything, she thought, except explicitly announce "I am a lesbian" to her class of twenty-five students. She dressed, walked, and sat in her usual manner; made reference to her "girlfriend"; assigned Adrienne Rich; and in general acted herself. A year later, a student from that inaugural class came out to her, and she—explicitly—to him. He explained how the class had been an eye-opening experience for him; he and others had even suspected that their instructor was gay. "I understand why you couldn't come out to us, though," he reassured her. "Don't worry. Just wondering about it was enough." Ouch! This strong and thoughtful young man would have made his own way regardless, but Kim could not forgive herself for leaving him and twenty-four other (straight—and gay?) students with the impression that their university was not a place where one could be out.

Coming out can take just a moment, but being out—in a way that empowers lesbian and gay students and asserts to straight ones the everyday actuality of lesbian existence—requires revisiting that revelation. Being out takes practice and intelligence. And like teaching, being out is work that must be rethought, revised, reconsidered. None of the suggestions we make here is made for all teachers in all situations for all time. In fact, we hope that in writing this essay we work to make such essays obsolete. By coming out on our barstools or behind our lecterns, we are making our presence felt where it is neither known nor welcome. We are pushing against people's nervousness about the conflict this country has always experienced when, in virtually every generation, a disenfranchised group has taken the Constitution literally and agitated for its civil and human rights. This lesson alone is worth teaching.

Notes

We write this essay, addressed to teachers, for the out gay students in our classrooms; their presence and their courage remind us of our own privilege and responsibilities— and, finally, of the cost of our silences.

We'd like to thank all the people who loaned us their coming-out stories and talked with us about this draft—especially Caroline Chung Simpson and Kathryn Baker. We'd also like to thank those lesbians who have written before us about coming out in the classroom. We refer interested readers to Sarah Hope Parmeter and Irene Reti, eds., *The Lesbian in Front of the Classroom* (Santa Cruz, CA: HerBooks, 1988), Margaret Cruikshank, ed., *Lesbian Studies: Present and Future* (New York: Feminist Press, 1982), and all the other essays in this book. We also acknowledge the editors of *The Alyson Almanac: A Treasure of Information for the Gay and Lesbian Community* (Boston: Alyson Publications, 1990), where we found our facts about Alan Turing and Peter Tchaikovsky.

5

Small-Group Pedagogy:
Consciousness Raising in Conservative
Times

Estelle B. Freedman

In the fall of 1988 I began teaching the introductory course in the feminist studies program at Stanford University. Introduction to Feminist Studies: Issues and Methods (FS101) had grown from a small discussion class to a medium-sized lecture course with separate section meetings for sixty-six students. The subject matter ranges from the origins of sexual inequality and the history of feminism to contemporary paid and unpaid labor, race and feminism, reproductive rights and sexuality, and violence against women. Because many of these topics raise both emotional and political sensitivities, I felt that FS101 required a forum in which students could discuss their personal reactions to classroom learning. Even more than the US women's history classes I had taught previously, Introduction to Feminist Studies permitted, and indeed necessitated, the integration of the personal and the academic.[1]

In preparing the course, I wondered how I might use consciousness raising (c.r.) in the classroom to achieve this end, and whether my 1970s experience of c.r. would work with the more conservative students of the late 1980s. By consciousness raising I mean the sharing of personal experience with others in order to understand the larger social context for the experience and to transform one's intellectual or political understanding of it. Once before, in a women's history class, I had experimented with the explicit use of c.r. in the classroom. On the day we discussed documents from the feminist movements of the 1960s and 1970s, I spontaneously turned the class into a consciousness-raising session. We formed a circle and spoke in turn about how one article or idea in the readings had affected each of us personally. The experi-

35

ment took over an entire week of the course, as students shared feelings of both anger and inspiration, revealed personal experiences with sexism on campus, and reacted to the differences that emerged in their views. The evaluations of the exercise were enthusiastic, so the next year I built a consciousness-raising session into the syllabus. Again, the students reported that they not only understood the historical experience of feminism more clearly, but that they made important connections between the past and the world around them.

In addition to this and other positive models, I had more defensive reasons for incorporating c.r. into the introductory course.[2] The preceding year, a hostile male student had tried unsuccessfully to disrupt FS101, and at the University of Washington, one male student had placed the entire women's studies program under attack by claiming that classes discriminated against men. I wanted to forestall such disruptions as much as possible by creating a place outside of the classroom where emotional responses might be shared with peers and not simply directed at faculty. Aside from hostile students, I worried about the feelings of alienation that students of minority race, class, ethnicity, sexual identity, or physical ability would experience in a predominantly white, middle-class, heterosexual, and able-bodied classroom.[3] Consciousness-raising groups might allow these students to acknowledge their feelings and make personal and intellectual connections between gender and other forms of social hierarchy.

To faculty who are veterans of 1970s women's studies classes, or who work in public universities or small liberal arts colleges committed to teaching, my rationale for incorporating consciousness raising into the classroom may seem unnecessary. But I work within an extremely elitist university in which pedagogy is rarely discussed and academic advancement depends almost exclusively on scholarship. At this university, opponents of the term "feminist studies" shudder at such a self-conscious reference to the political nature of knowledge and associate feminist scholarship with a political radicalism they consider anti-intellectual. Indeed, even a colleague at a feminist studies meeting reacted to my plans for setting up c.r. groups by warning that it was inappropriate and unprofessional for me to attempt to do "therapy" in my classes.[4] Students who signed up for FS101 arrived in a state of extreme fear of feminism. Most associated the term with an unpleasant militancy and refused to accept the label "feminist" even if they believed in the liberal goals of the movement.

In this setting, I feel that the use of c.r. has to be handled carefully not only for its pedagogical value but for the political well-being of the course and the program. Even on more liberal campuses, these conservative times might make faculty wary of the explicit use of consciousness-raising groups. I believe that now more than ever, however, we need to confront students' fears of feminism and of social change. As women's studies courses become part of general education and distribution requirements on many campuses, we can expect more conservative or nonfeminist students in our classes. From my experience teaching FS101, I believe that c.r. can be an extremely effective way to address the fear of feminism held by many of these students. This paper, then, is an effort to share my own and the students' experience with c.r. in the late 1980s in order to encourage the careful incorporation of personal experience into academic classes wherever this might be appropriate.

With advice from feminist colleagues, I devised a structure for making c.r. central to FS101. Required biweekly group meetings supplemented an already demanding course—three lectures, heavy reading, a discussion section weekly, and three papers during the quarter.[5] Thus, to make clear from the outset that the groups were not extracurricular but integral to the process of learning, I spelled out on the syllabus the rules for attendance and the format of sessions; and I stressed the importance of a final paper evaluating the groups. On the recommendation of several colleagues, this paper would not be graded, lest students feel judged for either their emotions or their politics. Knowing Stanford students' sensitivities about language and politics, I called the process "small groups." Although I referred to consciousness raising in my lectures, students continued to speak of their "small groups" rather than "c.r. groups."

The major dilemma I faced, however, was not about naming, but whether to create random groups that would mix students from various backgrounds or to create minority support groups—for women or students of color, lesbians and/or lesbians and gay men, disabled, male, ethnic, or working-class students. As much as I wanted to diminish minority alienation, I felt that it was more important for each group to confront the issues of difference with as much firsthand information as possible. In addition, many students had multiple or overlapping identities; constructing separate groups would force them to choose only one basis of support. For these reasons, the groups were formed by a random sorting of names into thirteen sets of four or five students each. (I hoped that the small size, compared to discussion sections of up to twenty-one students, would make scheduling easier, allow students to meet in a dorm room, and help to build friendships.) Each group had to meet five times during the ten-week quarter, for a session lasting about two hours, at a time to be arranged by group members.

I assigned readings for the first session only: Pam Allen's "Free Space" and Irene Peslikis's "Resistances to Consciousness."[6] I also recommended a rotating timekeeper, leaderless groups, and an uninterrupted five to ten minutes for each member to speak at the outset of sessions. Suggested topics paralleled the syllabus and attempted to link course readings and lectures with everyday life. "How does your personal experience of race, class, and ethnicity affect your response to what you are learning?" followed the lecture on race and feminism and coincided with a required "unlearning racism" workshop.[7] When we studied women and work, the suggested question asked students to relate readings and lectures to jobs, families, and campus life. I left one week open for student topics and closed with a question to parallel our reading of Marge Piercy's utopian novel *Women on the Edge of Time:* "What one thing would you most want to change about our current world?" Students were asked to keep private journals after groups but not to submit them. The final paper evaluating the groups was to draw heavily upon the journal.[8]

During the quarter, several incidents on campus, in the community, and in the classroom intensified the importance of c.r. and expanded it beyond the groups and into the lecture sessions. On campus, two white students posted racist slurs in the Afro-American theme house, igniting a year-long debate over the action and the administration's response, and heightening awareness of racism. Then, against the backdrop of the Bush-Dukakis campaign, a few antiabortion activists mobilized conservative women to join Operation Rescue's blockade of local abortion clinics, while campus feminists formed a prochoice alliance. Within the classroom, students responded to the readings on lesbian feminism with such a profound silence that I felt compelled to challenge their homophobia. Borrowing a technique from a colleague at an even more conservative university, I asked students to write hypothetical "coming out letters" to their parents, drawing on their readings about lesbianism and homophobia.[9] At the same time, the students' presumption of their instructor's heterosexuality made me extremely uncomfortable about passing as straight and raised my own consciousness to the point that for the first time I came out in a classroom as a lesbian.

Thus for me, as well as for the students, FS101 took unexpected turns. On two occasions, for example, students raised my consciousness about issues that personally affected them. First, shortly before my lecture on sexual violence, I received a call from an incest survivor in the course who had been distressed by the lack of reading on incest. I asked her permission to discuss the call, anonymously, in class, and used the episode to talk about my own preconceptions about violence.[10] Secondly, in anticipation of the lecture on women and food, a student volunteered to speak about her own struggles with anorexia and bulimia. Her moving, expert presentation provided both personal testimony and information about support groups on campus. Inspired by her offer, I invited other students in the class to speak about their personal involvement in issues we studied. Members of the Rape Education Project did so, and since no students came out in the lecture class, I invited representatives from the Gay and Lesbian Alliance to speak on available student support services.

Meanwhile, students managed the small groups independently. Every other week I asked for feedback on the groups during lecture. Although students made few concrete comments at the time, they suggested that the groups were going well and were important to them. Only at the end of the course, after I read the set of sixty-six papers describing and evaluating the groups, did I realize how critical they had been to the educational process. Several students felt that the groups were as important as the class itself; for some, they were "the best part," and for at least one, "the most personally enriching part of the class."[11] Not every group, however, succeeded in establishing a sense of purpose and facilitating growth. Several groups had difficulty finding meeting times or sharing personal experiences; their members felt disappointed when they compared their experiences with those of the majority of students. Generally though, papers from eleven of the thirteen groups testified to the power of the small groups for enhancing student understanding of issues raised in class and for contributing to both self-understanding and greater understanding of others.

As they did for second-wave feminists of the 1960s and 1970s, c.r. groups in FS101 functioned to move students from silence to speech, from isolation to community, and sometimes from political ambivalence to political commitment. Once empowered to explore ideas and feelings, a number of students were able to confront personal dilemmas, especially those concerning sexuality and race. As a result, their definitions of feminism expanded. By the end of the course, the majority of students reported that they had shifted from discomfort with feminism to enthusiastic embrace of the term and its complexity. A few made commitments to political activism. One small group continued meeting throughout the year to support the feminist activism of its members. [. . .][12]

Reflecting the feminist politics of the 1980s, when women of color moved feminism from its white, middle-class focus to a more inclusive political worldview, FS101 attempted to emphasize the intersections of race and gender inequality. Along with the readings on race and feminism, the unlearning racism workshop and campus incidents made race and racism highly charged topics within the class. Small groups offered a potential space for understanding racial difference and patterns of domination. The demographic composition of the groups, however, strongly influenced the tone and depth of their discussions of race. Because three-quarters of the students were white, minorities were either absent or rare in small groups. Predictably, all-white groups had the least insightful discussions; highly unbalanced groups placed the burden of education on the single minority student; and highly mixed groups had the most valuable sessions on race.

The all-white groups tended to focus on the shared experiences of women and on nonracial differences between members. A man in one of these groups regretted its racial composition. Although he enjoyed the comfort and intimacy of his group, he realized that it "felt more like a womb than a coalition," in the terms of Bernice Johnson Reagon's article "Coalition Politics: Turning the Century," which was included in the course reading.[13] Had the group been more diverse, he felt, members would have been forced to deal with differences in other ways. Often, these groups sought ways to resolve their discomfort over white privilege, with some interesting results. For instance, one white student used the concept of "simultaneous oppression" in her own way. Rather than referring to the multiple and simultaneous oppression of women of color (by gender, class, and race), she took the term to mean that white women were both oppressed and oppressors. With this interpretation, she identified through her gender with subordinate groups, while she accepted responsibility for her position of racial dominance.

For both mixed and all-white groups, the themes of white guilt and feelings of helplessness recurred in the papers.[14] White students in a mixed group felt immobilized by the realization, as one wrote, that "at one time in our lives we are all the oppressor." "Our group teeters on the brink of an intellectual abyss," she wrote of the unsatisfactory conclusion. "We say nice things to each other and depart." Or as the one black member of the group put it, the white women "all admitted to feeling guilty for being white." As another white member acknowledged, recognizing difference within feminism "was really very eye-opening and made some of us feel as though we had been pretty spoiled and blind." Similarly, a white woman in another group commented after listening to a Chicana describe the dual effects of racism and sexism: "It was hard for the white people in our group to accept that we would never be able to truly identify with the minority women's experience."

The racial imbalance in mixed groups placed a special burden of explanation on black, Asian-American, and Chicana members. "It seemed that [x] and I, who were the two people of color in our group," wrote one man, "did most of the talking on the subject of racism." The woman to whom he referred illustrated the educator role when the group discussed Betty Friedan's attitude toward housework. Other students, she explained, "felt sorry for housewives," but since her own mother had been on welfare and then struggled in a service job, she longed for "my mom to be a housewife and to live in a house like the 'Brady Bunch.' " The man in the group shared with her "the alienation minority children feel when they are taught by the media to value a white, middle-class lifestyle over their own."

[. . .]

The most successful discussions of race—that is, the ones that elicited deep responses, as well as conflicts—occurred in the most diverse groups. A group with two minority women, two white women, and one white man achieved a degree of safety in discussing difference and racism. As the Chicana member wrote, the group "seemed to me to be a microcosm of the feminist movement—where people work for many of the same goals for differing reasons." Having made her " 'foreign' experiences and ideas accessible to people through small group," she now felt ready to "move to this next stage of a potentially more hostile environment" in the world at large.

[. . .]

These episodes reflected the dilemmas of mixed groups. On the one hand, these groups did most to educate white students and sometimes helped alleviate their guilt. In the process, they risked relying on students of color as racial educators who explained differences among women, rather than addressing the deep personal and structural barriers to race equality. On the other hand, the few minority students in these groups learned a great deal about white attitudes toward race and how these attitudes affect them personally. Given the race and class stratification of our society, students of color will no doubt confront these views throughout their lives; small groups can serve as testing grounds for clarifying their responses. Overall, the racially mixed groups worked at identifying the dilemmas of difference better than the all-white groups; but they would have been even more effective if they had a greater proportion of students of color. That way the minority students would feel less isolated and less targeted as racial educators. At a more racially mixed campus, or in a course with greater minority enrollment, groups could go even further in raising consciousness about racism. In this setting, mixed groups can go only so far toward exploring the relationship between gender and racial inequality.

Whatever progress the lesbian and gay movement has made since the 1970s, for most Stanford students, lesbianism remains a frightening topic. In signing up for FS101, a woman student risked being labeled, in the words of one, as "the feminist dyke." Or, as another woman told her group, she "felt funny because people who knew she was taking the class would think of her as a lesbian." The association of feminism with lesbianism ran deep among students who brought to the class strong prejudices about homosexuality. Several expressed their religious opposition to gay sex, or, in response to viewing the film *Choosing Children,* to lesbians or gay men raising children. Even liberal students wanted to distance themselves from homosexuality by defending feminists against the label of lesbianism.

Not surprisingly, the coming out letter challenged the class enormously and proved to be "harder than we had thought." Everyone expressed discomfort about doing the assignment. Students who had thought they were tolerant of lesbians and gay men found themselves hiding the assignment from roommates; some wrote " 'Fem-Stud Assignment' across the top in big letters," in case friends passed by as they wrote. In the words of one student, we "were continually worried that somebody was going to look over our shoulder and misinterpret what we had written."

The small group following the letter-writing assignment was, for many, "by far the most tense of the quarter." One of the most highly political groups seemed to spend little time discussing the letters. One member was reportedly "speechless" and "couldn't imagine how others managed to do it." Another woman became "very depressed" writing hers, and for telling reasons: "I knew my parents would go off on another fit, and that once again I had to face the fact that their love and financial support is conditional." Fear of parental disapproval loomed large in the discussions and helps explain the tone of so many of the letters, well summarized by a freshman who wrote critically that several members of his group had made "a total emotional plea to their parents telling them of their misfortune and asking for acceptance." The members of another group "all agreed that it took a while to finally get around to actually saying 'I am lesbian' "—a term that many letters avoided altogether.

However difficult, the exercise, and especially the group discussion of it, brought home the depth and the costs of homophobia. "If we feared so much that someone might find our letter, did that indicate that we were homophobic?" The discussion of the letters led another group to realize that "by denying our feelings of homophobia, we were only perpetuating them." It also helped to undermine homophobic responses. During the discussion of hiding the assignment, for example, one woman "gradually realized that my fear of being stereotyped wrongly had greatly diminished since the beginning of the course."

For other students, the assignment brought homosexual feelings to the surface. The group discussion forced one man to "think about my own homophobic fears—did I harbor those feelings because being homosexual is not being a man?" Another group asked the question "Have you ever thought about being homosexual?" which produced "some defensive reactions." At least one woman admitted to the thought but found that she could not "envision a sexual relationship" with another woman. In response to the question, another woman contemplated her unsatisfactory relationships with men and wondered if she might be lesbian. At that point, she recalled, "Two of the other members looked like they thought I was going to come out right then and there and didn't know what to do, and the other member looked grateful that I had responded to her question honestly, and did seem to sincerely understand my confusion at the time." The speaker found it a "rewarding moment" because she was not ostracized for her honesty or her suspicions about her sexuality.

If the coming out assignment created the most tension, it also seemed to have had the most consciousness-raising effect. In one group, a woman who had recently "stopped identifying . . . as heterosexual" rated this session as the "best meeting" because it "produced the most consciousness raising." Other members (a straight man and two straight women) agreed that it was the "most rewarding," in part because the letter gave a "concrete experience" about which to relate feelings and "a bonding experience" for students who struggled with the assignment. In several groups, attitudes toward coming out seemed to have changed for many students. One group member "concluded that many more people would come out if there weren't such a stigma in society. We admired those who are strong enough to."

Only two students came out in their groups. In one case, a gay man was relieved to find that he was "among pretty gay-sensitive people." The group later turned to him to tell them what was and what was not "offensive" in their behaviors and whether their fear of having their coming-out letters seen constituted homophobia. Accepting the educator role, he both criticized and reassured his peers. "We all sort of agreed," he wrote, "that this was another form of homophobia but acknowledged, too, that individuals are forced to make choices under duress in a deeply homophobic society." In another group, a woman catalogued the responses when she "told the group that I am a lesbian": "Unfortunately, the person who I expected to have a negative reaction had to go to a funeral. . . . One seemed unimpressed. . . . One asked me what lesbians looked like, was obviously uncomfortable, but made a very noble attempt to pretend that she wasn't, and the other felt very comfortable and proceeded to ask me lots of questions." The discussion shifted when this same student also revealed that she was an incest survivor and explained that she was not alone among Stanford students. Group members, she reported, "were more shocked by this than the lesbianism, and had a hard time dealing with it. . . . As for myself, I didn't think I could deal with talking about either subject without being honest about it. I also felt I owed to other lesbians and to other incest survivors to speak out." In the small-group setting, she was able to do so.

Just as all-white groups had more superficial discussions of race, the overwhelmingly heterosexual groups often began with the question of homosexuality but soon moved to the general topic of sexuality and relationships. In two of the women-only groups, the coming out discussion turned to comparable fears of rejection or exposure among straight people. "Just as gay people are expected to be ashamed of their sexuality, fat women are supposed to view their weight as a transitory state," explained one student. Another group moved from discussing lesbians' fear of rejection by their families to memories of their own childhood rejections by other girls and the lasting fear of being different. The parallels gave them insight into homophobia in the absence of firsthand accounts from lesbian or gay male students.

I was surprised by how few lesbian and gay male students either took this class or came out in it; fear of disclosure by association with feminism may have kept them away or in the closet. Nonetheless, the predominantly straight groups learned more about homophobia than they had expected, in large part due to the letter-writing assignment. Despite their resistance, once students tried on a homosexual identity, they had at least a glimpse of the firsthand experience that was missing in most groups. Forced to identify with the sexual minority, students seemed to confront their homophobia more personally, and with less guilt, than they confronted their racism. Thus, although the presence of minority students within groups did not necessarily raise consciousness dramatically, an assignment that encouraged personal identification with minority vulnerability had strong potential to do so.

During the first lecture of the quarter, before I distributed the syllabus, I had asked each student to write a paragraph or two about how they defined and reacted to the term "feminist." The overwhelming majority of the class described the goals of liberal feminism positively, but they found the label "feminist" too frightening to adopt for themselves. At the beginning of the small groups, students addressed these feelings. "All of us stereotype a feminist negatively," one black woman explained, "that is, as a militant person." Or, as one student summarized the reaction to feminists voiced by each member of her small group: they "hated men," "did not want to appear attractive," and "were radical and rebellious."

In analyzing their prejudices in class discussion, many students credited the media with shaping their image of angry, militant feminists. I would add that Stanford's student culture not only emphasizes the importance of being attractive to the opposite sex, but also encourages conformity to a model of self-satisfaction (the "no one has problems at Stanford" syndrome, as a counseling center flier labels it). In this atmosphere, political rebelliousness—especially when it addresses personal issues rather than, say, US foreign policy—can be dismissed as a sign of personal failure.

[. . .]

I sensed from the student papers that the small groups were perhaps the most critical element in the process of unlearning earlier stereotypes. "I used to think that all feminists were either lesbians or militant man-hating women," wrote an Asian-American woman. "After taking this class, I am proud to say that I am a feminist and I also do not hesitate to inform others of my feminist views and beliefs." Similarly, another woman confessed that "I'm quite sure that I wrote one of the least flattering definitions of and reactions to feminism at the beginning of the quarter," and that she "would certainly never have said that I was a feminist." During the course she had adopted a definition of feminism that made her able to identify with the term: "a feminist recognizes differences between men and women, but does not always value either male or female attributes and qualities more than the other." She concluded her paper by embracing a new identity: "Now all I have to do to know how I respond to the word feminist is to look in the mirror and see someone whom I respect and like very much." One male student shifted from "a negative gut reaction" to a positive one: "I now consider myself a feminist, which I hadn't even considered before the class." Or, as another man reported, "for the first time, I openly consider myself a feminist—with pride."

The disappearance of defensive reactions to feminism recurred as a final theme in the small-group papers. [. . .] The final paragraph of a paper typically spoke of pride and even joy in the student's transformation into a feminist:

> When I see the word "feminist," I feel like celebrating and crying at the same time. I feel a sadness because I know that many people will react to it negatively. . . . I also respond with a feeling of happiness because I know that through education, the incredible ideas of feminism have and will break through the negative stereotype. . . .
>
> Now, when I see or hear the word feminist I invariably respond positively. I feel a bond with the person it is directed toward, and proudly feel a renewed women-centered identity.
>
> When I hear the word feminist, I think: this is a person I want to get to know.
>
> To be sure, when I see or hear the word feminist, I respond with a proud, warm, connective feeling. I myself am a feminist and it's nice to know that I have sisters and brothers who are the same.

Students from several groups echoed this last student's historical insight: "I now understand why feminist consciousness-raising groups in the 1970s were so effective in generating women's energies."

While most students claimed a greater willingness to identify as feminists, to themselves or to others, and a more complex definition of feminist constituencies and goals, others addressed the limits of their politics. Unlike the generation that initially adopted c.r. in an era when radicalism was fashionable, today's students shy away from any taint of political rebelliousness. "Even after having taken this class," a woman wrote, "I have yet to conquer my enduring uneasiness with the word 'feminist.' . . . I do still feel a deep and vague discomfort with the word . . . and continue to have difficulty saying 'I am a feminist' " because of the connotation of "radicalism, rebelling, and a touch of 'man-hating' that I am not yet able to accept or overcome."

In a different way, other students expressed how, by the end of the course, they had become acutely aware of their political limitations. As one woman of color reported of her group, "Each of us were entrenched in our inner conflict about our own capitalistic desires and urges." The most frequent conflict women addressed concerned standards of beauty. "We agreed that since taking this class we have often felt like complete hypocrites as we put on our makeup," one white woman revealed of her group. "I grapple with my difficulty of redefining beauty," wrote another woman, "perhaps I need to accept my silly definitions of beauty as dictated by the society I live in." The challenge of differentiating between the messages of the culture and their own beliefs confounded this woman's group, as it did other feminists of the 1980s. The free classroom copies of *Ms.* magazine drove home the point—today's political feminism came packaged with contradictory messages extolling traditional femininity and consumer capitalism.[15]

Whatever the limitations of student political consciousness, this experiment in the use of small-group, personally based learning proved even more rewarding than I had anticipated. I agreed with the student who wrote that, while she "expected these consciousness-raising sessions to change each of us, the rate and degree to which it occurred surprised and inspired me." Small groups had clearly played an important role in allowing internal, emotional shifts to occur gradually in students who had been resistant to feminism. Although the purpose of the groups was to enhance classroom learning and not necessarily to achieve political conversion, the two seemed to happen simultaneously. The intellectual challenge of readings, discussions, and papers certainly contributed to the process, but c.r. provided something that traditional academic work could not: a safe space for discussing personal difference and connecting these differences to gender inequality. Given the complexity of feminist identity that emerged in the 1980s, as well as the negative stereotypes of feminists that persist among students, c.r. offers a unique method for learning the very things feminism espouses.

Finally, in addition to emphasizing the importance of c.r. as a form of pedagogy and urging its adoption in other classes, I want to credit the students in this course with making c.r. work. Those who were willing simply to enroll in FS101 at a campus that was generally hostile to feminism had to be exceptional students. Revealing their own fears of feminism, their anger and guilt about racism, and their discomfort with homosexuality took courage and entailed risks. The requirement of attending c.r. groups may have motivated change, but the students themselves made possible the personal and political growth that their papers document. For a feminist teacher, their learning has been an inspiration and a source of faith that feminism will survive, even in these conservative times.

Notes

Reprinted with permission of Ablex Publishing Corporation.

1. In planning this course, I benefited especially from the experience of my colleague Jane Collier (Anthropology), who had previously taught FS101, and from my two graduate teaching assistants, Lisa Hogeland (Modern Thought and Literature) and Kevin Mumford (History). I thank them, along with the following other members of the feminist community at Stanford, for their responses to this paper: Laura Carstensen, John Dupre, Mary Felstiner, Regenia Gagnier, Patricia Gumport, Margo Horn, Susan Krieger, Diane Middlebrook, Adrienne Rich, Alice Supton, and Sylvia Yanagisako.

2. Two experiences outside my own classroom influenced my use of c.r. in FS101. I learned a great deal from sociologist Susan Krieger's example when she successfully incorporated small groups in a class of conservative prebusiness students. Her students wrote self-reflective papers about small-group dynamics, rooted in personal experience. If such groups could work with these students, the groups seemed to have great potential for feminist studies. Another model was an unlearning racism workshop I had attended at the Stanford women's center some years earlier, facilitated by the late Ricky Sherover-Marcuse. In order to require such a workshop of all FS101 students, the feminist studies program hired an experienced facilitator to conduct workshops for members of this class.

3. Of the sixty-six students who took this course for credit (not counting auditors), 74 percent were white and 26 percent black, Asian, or Chicana. Men constituted 17 percent of the entire class, 12 percent of minorities, and 18 percent of whites. Students tended to identify themselves in terms of race and gender. Similarly, in this paper I refer to students by gender and race, unless a student has indicated another identity.

4. On earlier resistance to the use of consciousness raising by women's studies faculty, and for a review of the theoretical basis for c.r. in the classroom, see Renate D. Klein, "The Dynamics of the Women's Studies Classroom: A Review Essay of the Teaching Practice of Women's Studies in Higher Education," *Women's Studies International Forum* 10:2 (1987): esp. 189–93.

5. I assigned the following readings: Johnetta Cole, ed., *All American Women: Lines That Divide, Ties That Bind* (New York: Free Press, 1986); Emily Honig and Gail Hershatter, eds., *Personal Voices: Chinese Women in the 1980s* (Stanford, CA:

Stanford University Press, 1988); Buchi Emecheta, *The Joys of Motherhood* (New York: George Braziller, 1979); Virginia Woolf, *Three Guineas* (1938; reprint, New York: Harcourt 1963); Marge Piercy, *Woman on the Edge of Time* (New York: Fawcett Crest, 1976); Alison Jaggar and Paula Rothenberg, eds., *Feminist Frameworks: Alternative Theoretical Accounts of the Relations between Women and Men* (New York: McGraw-Hill, 1984); and a thick course reader.

6. Pamela Allen, "Free Space," in *Radical Feminism*, ed. Anne Koedt, Ellen Levine, and Anita Rapone (New York: Quadrangle, 1973), 271–79; Irene Peslikis, "Resistances to Consciousness," in *Sisterhood Is Powerful*, ed. Robin Morgan (New York: Vintage Books, 1970), 379–81.

7. In this three-hour workshop, an experienced facilitator helped students to explore their personal class, race, and ethnic backgrounds and to dispel unconscious stereotypes about various groups. The workshop attempted to affirm the value of difference, address the costs of discrimination, and create a nonjudgmental space for students to acknowledge the racial fears and misinformation they had acquired in the past. Ideally, the students should attend a series of workshops, but because of time and budget limitations, the small-group meeting served as a follow-up to reinforce the workshop.

8. Despite my effort to make the group meetings required, several papers complained of members who appeared irregularly, because it seemed "almost like a luxury— and when it comes to a clash between 'real' classwork ... and therapeutic classwork, it's hard to break the Stanford mold and take the ungraded activity seriously." Evaluation papers suggested that attendance would improve if I scheduled group meeting times rather than leaving it to students. They also complained about the rigid format I outlined and convinced me that in the future the groups could determine their own process and discussion topics. After the second year of teaching this course with c.r. groups, I have decided that it is essential to structure the meeting times into the course schedule in advance. Doing so would be especially important for nonresidential schools, where it is even more difficult for students to find informal meeting times and places.

9. John D'Emilio constructed this exercise at the University of North Carolina-Greensboro, and it has been used by several other faculty members around the country. Several students discussed their letters with parents. One of my favorite responses was from the mother of a straight son; the son called to say he was writing a coming out letter to her, "hypothetically real," and wondered what she would say if he sent it. Her reply: "The same I said when you went to college: Always use a condom." I am grateful to such mothers for sending their daughters and sons to my classes.

10. After the lecture, which did discuss the problem of incest, two other incest survivors identified themselves to me privately, and one suggested readings for the next year. From this experience I learned about the importance of making sensitive topics visible on the syllabus in advance and not only in the lecture class.

11. In quoting from the student papers, I have corrected typographical errors but have left grammar and punctuation intact. Students did sign the papers, so they may have had an interest in presenting a positive evaluation of the groups in order to please the instructor. The papers, however, did not affect grades, and many students

offered criticisms about the structure or timing of groups, alongside their reflections on how groups influenced them.

12. Editor's note: A longer version of this essay appeared in *NWSA Journal* 2:4 (Autumn 1990): 603–23. Bracketed ellipses indicate editing for *Tilting the Tower*.

13. Bernice Johnson Reagon, "Coalition Politics: Turning the Century," in *Home Girls: A Black Feminist Anthology,* ed. Barbara Smith (New York: Kitchen Table Press, 1983), 356–68.

14. For example, a white woman who missed the meeting on race in her mixed group wrote: "I suppose I could have talked about the white guilt everyone tells me is not healthy to have but that I have anyway. I just don't understand why I can go to Stanford while other people are starving."

15. Editor's note: In the late 1980s, *Ms.* magazine still included advertisements. The new *Ms.* does not.

6

The Pocahontas Paradigm, or
Will the Subaltern Please Shut Up?

Maia Ettinger

An interesting thing often happens when people of color or queers speak up in class: everyone else feels silenced. I am tempted to define "everyone else" as most straight white people. In this case, however, race and sex categories are both over- and underinclusive. "Everyone else" really means People Lacking an Agenda (PLAs), people whose interest in race, class, and gender is grounded in something other than the need to survive in an alien culture and/or to assess in good faith their own position in the multiple systems of subordination that constitute the culture.

I have seen PLAs before. After a 1982 lecture by Barbara Smith at Yale's Afro-American Cultural Center, PLAs shot their hands up to express how excluded they felt because Smith's lecture, while broad in scope, clearly was addressed first and foremost to the women of color in the room. PLAs get sulky and petulant when traditionally marginalized people take the floor. What a remarkable sense of entitlement must drive their willingness to assert their experience of exclusion! If I wanted to raise my hand every time I felt excluded, I would have to glue my wrist to the top of my head. Yet in the few instances where a relatively multicultural environment should provide some respite—such as graduate-level class discussions revolving around race and gender—tensions inevitably soar as PLA anxiety surfaces.

Both classroom dynamics and broader theoretical concerns regarding communication among cultures must be examined to make fruitful the current trend toward an inclusive academy. It cannot be assumed, for example, that every participant in a diversely populated classroom is equally equipped to discuss race, gender, class, or sexual orientation on either a practical or a theoretical level. I would venture to say that in classes where such discussions regularly arise, the balance of "equipment" tends to tilt away from inhabitants of the mainstream. Not because people of color or queers boast superior intellectual faculties, but because, as marginalized people, we know a lot more about our situation than do PLAs, and—for once—our situation is central to the discourse.

The role of critical theory deserves special attention when contemplating the confrontation between PLAs and the unsilent Other. As I will discuss later, an unguarded affinity for theory is often a presenting symptom of PLA anxiety. When I express concern over the inaccessibility of most critical theory, over what Barbara Christian describes as "the sheer ugliness of the language, its lack of clarity, its unnecessarily complicated sentence constructions, its lack of pleasurableness, its alienated quality," academics usually justify its density and obfuscation as arising from the complicated nature of the issues it addresses.[1] I will grant that race, class, gender, and queerness are complicated issues. However, I suspect that the complications arising as the academy begins to grapple with the epistemological dimensions of oppression are as emotional as they are intellectual. While these emotional complications are many and varied, I would like to focus on one dynamic that arose repeatedly during my recent sojourn in graduate school. I call it the Pocahontas Paradigm.

Peter Hulme observes that a major feature of the Pocahontas myth is the ideal of cultural harmony through romance.[2] This ideal is systematically instilled in white North Americans through, among other things, the annual Thanksgiving Pageant. Year after year, a little white boy in a Pilgrim hat and buckled shoes clasps hands on stage with a girl in a leather dress with fringes. Little John Smith, who has ventured into uncharted territory populated by an unfamiliar Other, is rescued by a girl in braids whose spontaneous, unsolicited love transcends his foreignness and his whiteness and drives her to protect him from the more threatening elements among her own people.

No one seems particularly surprised that the sight of a white man under attack should awaken such a passion in Pocahontas; indeed, the myth of Pocahontas is concurrently the myth of John Smith's entitlement to protection. When his psyche is at risk, when the clubs of an alien consciousness are posed and ready to put a dent in his head, Pocahontas is guaranteed to intervene. The crux of the Pocahontas Paradigm is the promise of aid and comfort from the Other: cultural and racial harmony are accomplished not because John Smith makes any effort to redefine his own position in a new and unknown world, but because Pocahontas volunteers to bridge the gap with love. Her love not only reconfirms his desirable superiority, but implicitly absolves him of guilt over the impending genocide of her people.

The saga of the first settlers is reenacted today as members of the academy set sail into the uncharted waters that lie beyond the dominant discourse. While excitement and intellectual stimulation mark the genuinely radical discovery of a world in which traditional structures of status and knowledge are dismantled, alarm and disorientation also set in when a comfortable sense of self, situated in a familiar landscape, dissolves beneath scholars' feet. The world they are trepidatiously discovering is not, of course, uninhabited. The dominant discourse has never been home to people of color, queers, or those who combine racial and sexual otherness. As Angela Harris has written, "black women have had to learn to construct themselves in a society that denied them full selves."[3] Similarly, in order to claim an identity free of self-loathing, gay and lesbian people have created discursive strategies that reject and transform the categories produced by a hostile and hegemonic heterosexual discourse. Thus, my compass is calibrated by my need to speak, act, and love. My map charts the course for my survival.

People Lacking an Agenda also lack a map. As the direction of classroom discussions prompts meaningful participation by people whose experience lies outside the dominant discourse, as subordinated people generate a discourse which implicitly or explicitly critiques the established order of the classroom, PLAs begin to lose themselves, and the Pocahontas Paradigm erupts. I have heard complaints that the people of color in a certain class were trying to make everyone else feel guilty: "Can't we move beyond our differences? Can't we find some common ground? This is too depressing. Surely we can bridge the gap." We must question, however, for whose comfort the common ground is to be laid. Cultural harmony on whose behalf, accomplished by whom? It is worth remembering that the groundbreaking collection of writings by radical women of color is titled *This Bridge Called My Back*.

Queers are also subject to the Pocahontas Paradigm. Overhearing a comment made to me about how homophobia got little attention in a class about the politics of subordination, a fellow student grabbed my arm, smiled brilliantly, and said, "Oh yes, you should definitely bring that up! I'm just dying to discuss my fear of lesbians with you!" However great her fear of me and my kind, her sense of entitlement to my attention apparently outweighed it. Another classmate told me she felt too guilty to talk about oppression at all. Well, guilt is like that—paralyzing and immobilizing. As such, guilt is a convenient way to claim powerlessness in the face of responsibility. White people are responsible for racism, and benefit from it. Straight people are responsible for homophobia, and benefit from it. To take responsibility is to find your footing in the world outside the dominant discourse. To take responsibility is to acquire an agenda, and leave the legacy of John Smith behind.

Actually, the Pocahontas Paradigm is a relatively benign manifestation of PLA anxiety. The other PLA phenomenon I wish to address concerns theory, or rather, a certain attitude about theory. All theory, by its nature, stands at a distance from its subject. Postmodern discourse, with its extremely specialized vocabulary and its self-referential tendency toward criticism of criticism of criticism, turns this distance into a chasm. As a result, a purportedly progressive endeavor such as colonial-discourse theory—aimed, in the words of Edward Said, at ending "dominating, coercive systems of knowledge"—lacks a practical relationship to the masses of people whose lives and identities are directly burdened by these very systems.[4] While this distance may indeed reflect the complexity of the critical task at hand, it also reinforces the academy's stubborn refusal to confront the disorderly specificity of oppression as it operates in the world. If the Pocahontas Paradigm represents one response to the anxiety and disorientation produced when the Other speaks, the PLA's uncritical and possessive approach to theory represents the correlating response: namely, a refusal to hear what the Other is actually saying.

In classrooms and at conferences where critical theory figures centrally, people who raise concerns regarding the alienation, exclusion, and inaccessibility produced by theory often are met with impatience, condescension, and contempt nearing brutality. The academy's inexcusable complacency regarding the inaccessibility of theory is predicated on the assumption that people outside the academy, and especially subordinated peoples, have no significant relationship to the theoretical realm.

In fact, as bell hooks suggests, "theory is not an alien sphere" to the oppressed.[5] First, as I have previously suggested, the development of an identity at odds with the dominant discourse requires and generates a high degree of creative abstract thought on the part of both individuals and groups. As Ntozake Shange has written, "bein alive & bein a woman & bein colored is a metaphysical dilemma."[6] Second, communities that cannot rely on the state to regulate their internal

conduct often develop alternative institutions and systems of knowledge in response to such predicaments as a unilaterally hostile police
presence that protects no one or, in the case of gays and lesbians, the
absence of state-sanctioned mechanisms for validating, formalizing,
and regulating sexual and familial relationships.

In addition, communities engaged in struggles for liberation need
access to theory. Contrary to the prevailing assumption that our cher-
ished epistemological complexities need no popular dissemination, the
systems of knowledge addressed by critical theory often have direct
bearing on people's lives. To give but one example, epistemic violence
is more than a colorful phrase to thousands of gay and lesbian teenagers
who commit suicide at three times the national average. The absolute
hegemony of heterosexual discourse produces an understanding of
same-sex desire that, to paraphrase Said, is governed not by empirical
reality but by a battery of heterosexual desires, repressions, invest-
ments, and projections.[7] Internalized by the vulnerable adolescent
mind, this vicious and dehumanizing system of ideas suffocates the
healthy development of identity, leaving nothing but hopelessness in
its wake. The gay and lesbian community's need to understand the
operation of this system in all its complexities speaks for itself.

The need for dialogue both within the classroom and with the outside
world is, I hope, equally self-evident. Diversity and multiculturalism
will mean very little unless we are willing to locate ourselves within
the systems currently under deconstruction, and commit to examining
and unmasking the mechanisms that perpetuate silence, distance, and
epistemic violence at home and abroad.

Notes

1. Barbara Christian, "The Race for Theory," in Gloria Anzaldúa, ed., *Making Face, Making Soul/Haciendo Caras: Creative and Critical Perspectives by Women of Color* (San Francisco: Aunt Lute, 1990), 339.

2. Peter Hulme, *Colonial Encounters: Europe and the Native Caribbean, 1492–1797* (London: Methuen, 1986).

3. Angela Harris, "Race and Essentialism in Feminist Legal Theory," *Stanford Law Review* 42 (1990): 613.

4. Edward Said, "Orientalism Reconsidered," *Europe and Its Others,* vol. 1, Proceed-ings of the Essex Conference on the Sociology of Literature, University of Essex, 1985, 23.

5. bell hooks, *Yearning: Race, Gender, and Cultural Politics* (Boston: South End Press, 1990).

6. Ntozake Shange, *for colored girls who have considered suicide when the rainbow is enuf* (New York: Macmillan, 1977), 45.

7. Edward Said, *Orientalism* (New York: Vintage, 1978), 8.

7

Cultural Conflict: Introducing the Queer in Mexican-American Literature Classes

María C. González

Recently one of my students complimented me for having the courage to teach an author who is an out lesbian. I responded with a simple thank you, and yet I remained puzzled as to whether or not there really was anything courageous in my syllabus. I had included Gloria Anzaldúa's *Borderlands/La Frontera* in my Mexican-American literature class, a junior-level course in the English department at the University of Houston. The response from my students was consistent; most were quietly shocked. For many of them, my course was the first time they had come into contact with the concept that lesbianism is something other than a sin.

To understand their response, one needs to understand some simple demographics. The University of Houston is approximately 35 percent ethnic, a rather large percentage compared to most universities, and 11 to 15 percent Hispanic, mostly Mexican-American.[1] We have large Asian-Pacific and African-American student communities as well. The University of Houston is a commuter and urban university; many of our students' first priorities are family and job, and then school. In a typical junior-level Mexican-American literature class, the majority of students are Hispanic. Only this year, 1993, has the class shifted to reflect the diverse campus-wide demographics a little more accurately.

The Mexican-American literature course offered in the English department consistently draws students from a wide range of disciplines, especially sociology, psychology, and education. As with many classes where a large number of the students are Hispanic, the class is largely populated by students who are the first in their families to seek education beyond high school.[2]

There are many different factors that can explain some of my Hispanic students' responses to homosexuality. I begin with a specific incident to show the campus atmosphere that affects our discussion. There was a very large and vocal gay and lesbian presence at the 1992 National Association for Chicano Studies (NACS) conference in San Antonio. Many papers were presented that specifically dealt with queer theory, with the socialization and construction of gayness in the Hispanic community, and with literature and history by and about lesbians. Many of the students attending the conference were from California schools, and they appeared comfortable with, if not actually involved in, the open discussion and papers dealing with homosexual issues.

The students from Houston, I later discovered, felt overwhelmed by some of the discussions at NACS. Following the conference, I received a call from a colleague who advises the Mexican-American Student Organization (MASO), who told me that MASO students had requested more information on feminism, queer theory, and homosexuality in general. The MASO students felt unprepared to deal with many of the issues that were the focus of some of the liveliest discussion at NACS. They realized that the University of Houston had failed to educate them on many cutting-edge issues. Of particular discomfort to them was the fact that the university had completely failed to expose them to homosexuality, queer theory, and feminism. I was invited to speak to MASO on these topics.

Instead of the homophobic response I expected, the MASO students admitted to being unfamiliar with feminist and gay theory, and instead of running away, attacking, or dismissing the issues, they asked for knowledge. What is feminism? What is queer theory? What is homophobia? What is patriarchy? Who are these authors that people at NACS were tossing about in their lectures? The MASO students did not want condescending treatment (which I suspect they received at NACS). They wanted knowledge.

This was a refreshing experience for me because the University of Houston often lives up to its good-ole-boy reputation. The women's studies program was started only in 1991 after years of indifference and outright resistance. There is no women's center on campus. Only recently has the university begun to develop a nondiscrimination statement that includes sexual orientation. This is not a university where feminism is widely acknowledged as a legitimate philosophy. The students of MASO realized that there had been something missing in their education.

Many of our Mexican-American students come from a community

that subscribes to very rigorous and traditional definitions of gender and gender roles. For many, the university provides their first exposure to homosexuality that is not negative. These students were clearly overwhelmed by the NACS conference, but they were not paralyzed by the constraints of their families and communities. They took the initiative and simply asked the university to fill a gap in their knowledge. As an active and out lesbian among the Hispanic faculty, I was a logical choice to speak to their concerns.

My presentation was as informal as I could make it given the limitations of a lecture format. I offered some basic feminist terms, attempting a very general definition: feminism is the critique of patriarchy and an attempt to offer an alternative vision.[3] I pointed out that feminists generally agree about the investigation and dismantling of patriarchy; it is the process of reaching an alternative that consistently creates the differences among feminist theories. The students were very receptive to my discussion of feminism. The issue of homosexuality was a bit less comfortable for them to listen to and accept.

One of the first items I pointed out was the great debate raging around nurture versus nature. I carefully explained that there were two major schools of thought which seem to contradict each other. When I began this discussion, students asking questions were more obviously nervous, but at the same time they honestly admitted to their own puzzlement. Why had they been taught to condemn homosexuals? Why were there no conclusive answers to many of the questions I was addressing? Why did I qualify more carefully my statement about homosexuality, when I appeared so strident about feminism?

That final question was a catalyst to an understanding of my own assumptions. I explained that feminism as a philosophy, an area of study, an intellectual point of departure, is more accessible for most people. As a formalized area of study queer theory presently is still in its nascent stages. I pointed to two texts I had brought along, *Chicana Lesbians: The Girls Our Mothers Warned Us About*, edited by Carla Trujillo, and *Compañeras: Latina Lesbians (An Anthology)*, edited by Juanita Ramos, two compilations of queer theory by and about Hispanic lesbians. Most of the works compiled are some combination of essay, fiction, dramatic monologue, and poetry. As with Gloria Anzaldúa's *Borderlands/La Frontera*, these texts attempt to break out of the traditional essay genre and explore other means of communicating extremely philosophical questions about sexuality.

My interaction with the MASO students clarified for me many of the ideas I had only begun to investigate closely. My own work with authors like Anzaldúa or Ana Castillo was something I had developed into. I discovered that I would not have been emotionally and intellectually prepared as an undergraduate to investigate homosexuality. I, too, had been a product of a world that saw homosexuality as an immoral disease. My studies in feminism prepared me to accept my own lesbianism and also gave me an intellectual context for understanding my own resistance to and fears about it.

When I first began teaching Mexican-American literature at the University of Houston, I knew my responsibility included introducing concepts my students would be completely unfamiliar with. The Mexican-American literature class has been taught for approximately twelve years, mainly by individuals who were traditionally trained. Concepts such as postmodernism, feminism, and queer theory have, on this campus, only recently become included in courses.

I usually begin the course with an early classic of Mexican-American literature, Rudolfo Anaya's *Bless Me Ultima,* and the early works of the Chicano movement, mostly written by male authors. I then move the class to the works by women who question assumptions about gender and power structures, that is, to feminism. My formal lectures end with Anzaldúa's *Borderlands/La Frontera,* which is followed by individual student presentations on Hispanic texts they have discovered on their own. Anzaldúa brings to the class a further complexity in Chicana feminism by introducing lesbianism and postmodernism. She also provides a culturally defined understanding of homosexuality and discusses homophobia within the Hispanic community. Her text is especially useful in introducing culturally explicit perceptions of homosexuality from both a Hispanic and a Texan perspective. She writes, after Virginia Woolf,

> As a *mestiza* I have no country, my homeland cast me out; yet all countries are mine because I am every woman's sister or potential lover. (As a lesbian I have no race, my own people disclaim me; but I am all races because there is the queer of me in all races.) I am cultureless because, as a feminist, I challenge the collective/ religious male-derived beliefs of Indo-Hispanics and Anglos; yet I am cultured because I am participating in the creation of yet another culture, a new story to explain the world and our participation in it, a new value system with images and symbols that connect us to each other and to the planet. *Soy un amasamiento,* I am an act of kneading, of uniting and joining that not only has produced both a creature of darkness and a creature of light, but also a creature

that questions the definitions of light and dark and gives them new meanings (80–81).

My student's responses to my introduction of the queer into Mexican-American literature classes are many and varied. Fortunately, very few are outright hostile to exploring and discussing homosexuality in terms that are not pejorative. Those who are hostile put on a very civilized cover; they smirk only initially. I have had to make the following statement only once: "We are not here to continue the denigration of any individual." That statement from me to a student who was being vile quickly silenced and discouraged the mean language. I also make it clear that students have a right to hold their own opinions, but if they choose to express them, they have to be civilized and not use pejorative terms. No name-calling is necessary in an intellectual discussion.

A few students who believe homosexuality is immoral have been willing to express those opinions. I respond by asking what assumptions their opinions are based on. I make it clear that I am not out to change minds or moral assumptions, but that I intend to make sure that students understand the basis for their opinions. My standard statement to the class is: "You have a right to hold any opinion. Just know why you hold it and be prepared to respond when I ask you what concepts that opinion is based on." I make this statement very early in the course, when I am introducing students to the position papers that I require they write on a variety of topics. The position papers are short, half-hour, time-pressured writing exercises asking students to make one statement about a text and defend it. The assignment is a way for me to teach students how to defend their opinions about a text and to help them write a coherent, concrete argument. Because they are familiar with this assignment by the time I introduce *Borderlands*, they are not surprised when I ask about the assumptions behind their opinions about homosexuality.

A few of my students, influenced by religious fundamentalist teachings, simply point to the Bible as the source of their opinions. I acknowledge religion as a major influence on the development of values and opinions; I point out that the Bible has a great deal to say on many different issues and, depending on your religious community, many different interpretations. I have on occasion acknowledged my own Catholic training and how that has influenced my interpretation of the Bible, including the assumption that the Bible may be a place to begin but is not the only place to look. Because of the heavy Catholic and Baptist influence and the tension between the two in Houston, issues of religion are very difficult to address. My own response has been to draw an analogy between the concept of creationism in the Bible and how the academic curriculum directly contradicts that concept, pointing out that students do not reject issues in their physics or biology classes based upon biblical arguments. Usually students acknowledge this separation of issues, and we begin the real discussion of assumptions.

During one class, however, a student did challenge the dismissal of the Bible as the only basis for opinion. He was clearly threatened by the concept of homosexuality as anything other than wrong. I explained that all assumptions in my class have a right to be interrogated and that no text is challenge-proof. I acknowledged the position the Bible takes on homosexuality and asked the student if my interpretation was accurate: homosexuality is immoral. The student agreed. I then turned to Anzaldúa's text and asked him if my interpretation of her was accurate: homosexuality is not immoral. He agreed. I then turned to the class, inviting everyone into the discussion about authors who challenge traditional forms of authority. I had negotiated my students away from a discussion solely about the Bible to one exploring traditional forms of authority and those who challenge them. By keeping the discussion on a broader level and attempting an intellectual exercise, and by resisting the student's attempts to engage me in an argument between his personal belief system and mine, I was able to limit the threatening aspects inherent in a discussion of homosexuality among a homophobic audience.

While most of my students are initially uncomfortable discussing homosexuality, they do not want to appear threatened. I assume that they are mature and willing to approach all issues, and one thing I can say with certainty about University of Houston students is that they are a very polite community. They know how to disagree with each other without becoming verbally violent. Their basic sense of goodwill toward each other has helped whenever we have had heated discussions.

I trust my students' skills and my own to begin a dialogue that they will have to continue in order to understand current issues in Mexican-American literature. I do not expect to change opinions or minds. I expect my students to learn to acknowledge and understand their assumptions. For many, my introduction of homosexuality begins a process. I acknowledge that they may come away with opinions different from mine, but at least they will have learned to articulate why they hold them.

Notes

1. The terms used to identify Hispanics in the United States vary from region to region, culture to culture, and by political position. "Hispanic" is an umbrella term created by the US Census Bureau in order to identify individuals of the Spanish and Portuguese diaspora. "Latina" identifies women of Hispanic descent and also applies to women from Latin America. "Chicana" identifies Mexican-American women but is also a term some members of the Mexican-American community do not embrace. I use the terms Mexican-American and Hispanic interchangeably.

2. The Hispanic population in the United States has one of the lowest high school graduation rates of any ethnic group. Forty-nine percent of Hispanics receive a high school diploma (Kanellos 306).

3. This oversimplified but extremely useful definition of feminism is borrowed from a lecture given by Marlene Longenecker at Ohio State University, January 1988.

Works Cited

Anaya, Rudolfo. *Bless Me Ultima*. Berkeley, CA: Quinto Sol, 1972.

Anzaldúa, Gloria. *Borderlands/La Frontera: The New Mestiza*. San Francisco: Spinsters/ Aunt Lute, 1987.

Castillo, Ana. *The Mixquiahuala Letters*. Binghamton, NY: Bilingual Press, 1986.

———. *Sapogonia*. Tempe, AZ: Bilingual Press, 1990.

Kanellos, Nicolás, ed. *The Hispanic-American Almanac: A Reference Work on Hispanics in the United States*. Detroit: Gale Research, 1993.

Ramos, Juanita, ed. *Compañeras: Latina Lesbians (An Anthology)*. New York: Latina Lesbian History Project, 1987.

Trujillo, Carla, ed. *Chicana Lesbians: The Girls Our Mothers Warned Us About*. Berkeley, CA: Third Woman Press, 1991.

8

Collaborating with Clio:
Teaching Lesbian History
Cynthia D. Nieb

Teaching lesbian history never struck me as something unusual until someone asked me how my first class of the semester had been received. In all honesty, I had to say, "I don't know." Most of my colleagues are either shyly shunned or asked provocative questions after an initial presentation. I have never had that experience. Students respond in one or two ways: either they tell me that they are queer, or they inform me that they know somebody queer. It is an interesting experience that has a form to it, namely, the firm meeting of the eyes and a proclamation of related identity with a hint of soul-searching. I, too, have perfected a response which includes the mirroring of my students' actions and a welcoming smile. Would a teacher of economic history face confessions of Marxist tendencies? Somehow I doubt it.

As with all disciplines, teaching lesbian history requires a grappling with the student, the material, and one's goals as a teacher. My class, "Other" American Women: Lesbianism in Twentieth-Century American History, attracts another audience and asks questions different from anything that I have encountered in other classes, however. It serves another purpose. It is an affirmation of lesbian visibility and an introduction to the historical varieties of lesbianism.

Because I teach a Freshman Writing Seminar, most of my crew are first-year students.[1] During the initial year of teaching "Other" American Women, many students signed up for the seminar because it was one of the few courses offered in the evening. Their expectations varied. Some elected the course because they were les/bi/gay. One woman, a closeted lesbian, wanted to have contact with lesbian subcultures without "outing" herself. A gay ROTC student sought self-affirming scholarship while he struggled with the arduous task of releasing himself from the military and informing his conservative parents of his sexual orientation. As the semesters passed, students chose my course for other reasons. An out lesbian couple signed up for the class to revel in their coupled status while exploring their "roots" and to spend time together. Many women who suspected that they might be queer used the materials and discussion to explore questions that were not safe to examine in other venues. Our general theoretical and historical dialogues allowed students to place their ideas and feelings within a context of recognized historical categories including society, politics, economics, culture, ethnicity, gender, and race. In sum, I encourage the exploration of any concept connected to the study of lesbian history.

Although my lesbian and gay students received confirmation of their existence by tracing their ancestors in mounds of primary and secondary source materials, I think that "Other" American Women provided a far greater service to the straight community. I have seen the humanizing power of telling the tales of lesbian lives.

During the semester, the changes in attitude from homophobic resistance and curiosity to in-your-face militant activism and empathy among my straight students tell me that I am providing a worthwhile service. The reasons straight students elect to take "Other" American Women and the learning process they encounter differ greatly from those of les/bi/gay freshmen. One young heterosexual fraternity brother told me in his journal that he was a fan of Howard Stern and that he assumed that I, too, would show pictures of lesbians clad in teenie-weenie bikinis stuffing kielbasa sausages down their throats. Later, he apologized for his assumption. A straight woman, who comes from a very conservative religious background, took the class because she was taught that homosexuality was sinful, and she wanted to understand the sin. Two years later, she lectures on les/bi/gay issues at her church. One ROTC cadet signed up because he wanted to comprehend the furor over the ban of les/bi/gays in the military. Another straight man credits the readings and discussions with making him a "better heterosexual lover": he learned to see the world in more complex patterns. Perhaps the most moving transformation for me occurred in a straight man who told me at the beginning of the course that homosexuality made him "sick." In the middle of the fourteen-week course, he defended a gay man who was being beaten by a gang of students in a freshman dorm bathroom. He warned the thugs that if they wanted to attack the gay man, they would have to get past him to accomplish their task. The student said that taking "Other" American Women made him aware that the gay man had done nothing to deserve the violent treatment he was receiving. His knowledge humanized him.[2]

The materials used in my class differ from those of an economic history class as well. When was the last time you feared that your Keynesian reader would be stolen by your dorm-mates? Students have reported that their books tend to walk away by themselves, that is, their friends can't keep their hands off the likes of Lillian Faderman, Joan Nestle, Susie Bright, Sigmund Freud, Jewelle Gomez, Martin Duberman, George Chauncey, Jr., Julia Penelope, and a host of others. I choose materials with a very specific goal in mind: I want to show students that lesbians, even though they not unlike everybody else, are not like each other either. We possess varying needs, tastes, and desires. At times, we step on each other's toes. Often, we support one another. We, too, have children, parents, pets, mortgages, businesses, jobs, problems, and diseases. A past in which our love for each other has been criminalized and defamed has affected the choices that we have made over our lifetimes. What I am attempting to establish is that the amalgam that we call history—the interaction of our own selections and the choices that are institutionally available to us during a particular time period—influences who we have been and who we will become.

I begin my course by examining The Lesbian. Students read anthologies such as Judith Barrington's *The Intimate Wilderness* to test the multidimensionality of lesbian existence. They are guided through stories of intergenerational lovemaking, menopause, cancer, waning love, youth, urban and country living, fantasy, s/m, and violence against lesbians. From there, we discuss lesbian separatism, which seems to be a particularly difficult subject for European-American, middle- to upper-class young men to grasp. Julia Penelope provides the fodder for this discussion. The common complaint is: "How will I ever learn anything if nobody will talk to me? Separation creates separation. This is not right." When I point out to my students that they are learning through the class at that very moment, usually without the benefit of a "real live lesbian," the light bulbs usually click on.[3] In other words, we learn what we want to learn.

Next, we take a historical tour with Lillian Faderman, Joan Nestle, and Jewelle Gomez. In the final few weeks the class reads *Piece of My Heart*, a Canadian-produced collection of stories by lesbians of color. I leave this for last: I want students to exit the course fully aware that the same institutional and race-relation complexities that exist among heterosexuals can be found among lesbians as well. During the last two or three classes, students present their own original research.

All of this sounds well-organized and canned, as if I could hand anybody the syllabus and declare, "You, too, can teach this class." It is not so easy a task, nor so boring. I made a commitment to myself when I first began teaching that anyone who took my class would know the high, that rush of glory, that the historian receives when nagging philosophical or historical questions become a little clearer, or better yet, more complex. At first, I floundered in the hunt for my version of the Holy Grail. Finally, I asked myself why sharing the euphoric buzz of discovery was so important to me: I wanted to share my beliefs, my feminist thought and action with my young scholars. I wanted students to see the beauty of the Other rather than the threat, to get away from the hierarchical, institutionalized egocentrism we often confuse with teaching.

Two factors prevailed. I came to the conclusion that if I tried to cram the requisite amount of knowledge into students' heads, I would be protecting myself and shortchanging them. My false security would be tied to appearing in command—a performance model of excellence through which the active learning of the student is negated. In sum, it is the icon, the omnipotent professor who tells the students what is worthwhile to know, who appears to be important. To circumvent the system, I turn the class over to the students. They are presented with the syllabus that I have shared with you, and then they are told that the syllabus will be altered—that we can redirect, specialize, or broaden our focus—according to their interests.

That leads me to the second factor, my files. Over the years, I have collected hundreds of articles on everything from cross-dressing to xenophobia. I distribute photocopies of the clippings when students show an interest in a particular topic. I have discovered that this method keeps the class fresh for all of us, pays respect to the intelligence and inquisitiveness of the students, releases me from the dreadful model of the intellectual power broker, and presents an alternative model of learning in higher education.

Friends and colleagues have asked me how I do it, how I get up in front of a classroom full of les/bi/gay students, homophobes, ROTCs, and fraternity and sorority members and teach lesbian history. I tell them that my freshman writing seminar has been successful for numerous reasons. There is something wondrous about introducing students to new material and seeing them struggle and incorporate novel concepts into their thinking. More important, instructing has never been a one-way street for me. Given adequate background, encouragement, respect, and freedom, students do produce original work. My own scholarship improves when I teach because I am inspired by the dynamism of my students, their ability to take time-worn topics and to look at them anew.

One other important point should be made: I do not approach teaching lesbian history as an experience any more personal than the teaching of economic history. To get to the core of many questions, uncomfortable concepts (for me) must be discussed. That means honesty has to come to the forefront. "Honesty" might include statements from students like, "When I think of two men kissing, it makes me want to puke" or "Lesbians want to be men, right?" These types of statements upset me because I identify with the people whom my students defame. The stereotypes will not change, however, until we hear them and address each falsehood point by point. I must hear the words. A defensive response would only compound the difficulties.

This subtlety becomes problematic when les/bi/gay students do not understand why I am not verbally attacking the perpetrator of homophobic myths. They become frustrated until I explain later why I use the Socratic method. I do so for three reasons: First, it is not a natural response for me to go for the jugular when someone upsets me emotionally or intellectually; I have seen too many emotionally healthy graduate students who were crushed by the corrective zeal of faculty members or colleagues. Second, as the instructor in the course, serving in loco parentis, it is not appropriate for me to snarl at the student. I support snarling in the proper context (at Operation Rescue rallies?), but not in the framework of the classroom. Perhaps the most important reason for maintaining some decorum is the purpose of the class, namely, to aid students in learning about lesbians in the United States from 1900 to 1993. How many hours have been wasted despising professors because they shamed us and made us feel inadequate? While my goal is not to become Most Popular Professor, I do see the benefits gained by creatively leading students through difficult questions instead of saying "No! You're wrong!"

And how have I as a teacher collaborated with Clio? Muses, according to any dictionary definition, exist to inspire. Approximately twenty years ago, women's history and its champions demanded that the reality and relevance of this history be recognized by the profession. Historians did so with great caution as they continue to do today. Queer history occupies an even more precarious position. Although I have not been forced to battle with my department or the curriculum committee, I am aware that my subject matter and my application of nonhierarchical pedagogy do not mix well with current practices in the profession. Most of my colleagues hide themselves behind lecterns, thump their huge survey texts to emphasize their authority, and demand respect from their students. I wander among the students, change my syllabus according to their questions, and ask them to take some control of a class that belongs to them, not me.

As a historian, I am aware that our perceptions of history are as much colored by our present realities as the materials we uncover. As a dyke instructor who teaches queer history, I am different from my associates. It is important for me to support alternative teaching strategies as well as alternative histories. The women we study, the lesbians who duked it out in Buffalo's bars, attended dozens of consciousness-raising sessions, cross-dressed, and cared for AIDS patients, deserve more than a perfunctory lecture.

Notes

1. Freshman Writing Seminar students at Cornell University, where I teach, are required to complete two courses. These courses are assigned by lottery. Although students submit their preferences, these requests are not honored in all cases. Hence, an instructor might face a hostile student who really wanted to study the culture of baseball instead of lesbian history.

2. I have been granted permission by the students to mention their stories in this essay.

3. I am a "real live lesbian," but I stress that I do not represent all lesbians. I attempt to leave "me" out of the discussion as much as possible. Students are curious about my experiences, but I hesitate to spend too much time reviewing my life story; I am not that important. The variety of lesbian experiences is more valuable to their education.

Suggested Course Readings

Barrington, Judith, ed. *An Intimate Wilderness: Lesbian Writers on Sexuality*. Portland, OR: Eighth Mountain Press, 1991.

Faderman, Lillian. *Odd Girls and Twilight Lovers: A History of Lesbian Life in Twentieth-Century America*. New York: Columbia University Press, 1991.

Gomez, Jewelle. *The Gilda Stories: A Novel*. Ithaca, NY: Firebrand Books, 1991.

Nestle, Joan. *A Restricted Country*. Ithaca, NY: Firebrand Books, 1987.

Penelope, Julia. *Call Me Lesbian: Lesbian Lives, Lesbian Theory*. Freedom, CA: Crossing Press, 1992.

Silvera, Makeda, ed. *Piece of My Heart: A Lesbian of Colour Anthology*. Toronto: Sister Vision Press, 1991.

Suggested Films and Videos

"Before Stonewall: The Making of a Gay and Lesbian Community," produced by Robert Rosenberg, John Scagliotti, and Greta Schiller. 1984. Color videotape. 87 min.

"The Families We Choose," directed by Cheryl Qamar and Lisa Pontoppidan. 1985. Color videotape. 37 min.

"Lesbian Tongues." 1987. Color videotape. 90 min.

Thank God I'm a Lesbian, directed by Laurie Colbert and Dominique Cardona. 1992. 16mm film. 60 min.

"Tiny and Ruby: Hell Diving' Women," directed by Greta Schiller. 1988. Color videotape. 30 min.

9

There's No Place like Home?
Lesbian Studies and the Classics

Ann Pellegrini

Someone, I say, will remember us in the future.
—Sappho, Fr. 147

Make an effort to remember. Or, failing that, invent.
—Monique Wittig[1]

What's a nice girl like me doing in a place like this? The place is classical studies as institutionalized and practiced in the Anglo-American university. As it happens, this nice girl holds degrees in classics from two of the preeminent sites of western cultural conservatorship: Harvard and Oxford universities. Now when this girl is also an out and outspoken lesbian feminist, the place classics holds for her may become a site of contradiction and contestation. As Margo Channing said, in a vastly different context: "Fasten your seatbelts. It's going to be a bumpy night."

There were bumps aplenty in my six-year journey through classics and into lesbian and gay studies. Numerous detours, too. Other lesbians in the academy may recognize some of these landmarks: the homophobia so honed and institutionalized that it passes for "scholarly standards" or "methodological rigor"; the isolation, verging on another sort of closet, of libraries and late hours hunched over the word processor; the repetition compulsion to come out and come out again, as if we did not or could not get it right the first time or any time, as if they did not or would not register our meanings. Remember: The shortest path between two points is not always a straight line. My own route to the lesbian studies classroom has traced a circle. As if to say all roads really do lead to Rome—or at the very least to Lesbos—

70

my odyssey away from classics and toward lesbian and gay studies has actually landed me back in the mise en scène of classical antiquity.

When I was a baby dyke and also a baby classicist, just mentioning Sappho promised pleasures and not a little anxiety; this was definitely my hagiographic phase. I always imagined a dozen heads spinning quickly to identify just who had dared the S-word, as if it were the equivalent of farting in public. To my eternal despair, I was a Latinist, not a Hellenist, which made my attempts to read Sappho's difficult Lesbian (in the ancient sense!) dialect painful. Where other baby dykes might have cruised the women's studies or fledgling les/gay studies sections at bookstores, I used to stand in the classics section, flipping through all the available books with Sappho in the title or even just in the index. Really. I could not have known then that this was just the beginning of a circuitous journey toward lesbian and gay studies.

My four years studying classics at Harvard and Radcliffe Colleges were followed by two more years of classical studies at Oxford. By the time Oxford was through with me, I was convinced Harvard was a multicultural matriarchy. I was also convinced that there was no place for me within the conservative discipline of classical studies. I would like to think I was not lacking in the imagination to carry through a sustained feminist and queer-affirmative project in the classics. What I could not sustain was the energy required to keep my methodologies sufficiently disciplined, my politics polite, and above all, my closet tidy.

Ultimately, I decided to leave classics and returned to Harvard where I began a Ph.D. in religion and philosophy. As my research interests developed, however, it became clear that not only had I left classics behind, but my work in lesbian and gay studies had displaced me also from my latest institutional home. Finally, with the support of faculty from three different departments, I set up an ad hoc Ph.D. program in "cultural studies," where I might pursue research on twentieth-century representations of the lesbian body. This seemed to me a universe apart from my life as classicist. But one of the abiding ironies of my road trip through academe is that my first experience teaching lesbian and gay studies should have landed me back in the classics, back at Harvard.

In 1990, I was asked to develop and lead two lesbian and gay studies sections in Harvard's largest and, arguably, most popular classics course, The Concept of the Hero in Hellenic Civilization. The course, a semester-long introduction to the literature and culture of archaic and classical Greece, fulfills a literature and arts requirement in Harvard's core curriculum. Students attend two lectures and one discussion section each week. Discussion of lectures and assigned texts as well as grading of essays and exams takes place through these weekly sections, which are taught by graduate students. Annually, anywhere from 450 to 650 students enroll in "Heroes." In many respects, it is difficult to imagine a more mainstream site in which to introduce lesbian and gay studies at Harvard.

The invitation to add "gay" and (to a lesser extent) "lesbian" to "Heroes" and stir did not issue straight, as it were, from Zeus's ivory temple. Rather, it had something to do with my academic training and with the fact that I was out. In fact, I was the nearest approximation to an out classicist to be found at Harvard. I had even taken "Heroes" when I was a baby dyke, and I loved the idea of "queering" the course these many years later—thereby exacting something of my revenge on the straight and narrow of classics as discipline.

Certainly, the set texts for the course—Homeric epic, Sappho, Pindar and Hesiod, tragedies from the fifth-century Athenian stage, and a dollop of Herodotus and Plato—offered ample opportunity to queer the canon. Moreover, Professor Gregory Nagy and head teaching fellow Lynn Sawlavich gave me free rein to develop my own discussion topics parallel to (or, as would often be the case, askew of) the themes explored in the other sections. I could also offer a bibliography in feminist criticism and les/gay studies to supplement the required materials for the course. This was an offer I could not resist.

I did, however, suggest some subtle rewording. For reasons of historicity and classroom safety I insisted that the special discussion sections be officially designated under the rubric "gender and sexuality," and not, as had been initially suggested, under the identity sign "gay studies." The logic behind this shift was not, I hope, that of the closet; certainly I was going to be out in the classroom. Rather, my objections were political, historical, and pedagogical.

First, gay studies too easily leaves out the lesbian. The omission is no less marked when "lesbian and" decorates "gay studies"—as the recent history of the lesbian and gay studies movement too often attests. Classical scholars such as David Halperin and the late John Winkler have brought gay studies to bear on classical literature and culture, with important results.[2] However, if gay studies in the classics is, relatively speaking, a growth industry, lesbian studies is not. Even where feminist and gay-affirmative scholars are (re)writing the history of Greek and Roman sexualities, it is male bodies and male experiences of sexuality that generally take center stage. In those instances, moreover, where female sexualities are historicized, where the lives and experiences of women are the foci of study, the experience and representation of female homoeroticism generally drop out.[3] So, all the women are heterosexual, all the homosexuals are men, but some of us are brave? To be fair, nothing from classical antiquity survives in women's own voices except for fragments of Sappho's poetry. But numerous sources for what men thought, feared, and fantasized about female homoeroticism from this new generation of classical scholarship suggests how queering the canon may not go all that far to redress lesbian invisibility.[4]

I wanted to put the "lesbian" back into gay and lesbian studies for my students; but, I wanted to do so in a way which neither elided gender and sexuality nor erased the historical distance between classical western societies and the modern west. Some amusing confusions may arise when classical terms which have acquired distinctive and oh-so-modern meanings are retrojected onto the past. "Lesbian" is one such problem term. Strictly speaking, for a classicist, "Lesbian" means something or someone characteristic of the Greek isle of Lesbos. As an undergraduate classics major, I remember the titters of amusement, embarrassment, and (for this lesbian) hope which references to Lesbians in the Greek historians Herodotus and Thucydides would produce. I was always disappointed. For the Lesbians of these histories designate a national identity and a place of origin, not erotic love between women. To say of Sappho, for instance, that she was a "Lesbian" is correct in the geographic sense only; the facts of her personal biography—was she or wasn't she?—have been much debated from classical antiquity onward and remain much in doubt today.[5]

It is true that in ancient Greek texts, certain behaviors and proclivities are associated with the women of Lesbos. Evidently, Lesbian women were the caricature of wanton, sexually adventurous and lascivious women open to any and all comers, any and all acts. Among these acts could have been sexual acts with other women, but it was definitely not same-sex acts which centrally constituted ancient Lesbian stereotypes. In the fifth-century-BCE comedies of Aristophanes, for example, the verbs *lesbiazein* and *lesbizein* (literally, "to do as the women of Lesbos do") effectively mean "to perform fellatio"—an activity about as far from what is conventionally associated with "lesbianism" in the modern sense as possible.

This points to the more general historical problem that there just aren't classical equivalents for modern categories of sexuality, which too neatly translate the range of sexual behaviors into types of sexual beings: "homosexual," "lesbian," "bisexual," "heterosexual."[6] I am explicitly not claiming that individuals who desired and were sexually intimate with members of their own sex did not come into being until the term "homosexual" came into our language in 1869. Far from it. Rather, following Foucault, I am insisting that the category of sexuality is a modern invention, representing a historically and culturally specific set of assumptions concerning the proper alignment of gender, desire, and the anatomically sexed body. In ancient Greece and Rome, love between men is well attested, love between women considerably less so. But, generally speaking, individuals were not classified according to the anatomical sex of their object choice. If I was to convince my students of nothing else during our semester-long encounter with the Hellenic world, I wanted them to appreciate the contingency of contemporary western ways of organizing and classifying sexual desires and practices.

In addition to problems of historical and semantic accuracy, I was also aware that there were many students just coming out or closeted who might be hesitant to enroll in a section so visibly marked under the sign "gay" or "lesbian." I wanted to make it easier for them to take a queer-positive class. However awkward the locution "gender and sexuality," it would still be an easier mouthful to repeat to roommates and parents than "lesbian and gay studies." Keep in mind that "gender and sexuality" was only the official designation, my watchwords, if you will, against anachronism and parental anxieties. Elsewhere, the word was already out among Harvard/Radcliffe's lesbian, gay, and bisexual community that a "lesbian and gay studies" section was being offered for the first time in a core course. Not only did I not act to correct that nominal misapprehension, I encouraged it. This only goes to show that out of earshot of the conference room, even dyed-in-the-wool constructionists such as myself may use "gay" and "lesbian" as a shorthand for the thicket of theoretical and political controversies that swirl around the meanings and histories of same-sex sexual practices.

Is there such a thing as being too historically correct? In the ivy-choked atmosphere of a place like Harvard, there is a pressing political and pedagogical need for the clarion cry of the words "gay" and "lesbian." Perhaps "gender and sexuality" was too polite and too quiet. In my respect for historical categories and in my tacit concern for closeted students, had I unintentionally reinforced the closet for students who wanted and needed to hear "lesbian" and "gay" uttered in a crowded lecture hall? If so, those students would get their hearing.

On the third day of lecture, Professor Nagy gave me the floor to talk up the special sections. I had five minutes to make my pitch, and I had a lot to say:

> Timelessness and Classics. Studying the classics may teach us much about our present condition—and not just because we may recognize ourselves in the concerns and fears of the ancients, but because we may not recognize ourselves at all. We may feel decentered and disoriented, and it is these moments of disorientation and discontinuity which may best point out the contingency of contemporary western ways of reckoning the universe and human nature. One of the places where contemporary western categories do not find classical corollaries is sexuality. There just are no classical equivalents for "gay" or "lesbian," "homosexual" or "heterosexual." In part this has to do with the different ways classical Greek cultures had of understanding gender and its relations to desire. In my sections, we'll be reading the required texts for this course with an eye to tracing these discontinuities and challenging some deeply held views about the present. In doing so, we'll try to gain a more appreciative, historicized reading of these ancient texts. The reading strategies employed in this section will be heavily influenced by feminist theory, recent developments in lesbian and gay studies, and the historical work of Michel Foucault. As a lesbian feminist [this is the part where some jaws fell open, some faces fell into broad appreciative grins, and some male undergraduates laughed in open, adolescent ridicule], I also bring political questions informed by my own experiences to my reading of these texts. I assume that you too will bring your own concerns and your own histories to your readings. All I ask is that you be open to new readings and open-minded to your fellow and sister students.

When I finished there was sustained applause. My colleagues told me that I had looked supremely calm and composed, that I had spoken with great clarity. Evidently, the lapel microphone did not register the urgency of my heartbeat. I know that my pulse had been racing with the adrenaline of coming out to 430 students. I am sure it was the first time most of these students had witnessed a teacher coming out to them in a Harvard lecture hall.

The novelty of my very public coming out was brought home to me about one week later. A young woman on a bicycle quite nearly ran me down as I was jogging along the Charles. She wanted to know if I was "that section leader for 'Heroes.'" I knew what she was getting at, but I wanted to make her say it. "Which one?" "The one doing that special section." "Yes." "Can I ask you a question?" "Yes." "Why did you tell us you were a, uh, radical lesbian feminist?" "I never said I was 'radical,' although I could have." "Okay. 'Lesbian feminist.' But why did you tell us that? I have never heard any other lecturer make a similar announcement." "Exactly." What followed was a long, and in many ways predictable, discussion about the politics and experience of coming out. The young woman did not enroll in my section. For the remainder of the year, whenever I ran into her on campus, she looked straight through me.

In retrospect, I suspect that what I called the section—"gender and sexuality" versus "gay studies"—had less of an impact on who enrolled than that signal five-minute declamation. Roughly the same number of students, thirty, signed up during each of the two years I offered the special sections.[7] In addition to the regular course material, my students wold read, on average, one twenty-five page article in feminist or lesbian and gay studies criticism in classics a week. Yes, such criticism does exist, in small but growing quantity. The extra course work may also have had the unintended, but welcome, advantage of selecting out those very few students who fleetingly expressed interest in enrolling for the sole purpose and pleasure, it seemed, of my lesbian-feminist discomfort.

That thirty students were undeterred by extra coursework and did sign up for the special sections in gender and sexuality suggests that a strong demand for feminist and lesbian and gay studies classes exists at Harvard. This intuition is corroborated in the anonymous evaluations students wrote at the end of term. "The section on gender and sexuality is a wonderful addition to the other sections and actually the reason I chose to take 'Heroes.' Other courses should imitate 'Heroes' and do the same," wrote one student. For another student, the "gender/sexuality section was the best section [he'd] had in 2 and a half years." A third said that the gender and sexuality section constituted "a class in itself well worth taking."

Course-wide, the majority of students enrolled in "Heroes" were male undergraduates. My sections, in contrast, were disproportionately female, with undergraduate women making up roughly 75 percent of my enrollment. How disproportionately "queer" my sections were is an open question. The majority of my students were not out— at least not to me—as lesbian, gay, or bisexual during the time I was teaching them. That so many heterosexually identified students signed up for these special sections indicates that it is not only "sexual minorities" who benefit when the classroom closet swings open. I did have at least one openly les/gay/bi student in each of my three sections—probably an improvement by one on the number of students out in the other sections for the course. Several of my former students have come out since taking "Heroes." I would love to claim credit. But I won't.

Some of my students had backgrounds in women's studies; a few were familiar with recent texts in the history of sexuality. For other students, the section was to be their first introduction to feminist critical practices, never mind to gay and lesbian studies. In fact, some of the men who signed up specifically cited as their reasons for enrolling their lack of previous exposure to women's studies and their feeling that it was about time they got on board. One male classics undergraduate said he wanted to get a perspective on Greek literature not on offer in the mainstream of the classics department. He could say that again!

Throughout the semester's weekly meetings, students tried out different interpretations of the texts, exchanged ideas, and asked questions right up to the end of the hour. One of the nicest compliments I received from students in their anonymous evaluations was that "sections [were] too short!!!" Another student wrote that "we were usually hesitant to leave, but we had lecture right after class."

Because I wanted to resist the urge to bludgeon texts in a programmatic search for queer subtexts, some weeks' discussions took more of a women's studies approach. Together we looked critically at the representation of women in the text and considered what that might mean for the role of women in the larger culture which produced and consumed that text. Some of the assigned texts were more obvious candidates for les/gay studies. Sappho, for instance. Or, perhaps less obviously: the *Iliad*—where the relationship between Patrocles and Achilles would become fodder for heated arguments among fifth-century-BCE Athenians (some three centuries after the *Iliad* was first composed); or Aeschylus's *Oresteia* trilogy, where the adulterous lovers Clytemnestra and Aegisthus would be punished for, among other things, transgression of appropriate gender norms. The last also provided opportunity for one of the more popular discussion exercises. We did a mock staging of Orestes' trial for matricide in the *Eumenides*, the third play in the *Oresteia*. Students signed up one week in advance to speak in class only from the perspective of one of the play's characters. As a classroom exercise, it did seem to increase appreciation for the play and promote closer readings. It was also a good laugh as everyone tried not to step out of character and gang up on "poor" Orestes.

Sappho provided the most obvious opportunity to bring lesbian and gay studies to "Heroes." Unfortunately, this was an opportunity lost on many of the other sections, where students were coming away with no appreciation for Sappho's poetry nor with any sense of the cultural politics in which her life and work have been embroiled for millennia. On the end-of-term evaluations for the course as a whole, Sappho was often cited as the least valuable text. I discovered quite by accident just how uneven exposure to Sappho had been in the other sections. Two days before the final exam, two undergraduates enrolled in other sections rushed up to me, anxiously inquiring whether Sappho was a woman or a man; how were they supposed to know? When my jaw returned to its normal position at the lower edge of my face, I replied that Sappho was a woman, and that there is a voluminous literary and artistic history dating to classical antiquity which attests to this fact, if to little else. To my own query whether they had ever heard of Sappho before taking "Heroes," the two sophomores said no. Never heard of Sappho? How to shatter a lesbian's assumptions about cultural literacy!

This was decidedly not the case in my sections, where the hour devoted to Sappho was among the most popular discussion topics both years I taught the course. At the suggestion of Julia Dubnoff, who also taught a gender and sexuality section in 1990, I distributed six articles on Sappho and her poetry. These six articles presented widely divergent readings of Sappho's poetry and its relationship to her biography, real and imagined; they also took very different stances with respect to feminist and lesbian-affirmative critical approaches.

One article, for example, was at such pains to criticize the "biographical fallacy" of searching for Sappho's life through her poetry that it called even more attention to what the author was seeking to explain away. Another, in a similar vein, provided an alternative, and explicitly desexualized, reading of just what was and was not involved in Sappho's tutelage of the young girls of Lesbos. A rebuttal to this article's intended-to-be-comforting reading of Sappho, schoolmistress of Lesbos, was provided for balance. Three of the articles concentrated more on Sappho's artistry, including a subtle, feminist and lesbian-positive reading of Sappho's "double consciousness" by John Winkler.[8]

During the course of the discussion, as students gave their five-minute summaries in turn, the oral presentations quickly began to challenge, contradict, and reinterpret each other. It was exciting to watch the students realize that their own accounts of Sappho were necessarily partial and limited—precisely because they had only read one, maybe two, of the six articles, precisely because they had only gotten a fragment of the larger story. But this was itself a metaphor for Sappho, whose work survives only in fragments, and whose biography has been a source of controversy and contestation from as early as the fourth century BCE (two centuries after her death) to the present. Did she "do it" with women? Only with women? What would count as "proof"? And why does it matter? And if it does not matter—as some Sappho scholars argue and argue and argue it does not, until they are almost blue (never lavender) in the face—why do these same naysayers go on and on with the same argument? Whom are they trying to convince?

These are the questions that arise again and again around the figure of Sappho, obscuring the genius of her lyrics. They are also questions that have their own history, a history that might trace moments in the genealogy of modern understandings of sexuality in general and female sexual deviance in particular. Instead of taking Sappho's poetry as factual evidence for her life, I suggest a (dare I say it?) postmodern turn toward Sappho-as-text. An investigation of the relations torturously asserted and variously denied in two millennia and counting of Sappho criticism between her "life" and her fragmentary literary corpus might open a (partial) literary and political history of lesbianism in western literature, literary criticism, and culture. The history of lesbianism in western civilization is, in many respects, a history of inventions. And Sappho of Lesbos is perhaps the greatest and most versatile of these inventions.

To me, it is perversely appropriate that the very western classics which the new right is anxiously claiming and holding forth as antidotes to politically correct pedagogy, so-called, may themselves be reappropriated by and opened up to lesbian and gay critical practices and pedagogies. Sometimes, this reappropriation amounts to little more than hagiography, a tendency much on display in the lesbian apocrypha which have grown up around Sappho, that "right-on woman." But even reappropriation has its political value, as in that litany of "gay [or lesbian] self-justification . . . 'Sappho, Michelangelo, Shakespeare . . . and me.' "[9] Following this line of approach, queering the canon becomes the literary-historical equivalent of a gay cultural archaeology: recovering and reclaiming "gay" and "lesbian" figures from history.

However, this is not the only strategy available to lesbian and gay studies, nor is it the only politically viable route. Perhaps we can contest the canon precisely where and as we contest the sexual imperatives of modernity: "homo" and "hetero." What Diana Fuss writes of these much-contested terms might be said equally well of attempts to contest and queer the canon: "The dream of either a common language or no language at all is just that—a dream, a fantasy that ultimately can do little to acknowledge and to legitimate the hitherto repressed differences between and within sexual identities. But one can, by using these contested words, use them up, exhaust them, transform them into the historical concepts they are and have always been. Change may well happen by working on the insides of our inherited sexual vocabularies and turning them inside out, giving them a new face."[10] Because the literature of Greece and Rome constitutes the canon's western foundation, it proves rich ground from which to turn the classroom inside out.

On the left, it may be off with Plato's head. After the revolution, the dead languages may be laid to their final rest. But my own experiences introducing students to lesbian and gay studies in and through the classics indicate the abiding value of learning about these supposedly "dead" letters. Through their concentrated study of the literature and culture of a very different and very distant past, my own students learned much about the present, in particular about the contingency of contemporary ways of organizing and policing categories of gender and sexuality. From all indications, this was an opportunity that my students valued; during the two years I offered gender and sexuality sections, they received the highest cumulative ratings course-wide. I offer this not as an exercise in self-congratulation, but as students' own testimony to their desire to have lesbian and gay studies integrated into the mainstream of their liberal arts education. *What's a nice dyke like me doing in a place like this?* Plenty.

Notes

Many people have contributed to this article; however, they have no share of any errors, omissions, or prejudices expressed in it. Nancy J. Shumate, friend and teacher, encouraged my classical fancies before it was fashionable, and I dedicate this essay to her. Bernadette Brooten and David Halperin both generously shared their time and considerable knowledge of classical texts with me. Gregory Nagy and Lynn Sawlavich laid the groundwork for this article when they invited me to integrate the analytics of gender and sexuality into a large classics course. I thank my students for their energies and talents; they will never appreciate how much I learned from them. Finally, the debts I owe to Linda Garber are inestimable; I only begin to repay them here.

1. Monique Wittig, *Les Guérillères*, trans. David Le Vay (Boston: Beacon Press, 1985), 89.

2. See David Halperin, *One Hundred Years of Homosexuality* (New York: Routledge, 1990), and John J. Winkler, *The Constraints of Desire: The Anthropology of Sex and Gender in Ancient Greece* (New York: Routledge, 1990).

3. Important exceptions here are the work of Judith P. Hallett, Bernadette B. Brooten, Marilyn B. Skinner, and Eva Stehle. See Brooten, "Paul's View on the Nature of Women and Female Homoeroticism," in Clarissa Atkinson, Constance H. Buchanan, and Margaret Miles, eds., *Immaculate and Powerful: The Female Sacred Image and Social Reality* (Boston: Beacon Press, 1985); Brooten, "Women with Masculine Desires: Ancient Medical Treatments," unpublished paper delivered October 16, 1991, Seminar in Lesbian/Gay Studies, Center for Literary and Cultural Studies, Harvard University; Hallett, "Female Homoeroticism and the Denial of Roman Reality in Latin Literature," *Yale Journal of Criticism* 3:1 (Fall 1989): 209–28; Skinner, "Sapphic Nossis," *Arethusa* 22:1 (1989): 5–18; and Stehle, "Sappho's Gaze: Fantasies of a Goddess and a Young Man," *differences* 2:1 (Spring 1990): 88–125.

4. Nor can the disproportionate focus on male subjects in these new studies be put down wholly to the fact that sources about men's lives, many of which address male same-sex desire, greatly outnumber sources about women's lives. For there are, in fact, numerous classical references to female same-sex desire. Allowing that there are fewer sources for female sexual experience is not the same thing as saying there are no sources.

5. Sappho lived in the late seventh and early sixth centuries BCE. Within two centuries of her death, the historical Sappho had already passed into myth. On the stage of classical Athens, she was the titular figure in six comedies; fragments survive from only two of these. In the *Sappho* of Diphilos, the Ionian poets Archilochus and Hipponax are her *erastai* (lovers), and there is no hint of any erotic ties to women. In later literary histories of the classical period, the "facts" of Sappho's personal life would be held up to examination and scandalous report: among the rumors were her purported life as a courtesan, or high-class prostitute, and her purported "fondness" for other women and young girls. Of less import than the truth or falsity of either of these claims is their effect: at either extreme—heterosexual prostitution or lesbianism—Sappho's sexuality is held up as a means of discrediting her artistic genius.

6. For a contrary and influential view, see John Boswell, *Christianity, Social Tolerance, and Homosexuality: Gay People in Western Europe from the Beginning of the Christian Era to the Fourteenth Century* (Chicago: University of Chicago Press, 1980). See also Amy Richlin, "Not Before Homosexuality," *Journal of the History of Sexuality* 3:4 (1993): 523–73.

7. On both occasions, after the mechanics of fixing meeting times convenient to as many students as possible, I was left with two sections of eight to twelve students. In 1990, I was only able to teach one section myself. Julia Dubnoff, a classicist of great imagination and talent, taught the second section that year. Julia is a wonderful teacher, not just of her undergraduates, but of her teaching colleagues as well. I am indebted to Julia for many of the classroom exercises I have since tried out on my own students.

8. John Winkler, "Double Consciousness in Sappho's Lyrics," in *Constraints of Desire*, 162–87.

9. Andy Medhurst, "That special thrill: *Brief Encounter,* homosexuality and authorship," *Screen* 32:2 (Summer 1991): 205.

10. Diana Fuss, "Introduction," *Inside/Out: Lesbian Theories, Gay Theories* (New York: Routledge, 1991), 7.

10

Straight but Not Narrow: A Gynetic Approach to the Teaching of Lesbian Literature

Sally L. Kitch

Although I am a straight woman, I teach about lesbians; and I choose to use literature by lesbians in my classes. I make that choice for two reasons. One reason has to do with my ever-strengthening belief that identity politics—that is, the equation of personal experience with the authority to speak, write, or teach about a subject—cannot control the women's studies curriculum. I believe that every women's studies class, and everyone who teaches, must be prepared to deal with the variety of women's lives. I believe we must model the value of diversity by attempting to achieve diversity within our own consciousnesses, even if we cannot achieve it in our experience. As we develop approaches to lives that are very different from our own, we not only expand our perceptual powers, we also decenter our own experience in the learning process. Such decentering is especially informative if we have been raised to consider our own experience "normal." Walking a mile in the perceptual shoes of those excluded from our own dominant group reveals the politics of both inclusion in and exclusion from categories of normalcy, and reduces complacency about our own designation.

Such decentering of dominant experience among women is consistent with the long-standing demand in women's studies scholarship and pedagogy that an androcentric world decenter male experience and expand its perceptual universe, as well as its systems of opportunity and rewards, beyond the limits of that experience. Now the discipline must demand that women decenter dominance among them(our)selves, that we see beyond the perspectives of white, middle-class, and/or heterosexual women.

My second reason for teaching lesbian literature is my interest in analyzing it as part of a larger theoretical project I have undertaken in recent years. I first developed interest in lesbian literature, as well as literature by women of diverse ethnic and racial backgrounds—women who felt and were often marginalized by the white, heterosexual mainstream—because of its cultural significance, according to poststructuralist, postmodern psychoanalytic feminist theory. As I explored the relationship between the literature and the theory, I decided to teach using that theoretical perspective. In the process I discovered that, despite its complexity, the poststructuralist, postmodern psychoanalytic feminist theoretical perspective facilitates the teaching of what I came to call the literature of women's diversity, including lesbian literature. Among its helpful aspects is the theory's ability to situate learners who cannot approach particular literature on the basis of their own experience.

Demystifying the Mysterious

This essay will explore an approach, based on poststructuralist, postmodern psychoanalytic feminist theory, to teaching lesbian literature in a women's studies classroom composed primarily (though not exclusively) of straight women. I embark on this exploration understanding full well that many students and teachers find the complexity and arcane terminology of such theory daunting and worry that its incorporation into the teaching of literature might overwhelm the learning process. Despite those legitimate concerns, I believe that theory can become a key to unlocking and analyzing the literature if it is presented less for its own sake than for the sake of situating both the literature and the student's approach to it. Such issues of standpoint and contextualizing are especially important in the teaching of lesbian literature because of the difficulty some students have in abandoning, even temporarily, the homophobia they bring with them to their studies.

My goal in teaching the lesbian literature I selected for a class on the literature of women's diversity was to help students consider the cultural and literary value of such noncanonical literature on its own terms. I wanted to forestall hasty, generally negative judgments of literary work students might find unfamiliar and threatening because of its language and setting, as well as its views on race, class, and sexuality, by establishing a new foundation for analysis. I turned to poststructuralist, postmodern French theorists to provide that foundation because in their writing I found a model that explained unfamiliar language and content in terms of cultural and personal psychosexual structures. Indeed, theories connect the marginalization of certain persons and groups, including all women, with the suppression of particular expressive and linguistic modes. In addition, they connect the processes of individual gender-identity formation with the cultural repression of femaleness, as concept and experience. That repression marginalizes women as well as other cultural "females," such as racial, ethnic, sexual, and class minorities.

Implicit in the theories' vision of marginalization, however, is an "escape clause," a way to undermine and potentially reverse the forces of personal repression and cultural marginalization. For even as they describe the powers of domination, the theories hypothesize the mechanisms for the assertion of difference and the disruption of forces that would suppress that difference. They also identify the liberating potential of such nonhegemonic expressive modes as the language of the body, poetry, female sexual *jouissance*, and dream and mystical imagery. These mechanisms have particular significance for women's literary texts.

Delving Deeper

As background to using the theories in teaching, I recommend Alice Jardine's 1985 book *Gynesis*. I have found it a very useful summation of the various French philosophers whose work constitutes what I am calling poststructuralist, postmodern psychoanalytic feminist theory. Although others (Jane Gallop, for example) are better at presenting the personal psychosexual process through which gender identification presumably occurs, Jardine explores well the cultural significance of that process, especially the role of the phallus as the key symbol of Western cultural structures. Through her approach and terminology, the phallus is understood not just as a physiological attribute but also as a sign of normalcy against which all else appears deficient (lacking). (The phallus defiance of lesbianism becomes especially problematic in this scenario.) Such deficiency is considered "feminine," a term that indicates the cultural appropriation of gender as a symbol of otherness in the guise of sex-linked behavioral and psychological characteristics. To be outside the phallic metaphor—that is, to be deemed "feminine"—is to be marginalized and silenced. Because the phallus entails both hegemonic power and maleness, one need not be female to be feminine.

Building on the theories of French philosophers such as Jacques Derrida, Jacques Lacan, and Julia Kristeva, Jardine further explains that the feminine signifies the locus in discourse of the Other, that is, the marginalized place from which the Other must speak in the phallic or symbolic realm, which privileges reason, linear thinking, and unitary symbolism. The discursive role of the feminine combines individual and social processes. On the personal, psychosexual level, repression of the feminine occurs during the Oedipal period, when the symbiotic, libidinal mother-child dyad is interrupted through paternal mediation, and the imposition of patriarchal family structure and relationship boundaries occurs. On the social level, the Oedipal passage signifies a child's entry into the symbolic realm of social rules and linguistic structures (the Law [and language] of the Father) that honor the phallus and replace pre-Oedipal, semiotic, feminine expressiveness—characterized by nonlinear, multivocal, rhythmic, and imaginary modes—with linear, sequential, and rational expressive modes. Passage into the symbolic renders the child a speaking subject precisely because he/she has repressed desire for the mother and all feminine or semiotic affects and associations (Moi 99).

Of critical importance for literary theory is the connection between the repression of the feminine and the repression of certain modes of expression, including preverbal sounds and rhythms, dream imagery, the infant's memories of the maternal body and its nonphallic, sexual joy, or "jouissance," and the primal physical world of mucus, excrement, and blood. Jardine explains that repressed feminine/semiotic material is a reservoir of "mad, unconscious, improper, unclean, nonsensical . . . [and] profane" discourse; when released, it reveals "unknown, terrifying, [and] monstrous" spaces, hitherto unexplored (73). Dreams represent a common release of such material; according to many Lacanian theorists, including Julia Kristeva; poetry represents another. Both have the power to disrupt the symbolic order. Similarly, the "improper" discourse of marginalized peoples has the power to disrupt the symbolic order.

The disruptive potential of the semiotic represents the most important source of its revolutionary power and, ultimately, the most important source of power for the groups that have been marginalized and silenced because of their feminine discursive status. Jardine dubs this revolutionary power "gynesis," or "the putting into discourse of 'woman' . . . the valorization of the feminine, woman, and her obligatory, that is, historical connotations" (25). Gynesis represents the inclusion in the concept of the feminine of all who have been silenced and marginalized, including racial and ethnic minorities, lesbians and gays, the physically disabled, and the elderly.

Understanding the division of Western cultures into categories of linguistic/artistic acceptability and unacceptability based on tacit and often unexamined premises prepares students to explore from a fresh perspective literary works they may initially define as unacceptable. As they identify such works' capacity to disrupt and rearrange the symbolic structures responsible for their previous silencing, students learn to appreciate the feminine's ability to validate "that which has been 'left out,' de-emphasized, hidden, or denied articulation within Western systems of knowledge." They also come to appreciate the role of gynesis—the expression of the hidden, unknown, and unexplored—in challenging "the very foundations of Western culture and philosophy: Man, the Subject, History" and in disrupting "the discursive truth of the dominant order" (Jardine 36, 73, 44). Often students begin to identify previously unexplored expressive modes within themselves that gynesis gives them permission to release.

Effective teaching of gynesis requires the analysis of its various levels of meaning. On one level, gynesis defines a text's or writer's practice, a giving voice to personal and social entities that cultural processes seem routinely to suppress. On this level, gynesis signifies the disruption of hegemonic views of normalcy, views that serve a dominant and dominating group and may disserve those whose bodies, skins, or backgrounds do not reflect those views. Lesbian texts are gynetic in this sense because they decenter the heterosexual norm and the practices and institutions that accompany it—family, conventions of femininity—and expose their political agendas and strategies. On another level, gynesis designates a process within the mind of a reader. Confronted with a gynetic text, the reader may find her own identity decentered and her own tacit assumptions about the world challenged. Gynesis also presents the opportunity for readers to explore the relationship of sexism to other repressive processes. Without denying the specificity of oppression because of racial, ethnic, and other characteristics, gynesis suggests the links among mechanisms that marginalize and silence all who deviate from the phallocentric norm. It also supports the celebration and "valorization of the feminine, woman, and her . . . historical connotations" in a world in which the phallic metaphor has failed and become "complicitous with . . . ways of oppressing" through "reified and naturalized categories" that are, finally, imperialistic. In this sense of gynesis, lesbian texts do not simply represent an alternative lifestyle, they encode the disruption of Western master narratives, "a questioning and turning back" upon the dominant discourse "in an attempt to create a new *space* or *spacing within themselves* for survival" (Jardine 24–25).

Also contributing to the pedagogical importance of postmodern theories are their concepts of identity. Having established that language constructs the culture as well as the psyches of individuals, postmodernists like Judith Butler have argued that all identities, even those conforming to mainstream or dominant norms, are fractured or splintered, characterized by double and sometimes triple consciousness, and fabricated by political structures and operations that conceal the mechanisms through which they function. Furthermore, postmodernists insist that identity is ultimately unknowable because the very terms used to explore it are limited and predetermined (Butler 4, 9). Such messages about the multiplicity and instability of identity invite students not only to tolerate diversity—having recognized it within themselves— but also to experiment with novel standpoints as they experience and interrogate representations of diversity in literary texts.

From Theory to Classroom

Surprisingly perhaps, the complex theories outlined above devolve into a relatively straightforward gynetic reading strategy. Having learned the relationship between language/text and culture, students can be encouraged to approach a particular literary work as an artifact of culture and to consider the identity/ies embedded in the text and their interaction with hegemonic identities (including, perhaps, their own) as well as with hegemonic cultural norms and representations. Students can also be encouraged both to comprehend and to transcend the feminization/marginalization processes affecting the literary canon, as well as their own and others' aesthetic judgments and literary analyses. These goals can be facilitated by the exploration of texts in three basic steps: (1) identifying in a particular text the "norms"—that is, the representations identifiable as conventions and traditions of Western culture—against which it has apparently been written; (2) elucidating the alternative representation(s) provided in the text; and (3) exploring the means, that is, the narrative strategies, by which hegemonic norms are challenged and decentered in the text.

The analysis of a simple short story, "Right Off the Bat" by Lesléa Newman, can serve to illustrate the gynetic strategy. Newman's text represents lesbian identity as both a challenge to convention and a benign alternative voice from the cultural margins. While exposing the often hypocritical cultural norms against which it is set, the text successfully demystifies the cultural phenomenon (or space) referred to derisively in the story as the lesbian lifestyle by representing it as a harmless, even preferable, substitute for so-called normal family life.

The story is told in the voice of a twelve-year-old girl, Ronnie, who speaks to an unnamed new acquaintance standing outside the narrative frame. Ronnie is hoping to become friends with this acquaintance, but before she starts the relationship she wants the new person to know about her unusual family situation: she was born of a lesbian mother; her father was an anonymous sperm donor; the alternative (not artificial) inseminating instrument was a turkey baster; Ronnie now lives with her mother and her mother's lover, Linda. Ronnie is also Jewish. Her family arrangement had once shocked and alienated another friend, Brenda, whose mother told her she couldn't talk to Ronnie anymore because her mother was a dyke. (Whether anti-Semitism played a role in the prohibition against friendship between Brenda and Ronnie is unclear.) So Ronnie wants the new acquaintance to know the full story "right off the bat" so she doesn't risk having the new friend "pull a Brenda" on her (Newman 13, 21).

The first step in reading the story gynetically is identifying the conventions and traditions it highlights, addresses, and (eventually) replaces. This process requires a level of abstraction students may need help achieving, but the simplicity of this particular story makes the process easier. Ronnie's explanations to her friend about herself, her background, and her mother are clues to the traditions and conventions the story addresses. In addition, the story presents explicit commentary on conventions that block the lives of its characters.

Students will easily identify the first of the conventions the story addresses: the nuclear family model of mother, father, and child as the core of a good and decent home. With some prompting (and reference to psychoanalytic theory) they will also identify the implicit accompanying belief that children without fathers suffer both economically and (according to Freudian conventions) emotionally, because there is no one to mediate the emotional intensity of the mother-child relationship. They will further recognize the nuclear family model's implication that fathers are heads of families and households, that mothers and children rightly submit to paternal rule and control, and that families without fathers (and conceptions without penises) are inauthentic or "artificial" (as in "artificial insemination").

Also easily identified in the story is a second cultural convention:

the norm of heterosexuality, in which women love men and in which lesbians are generally represented as perverts. Lesbians' negative status is represented in the text by the term "dyke," which Ronnie explains "is a bad word for lesbian" (13). Students will also recognize that the heterosexual norm represents mothers as conventionally feminine and lesbians as, at best, disinterested in, and, at worst, perverters of children.

A third obvious cultural convention is a Christian-centered view that constructs Jews as outsiders or, in some cases, as enemies. Jews' negative status is represented in the story by the term "Yids," which is a clear parallel to "dyke" (13). An allusion to Nazi persecution of Jews toward the end of the story suggests the deeper level of threat that Jews, like lesbians, have sometimes represented.

Also evident in the text is the recognition of a few acceptable deviations from these norms in mainstream culture. Single mothers are acceptable, for example, as are their boyfriends. Ronnie uses that deviation to introduce the concept of a lesbian lover as a parallel to a heterosexual mother's boyfriend. Because she recognizes that such a relationship still occupies only shaky cultural ground, however, Ronnie hastens to assure her new friend that Linda's designation as her mother's lover does not mean she is a "Casanova," that is, someone overtly or embarrassingly sexual or even promiscuous (14). The text also represents Judaism as an acceptable deviation, but like lesbianism, Judaism requires explanation.

Other conventions implicit in the story include the mainstream American values of freedom, individualism, and middle-class levels of consumerism and child-centeredness. A complete analysis of the story requires an exploration of the many implications of those values, including the presumption that they produce a good society and happy, healthy people.

A gynetic reading of Newman's text cannot ignore the phallic implications of many of the norms and conventions against which it is written. Here the symbolic/semiotic model helps students see, for example, that the norm entails male control of women's sexuality and posits a family model dependent for its legitimacy upon the presence of a man and the phallic symbolism of his domination. That any explanation is required to legitimize a different pattern—lesbianism, Judaism—is testament to the hegemony of patriarchal and Christian values and principles as well as to the difficulty of asserting alternatives. Thus, the conventions that emerge in the text illustrate the mechanisms gynesis is designed to challenge and disrupt.

The second phase of the reading process is the identification of alternatives to such conventions presented in the story. In Newman's text, those alternatives are represented on several levels. On one level, they are almost revolutionary: Ronnie's mother is a dyke; her father was a turkey baster; her mother has a female lover who could also be considered her "father"; no one would be upset if Ronnie became a lesbian. Postmodern psychoanalytic theory suggests that such practices upstage the phallus, place women in control—indeed, replace father- with mother-rule—and give a woman, Linda, the mediating role between mother and child that has rendered fathers so powerful. Furthermore, those practices mean that, unlike daughters in conventional families, Ronnie need never leave a world of female identification that may lead to her own lesbian identity. (She wonders about her sexuality in the story without reaching a conclusion.) Ronnie's alternative familial relationships signify her closer identification with the pre-Oedipal mother-child symbiosis and female sexual *jouissance* than that of "normal" women, whose Oedipal passage is more complete.

On another level, however, the alternatives presented by the text are familiar and nonthreatening: the lesbian family lives in a comfortable house with a yard; Ronnie has her own room, a cat, books, and records; Ronnie's parents lavish care upon her by fussing over what she eats, whom she might date, and other matters typical of family life. Indeed, on the surface, the story represents Ronnie's revolutionary world as a comfortable one. As she retains her feminine attachments in a nonphallic world, she remains affable, cheerful, and "normal" in her tastes and desires. The lesbian world of her mother is also represented as comfortably diverse, encompassing women as weirdly "butch" as Ronnie's mother, who wears only "nerdy jeans," T-shirts emblazoned with embarrassing slogans, and sturdy footwear, and as familiarly feminine as Linda, who wears dresses, jewelry, and high heels (17–18). Linda represents the possibility of bridging the heterosexual world of Ronnie's school and friendships and the world of openly lesbian identity and sexuality. Linda also translates the hegemonic culture for Ronnie's mother and helps her see her connection to it by, for example, urging her to be patient, not to lay her "own trip on [Ronnie], the same way [her] mother laid her own trip on [her]" and to allow Ronnie "to make her own decisions about things" (17).

Related to the text's alternative representation of family is its alternative to heterosexual normalcy, the lesbian couple. Ronnie explains lesbianism at the story's beginning: "Being a lesbian means my mom loves women instead of men" (13–14). The story constructs Ronnie's mother as a parallel to a single heterosexual mother who dates, and since Linda is not a Casanova, she seems even less threatening than the boyfriend of such a mother, who might be one. The lesbian couple's butch/femme complementarity also reinforces their social acceptability. Indeed, a student who squints while reading Newman's story sees an eerily familiar husband-wife picture. As with the story's depiction of the family, however, there is another level of interpretation. Students appreciate the irony of the couple's complementary roles as a challenge to maternal conventions of femininity, in their attribution of maternal desires and commitment to the more butch of the pair, Ronnie's mother, and their location of the paternal function in its femme member, Linda.

Another obvious alternative to convention in the text is Judaism, which, like lesbianism, is presented, at least on one level, as a harmless parallel to the norm. Ronnie explains that "being Jewish means I go to temple instead of church . . . and we have Chanukah and Passover instead of Christmas and Easter" (13). Students will see that the Jewish parallel, like the parallel couple and family configurations, is designed to familiarize deviance by exploring the relatively safe area of religious diversity (a truism—if not a fact—of the American value system), in order to demystify deviance in more dangerous areas. Ronnie reinforces such a project by explaining that the more socially acceptable intolerance of lesbians—calling them "dykes"—is just as bad as the less socially acceptable intolerance of Jews—calling them "Yids."

Less evident is the story's presentation of alternative values, but having established the conventional values against which the story is written, students will easily find them. Throughout the story are examples of the lesbian family's concern for health and the environment, for example, and toward the end the text's most "deviant" lesbian delivers its most explicitly value-laden speech. Students will again appreciate the irony of the text's association of the mainstream values of individualism and self-determination with what much of mainstream society might consider a deviant character. But the association works. Ronnie's mother's admonition that everyone's first duty is to "be yourself" rings true. When she continues, "Be straight, be gay, be a drag queen in heels, or a bulldyke like your old ma, but be whoever you are and be proud of it," students will likely follow her logic (19).

The third exercise in interpreting the text gynetically is the discovery of the narrative strategies it employs as it decenters convention and transforms deviance or marginality into a new kind of normalcy. To discover these strategies, students must ask themselves how the story attempts to convince its (probably straight) readers that lesbianism is nonthreatening, and that, while challenging normalcy, these voices from society's margins are more like their own than they originally thought. They will identify one such strategy as the use of the twelve-year-old Ronnie to narrate the story. Ronnie is an engaging child who exhibits all the signs of normalcy, either despite or because of her role in a lesbian family. That she is clearly unharmed and uncorrupted by something the dominant society has labeled harmful and corrupting both defuses anti-lesbian prejudice and renders invalid the judgment of adults who cannot demonstrate Ronnie's level of tolerance.

Ronnie also plays the role of the straight reader, thereby bridging the heterosexual and lesbian worlds. As many readers might, she sometimes considers her mother and other lesbians weird. She admits that her mother "is not like anyone else's mother I've ever met" (14). She also empathizes with people who would reject her mother and Linda. After explaining how the couple were dressed to celebrate their anniversary, Ronnie concedes that "you probably think that's really weird, a woman wearing a tie, but lots of my mom's friends do." But then she teaches the reader how to deal with the weirdness as she does. By saying "I'm kind of used to it I guess," she teaches tolerance. By admitting that she "can't imagine my mother in a dress," she validates the legitimacy of real differences among people and the inappropriateness of a single standard for all (18). As we identify with Ronnie and develop affection and respect for her, Ronnie's approval and acceptance of her mother, Linda, and their lives together is transformed into readers' approval of the lesbian family as well as their diminished acceptance of the "normal" world that would oppress them.

Students are likely to identify the text's use of the Jew/lesbian analogy as the second major narrative strategy for transforming reader sentiment. The analogy locates lesbians within the more acceptable marginal category "Jews" and thereby establishes lesbianism as a more acceptable deviance. This device culminates in an incident that explicitly intertwines a story of homophobia with a story of anti-Semitism. The story of homophobia is a central motif in the text: Ronnie's mother and Linda go to a fancy restaurant to celebrate their anniversary, and their tires are slashed in the parking lot, where their "old pick-up with all [the] bumper stickers stuck out like a sore thumb . . . with all the Mercedes Benz and Cadillacs, and whatever other kinds of cars rich people drive" (18). The incident initially focuses Ronnie's anger at the "punks, or whoever it was" who slashed the tires, but then (like many straight readers) she becomes angry with her mom: "I mean if she would just shave her legs or put on a dress or quit holding Linda's hand on the street . . . these things wouldn't always be happening to her" (19). Ronnie's act of blaming the victim elicits her mother's memory of the other story: "Your Great Aunt Zeldo and your Uncle Hymie thought the exact same thing with their fancy Christmas tree on their front lawn," she reminds Ronnie, "and still their neighbors in Poland turned them in to the Nazis for a buck fifty apiece" (19). The emotional impact of the second story rehearses us for the emotions appropriate to the first. We are instructed to despise bigotry against lesbians just as we despise it against Jews.

The Utility of Theory

I have found that students respond well to the poststructuralist, postmodern psychoanalytic feminist reading of the literature of women's diversity, including lesbian literature. At first, they need help abstracting from the specifics of a literary text the cultural and developmental components underlying them, but with practice they become quite good at it. White, heterosexual, European-American students come to the process equipped with tacit knowledge of Western conventions; lesbians, students of color, and international students often have explicit ways of articulating those conventions, since they cannot survive on the same assumptions and blind spots common to the worldviews of their dominant-group counterparts. All students seem to enjoy schematicizing their cultural knowledge and applying it to the texts. I have found that composing a chart of the three stages of reading each text is a helpful exercise. For the first few texts in the course, we compose the chart as a group. Thereafter, students are able to do the charts on their own, in preparation for class discussion.

As students do gynetic readings of lesbian texts, they begin to question the representations that constitute their own identities and to separate those representations from something they might call real. As they explore the multiple components of the entity called "self," they start to value the hidden "deviations" in their own identities, and they revalue what they have learned to call deviance in the identities of others. As they learn to critique the culture that might have privileged them, they learn that dominant standards can be wrong. They consider the danger, as well as the injustice, of silencing the voices the dominant culture does not want to hear. Finally, they learn to see gynesis, the putting into discourse of that which has been hidden, left out, and despised, as an act of social responsibility that ensures there will never be another deadly silence again.

Works Cited

Butler, Judith. *Gender Trouble: Feminism and the Subversion of Identity*. New York: Routledge, 1990.

Jardine, Alice. *Gynesis: Configurations of Woman and Modernity*. Ithaca, NY: Cornell University Press, 1985.

Moi, Toril. *Sexual/Textual Politics*. London: Methuen, 1985.

Newman, Lesléa. "Right Off the Bat," in *Speaking for Ourselves: Short Stories by Jewish Lesbians*, Irene Zahava, ed. Freedom, CA: Crossing Press, 1990.

11

Heterosexual Teacher, Lesbian/Gay/Bisexual Text: Teaching the Sexual Other(s)

AnnLouise Keating

> *"I'm straight; what do I know about homosexuality? If I try to discuss it, I might offend my lesbian/gay students."*
>
> *"But what will people think? What if my chair finds out? What if parents complain? This is a conservative school . . ."*

The questions in epigraph above represent two of the major objections heterosexually identified teachers give when asked why they don't include writings by or about lesbians, bisexuals, and gays in their syllabi. The first obstacle—lack of personal experience—is based on the underlying belief that "only lesbians [or gays or bisexuals] can teach lesbian [or gay or bisexual] writing." Although this belief is motivated by the desire not to appropriate or misrepresent the experiences of sexual minorities, it relies on a simplistic form of identity politics that prevents us from acknowledging the complex interconnections between apparently dissimilar peoples. As instructors, we're often called upon to teach material that lies outside our daily frame of reference. Why should it be more difficult to learn about homosexuality than it is to learn about life in Victorian England?

The second obstacle—fear of public censure—is equally understandable, given the recent resurgence in conservative interest groups. Yet the only way to effectively challenge the heterosexism and homophobia underlying this fear is to speak out. As Audre Lorde asserts in "The Transformation of Silence into Language and Action," our silences do not really protect us from the oppressive social systems we fear; they only keep us paralyzed and divided: "It is not difference which immobilizes us, but silence. And there are so many silences to be broken."[1]

No matter how we identify ourselves sexually or culturally, as feminists and as teachers we have the responsibility to begin breaking the many silences that seem to divide us. But in order to do so, we must introduce our students—as well as ourselves—to a wide variety of worldviews and experiences. As Marilyn Frye points out, "Most of the students and faculty members in US universities in the present era need to be vastly more informed and appreciative of multiplicity, plurality, and diversity, both among and within cultures."[2]

For the past several years I've worked as an untenured assistant professor at a fairly small, predominantly Anglo university located in the Southwest's Bible Belt, and in all of my classes—from the expository writing courses required for all freshman, to introductory women's studies classes, to graduate-level literature seminars—I include material written by and/or about self-identified lesbians, gays, and bisexuals.[3] Despite my initial fears, students' responses have been surprisingly favorable; indeed, they're often delighted to encounter positive portrayals of homosexuality. In this essay I want to discuss some of the strategies I've found most effective in teaching lesbian/gay/bisexual material.

Self-Education

Whenever I incorporate new material into my syllabi, I try to learn as much about the subject as I possibly can. Thus, before I began teaching lesbian/gay/bi issues, I read a number of books on related topics. My goal was not to become an "expert" on homosexuality, but rather to acquaint myself with the numerous ways lesbians, gay men, bisexuals, and heterosexuals have defined themselves. (Not surprisingly, however, members of the latter group seldom define their sexuality.) I found Audre Lorde's *Sister Outsider* (Crossing 1984), the personal narratives in *The New Coming Out Stories* (Crossing 1989), Shane Phelan's *Identity Politics: Lesbian Feminism and the Limits of Community* (Temple University 1989), the essays on "queer theory" collected in Diana Fuss's *Inside/Outside* (Routledge 1991), and Warren Blumenfeld's anthology, *Homophobia: How We All Pay the Price* (Beacon 1992) especially useful.

Classroom Performance

Whether I'm teaching a survey of US literature, composition, women's studies, or graduate-level seminars, I emphasize the political, potentially transformative (and therefore disconcerting) nature of the course. Instead of treating homosexuality as a highly sensitive, forbidden topic, I make a point of always mentioning it in my introductory lectures. I inform students that my pedagogy is shaped by what Henry Giroux calls a "politics of difference," an exploration of the ways sexuality, gender, culture, ethnicity, and other variables "are shaped within the margins and centre of power."[4] I distinguish between a benign pluralism that incorporates diverse perspectives without interrogating the status quo—the heterosexual, Eurocentric, masculinist "norm"—and a politics of difference that examines the many power struggles informing US culture. By exploring a broad range of worldviews, issues, and experiences, we examine how hegemonic definitions create hierarchical, oppressive social systems. Because one of the power structures I want to destabilize is the teacher/student paradigm, I emphasize that I will not adopt the role of the "expert" who tells students what to think about sexual, gender, racial, or class issues. Instead, by problematizing the conventional conceptions of terms like "homosexual," "heterosexual," "masculine," "feminine," "race," "man," and "woman," I hope to encourage students' own critical thinking. Rather than accept the dominant culture's inscriptions, I want them to begin (re)defining these terms for themselves.

In fact, I even problematize my own sexuality by engaging in what I call "strategic nonnaming." That is, I make a point of not identifying as heterosexual, bisexual, or lesbian, and I inform students of the rationale behind my decision. Last semester, for example, I told my introductory women's studies class that I had consciously chosen not to discuss my own sexual preference, and I explained that by doing so I hoped to avoid what I see as two possible dangers in teaching lesbian/gay/bi material: On the one hand, if I identified as straight, it would be difficult not to establish an us/them polarity where "we" heterosexuals examine the sexual Other(s); on the other hand, if I identified as lesbian, I might be expected—or tempted—to speak for all lesbians and give students an insider's view that ignores the diversity among contemporary US lesbians. I discussed other issues related to incorporating homosexuality into the course material, including the importance of lesbian-identified role models, the academic community's homophobia, my own fears that I'd be labeled as lesbian (whether or not I actually was), and the temptation to refer to a fictionalized or real-life boyfriend, male lover, or husband. This staged (non)confession led to an intense discussion of homophobia and other internalized and external forms of oppression.

Let me emphasize: I'm not advocating that instructors should never disclose their sexuality in the classroom. As the term "strategic non-naming" implies, the decision to remain silent concerning my own sexual preference was a carefully chosen tactic based on my assessment of the students who sign up for my introductory women's studies courses. Many of them are rather conservative education majors, and I wanted to encourage them to incorporate lesbian/gay/bi material into their teaching in nonhomophobic ways. Thus I prefaced my own strategic (non)naming with a discussion of homophobia in the classroom. All too often I have seen heterosexually identified women (and others passing as straight) nervously preface their remarks on homosexuality with comments intended to assure their listeners of their own heterosexuality. These disclaimers strike me as homophobic, and I wanted my performance to serve as an alternate model. However, as I explain to my students, my point is not that instructors should never identify their sexuality but rather that different contexts require different tactical positions; strategic nonnaming is one strategy among others.

Focus on Multiple Issues

Probably the most useful strategy I've employed involves exploring diverse sets of issues simultaneously. By discussing sexualities in conjunction with culture, ethnicity, class, and/or gender, sexual preference becomes one aspect of the complex systems of difference that construct social actors in contemporary US cultures.

This emphasis on multiple systems of difference involves three interrelated techniques. First, I avoid focusing exclusively on homosexuality by encouraging students to examine the similarities and differences between all forms of sexuality. At times, I juxtapose "straight" and "queer" texts in order to stimulate comparative analyses. I've taught Mary Helen Ponce's *The Wedding* (Arte Público 1989) in conjunction with Rita Mae Brown's *Rubyfruit Jungle* (Bantam 1983); Paule Marshall's *Praisesong for the Widow* (Putnam's Sons 1983) with Audre Lorde's *Zami: A New Spelling of My Name* (Crossing 1982); and Dorothy West's *The Living Is Easy* (Feminist Press 1982) with Terri de la Peña's *Margins* (Seal 1992). I like to include works—such as those by Ana Castillo, Cherry Muhanji, and Alice Walker—that present a variety of sexualities.[5] I find Denise Chávez's *Last of the Menu Girls* (Arte Público 1986), Toni Morrison's *Sula* (Plume 1987), and Sarah

Orne Jewett's *Country of the Pointed Firs* (Norton 1982) to be especially effective in problematizing students' rather simplistic definitions
of lesbianism; these texts' ambiguous depictions of women's sexualities, coupled with their portrayal of autonomous female characters,
have provoked fascinating classroom discussions. By thus interrogating
same-sex and male-female relationships simultaneously, heterosexuality is not privileged. (It is, in fact, almost the reverse: as I will explain
later, by examining heterosexuality as one sexual preference among
others, we denaturalize it.)

Second, I rarely discuss sexualities in isolation from other systems
of difference. Instead, I structure my syllabi in ways that enable us to
examine lesbian, gay, bisexual, and heterosexual identities in the context of other issues, such as definitions and stereotypes; the importance
of self-naming; and the various forms of oppression (internalized,
horizontal, and vertical) often experienced by members of so-called
minority racial groups and women of all colors. For instance, when I
teach Introduction to Women's Studies I don't include a unit or readings that focus exclusively on homosexuality or lesbianism. Instead,
we discuss homosexuality in conjunction with related themes, including the ways peoples' sexual identities and self-perceptions have been
shaped by feminist movement,[6] gender roles, US sexual mores, and
identity politics. Similarly, in a recent "Race," Gender, and Literature
seminar I integrated issues related to lesbian and gay writing into our
examination of African-American, Native-American, Chicano/a, and
Euro-American texts. We explored both the lesbian subtexts and the
critiques of heterosexual relationships in writings by Sarah Orne Jewett, Alice Dunbar-Nelson, and Mary Wilkins Freeman; analyzed the
ways lesbian-identified writers like Gloria Anzaldúa and Judy Grahn
create characters who can pass as straight; and applied Eve Sedgwick's
theory of homosocial desire to works by Rolando Hinojoso, Scott
Momaday, and William Faulkner.[7]

Third, whether I'm teaching Freshman Composition, Introduction
to Women's Studies, or graduate-level US literature seminars, I select
texts that explore complex, overlapping issues from a wide range of
cultural and sexual perspectives. I frequently use writings by Gloria
Anzaldúa, Cherríe Moraga, Becky Birtha, Audre Lorde, and other self-
identified US Third World lesbians, because they illustrate Moraga's
assertion that the lesbian of color's "very presence violates the ranking
and abstraction of oppressions."[8] Similarly, the stories, essays, and
poems collected in anthologies like *This Bridge Called My Back: Writings by Radical Women of Color* (Kitchen Table 1983), *Making Face,*

Making Soul/Haciendo Caras: Creative and Critical Perspectives by Women of Color (Aunt Lute 1990), and *Brother to Brother: New Writings by Black Gay Men* (Alyson 1991) don't separate gender from sexual preferences, cultural identities, or class. These works provide students with concrete examples of the interlocking systems of oppression that marginalize people who—because of their sexuality, gender, ethnicity, and/or economic status—do not belong to the dominant cultural group.

This multiperspective approach shapes students' perceptions in significant ways. To begin with, introducing them to a broad range of worldviews—including the experiences of African-American, Anglo, Chicana, and Native-American lesbians and heterosexuals—effectively challenges their preconceptions about the sexual, cultural, or class Other(s). It becomes difficult, if not impossible, for students to accept monolithic definitions of gender, sexuality, and culture. They recognize that, just as there's no unitary, all-encompassing description of "woman" or "Hispanic," there's no single definition of "lesbian" or "gay."

Perhaps most important, this emphasis on a multiplicity of differences prevents us from equating difference with deviation. An exclusive focus on any single category—whether it's sexual preference, gender, culture, ethnicity, or class—inadvertently reifies the unexamined ("white,"[9] male, heterosexual) norm and, by extension, implies the abnormality of the (nonwhite, nonmale, nonheterosexual) group under examination. As Paula Rothenberg asserts, "Where white, male, middle-class, European heterosexuality provides the standard of and the criteria for rationality and morality, difference is always perceived as deviant and deficient."[10] Discussing same-sex relationships in the context of all forms of sexuality makes it difficult, if not impossible, to dismiss the former as abnormal. And by examining diverse forms of sexuality in conjunction with culture, ethnicity, class, and/or gender, sexual preferences can be seen as one aspect of the complex systems of difference that construct social actors in contemporary US cultures.

Problematize Definitions

Frequently, students' unthinking acceptance of heterosexuality, as well as their conceptions of lesbian, gay, and bisexual identities, are based on false information and homophobic stereotypes: "Heterosexuality is natural," "All lesbians hate men," "All gay men are effeminate," and so on. In order to challenge these inaccurate assumptions I attempt to denaturalize all forms of sexuality—including the heterosexual norm—by discussing the ways sexualities are constructed in contemporary US culture. The issues we explore include the following: How have the media and religious institutions portrayed homosexuals? How have they portrayed heterosexuals? What are the consequences of these images? Why has AIDS been defined as a gay disease? How has this media-constructed image adversely affected AIDS research and treatment? Given other cultures' more lenient attitudes toward same-sex relationships, why do contemporary western societies see homosexuality as so threatening?[11] How does homosexuality jeopardize the status quo? How does heterosexuality reinforce it? How does heterosexual privilege reward those who conform to the dominant culture's proscriptions? How does homophobia lock all people into rigid gender roles? How do accusations of lesbianism prevent women from forming bonds with each other, or from identifying as feminists? Suzanne Pharr's *Homophobia: A Weapon of Sexism* (Chardon 1988) and the essays collected in Warren Blumenfeld's *Homophobia: How We All Pay the Price* provide thought-provoking discussions of these issues.

Often students assume that homosexuality and heterosexuality reflect innate character traits: each person is born with an unchanging sexual identity. Although some lesbians and gays would agree with this view of sexual orientation, I stress that no one knows for sure how sexual identities develop, and often sexual preferences change within the course of a person's life. Students are surprised to learn that many theorists see heterosexuality, as well as homosexuality, as a matter of personal choice. Marilyn Frye, for example, challenges self-identified heterosexual feminists to reflect on their own sexual preference, to be "as actively curious about how and why and when they became heterosexual as [she has] been about how and why and when [she] became Lesbian."[12] Essays, stories, and poems by Cherríe Moraga, Gloria Anzaldúa, Audre Lorde, Adrienne Rich, Becky Birtha, Paula Gunn Allen and other self-identified lesbians further challenge students' assumptions by illustrating the diverse ways lesbians reconstruct their own sexual identities. For example, Anzaldúa claims that she "made the choice to be gay" and refers to a time in her life when she was heterosexual, while Moraga maintains that she's always been queer.[13] Similarly, in *The Woman Who Owned the Shadows* (Spinsters/Aunt Lute 1983) Paula Gunn Allen depicts her protagonist's uncertainty concerning her own sexuality as she explores relationships with both women and men.[14]

I problematize students' conceptions of homosexuality even further by mentioning some of the unresolved (and probably unresolvable) theoretical issues queer theory explores: What does it mean to be lesbian, bisexual, or gay? Is it simply a matter of sexual object choice? Or do the terms refer to specific lifestyles? Is there, for example, a "gay sensibility"? a "lesbian" worldview? a "lesbian ethics"? Diana Fuss's introduction to *Inside/Outside* and Teresa de Lauretis's "Queer Theory: Lesbian and Gay Sexualities/An Introduction" provide useful overviews of recent debates in lesbian/gay theory, especially when read in conjunction with "To(o) Queer the Writer," Gloria Anzaldúa's critique of academic queer theory.[15]

It's important to emphasize that there are no set definitions of lesbian, gay, or bisexual identity. Indeed, the word "lesbian" is itself extremely problematic. Often, people automatically believe the term indicates a unitary, essentialized core identity, yet this interpretation is too restrictive. As Ruth Ginzberg implies, it overlooks specific *"acts, moments, relationships, encounters, attractions, perspectives, insights, outlooks, connections,* and *feelings"* that could also be considered "lesbian." Not surprisingly, then, some lesbian theorists like Sarah Hoagland and Marilyn Frye refuse to define the term, claiming that "lesbians" don't exist in phallocentric conceptual systems. By thus locating lesbians outside patriarchal structures, they can claim that lesbians represent a new nonmasculine subjectivity. Monique Wittig makes a similar point in "The Straight Mind" when she distinguishes between "woman" and "lesbian." She asserts that " 'woman' has meaning only in heterosexual systems of thought and heterosexual economic systems. Lesbians are not women." I further underscore the diverse—and often conflicting—ways lesbians have defined themselves by discussing the positive and negative implications of the "woman-identified woman" and Adrienne Rich's "lesbian continuum," as well as the debates between nonlesbian feminists and feminist lesbians.[16]

Many self-identified lesbians of color take this interrogation of lesbian identity even further by exposing and rejecting its Eurocentric bias. Gloria Anzaldúa, for example, dismisses the words "lesbian" and "homosexual" as "white," middle-class labels and adopts expressions like *"tejana tortillera," "mita' y mita,' " "patlache,"* and *"mestiza queer"* to describe herself. As she repeatedly emphasizes the cultures and class-specific dimensions of her sexuality, she destabilizes ethnocentric (Anglo, middle-class) definitions of homosexuality and (re)defines herself and other dykes as "forerunner[s] of a new race, / half and half—both woman and man, neither / a new gender." And in.

a 1990 interview Paula Gunn Allen draws on her Native-American worldview to redefine lesbianism as "perversity (transformationality) ... the sacred moment, the process of changing from one condition to another—*life-long* liminality."[17]

Historicize Sexual Identities

I further problematize students' conceptions of lesbian, bisexual, and gay identities by challenging their ahistorical notions of sexuality. Generally, they assume that contemporary definitions of sexuality and sexual identity—especially the rigid hetero/homo binary opposition—are unchanging transhistorical categories. Yet these terms, as well as modern western culture's interpretations of sexuality itself, are fairly recent inventions. As David Halperin asserts, "Homosexuality, hetero-sexuality, and even sexuality itself [are] relatively recent and highly culture-specific forms of erotic life—not the basic building-blocks of sexual identity for all human beings in all times and places, but peculiar and indeed exceptional ways of conceptualizing as well as *experiencing* sexual desire."[18]

Students seldom realize that the words "homosexuality" and "het-erosexuality"—as well as the practice of classifying specific types of people according to their sexual preferences—didn't exist before the 1890s. As Arnold Davidson persuasively argues, until the second half of the nineteenth century sexuality was defined exclusively on the basis of anatomical sex; it wasn't until the "emergence of the psychiatric style of reasoning" that the concept of sexual identities, defined as "a matter of tastes, aptitudes, satisfactions, and psychic traits," developed. It's not that people weren't engaging in homosexual acts before this time but rather that these practices or behaviors did not indicate specific personality types or psychosexual identities. For example, sodomy—which had been perceived as a specific sex act that could involve people of any gender—was transformed into a type of person with distinct psychological traits: the sodomite or homosexual.[19]

Speak Out

I began this essay by mentioning two obstacles self-identified hetero-sexuals often confront as they consider incorporating lesbian/gay/bi issues into their syllabi: (1) lack of personal experience, and (2) fear of public censure. I've devoted most of the preceding pages to a discussion of the former, and to some extent, this focus has been intentional. After all, it's easier to compensate for your own lack of personal knowledge than it is to deal with other people's homophobia and heterosexism. However, the two issues are intimately related. As Audre Lorde suggests in "The Transformation of Silence into Language and Action," both have their source in the fears of the socially constructed differences that so often prevent us from establishing bonds with the sexual, cultural, and/or class Other(s). Unfortunately, speaking out dos not automatically make our fears go away. It does, however, enable us to begin forming political alliances with each other. Thus Lorde challenges her audience to overcome

> the mockeries of separations that have been imposed upon us and which so often we accept as our own. For instance, "I can't possibly teach Black women's writing—their experience is so different from mine." Yet how many years have you spent teaching Plato and Shakespeare and Proust? Or another, "She's a white woman and what could she possible have to say to me?" Or, "She's a lesbian, what would my husband say, or my chairman?" . . . And all the other endless ways in which we rob ourselves of ourselves and each other.[20]

As a black feminist, I am firmly convinced that we must challenge the oppressive social systems and the culturally constructed boundaries that blind us from recognizing our complex interconnections with apparently dissimilar women and men. But in order to do so, we must risk speaking out—despite our fears. Only then can we begin bridging the differences that seem to divide us.

Notes

Thanks to Renae Bredin, Cynthia Hogue, and the students in my spring 1993 Introduction to Women's Studies class for their comments on the ideas in this paper. Special thanks to Debra Miller for her suggestions on earlier drafts.

1. Audre Lorde, *Sister Outsider: Essays and Speeches* (Freedom, CA: Crossing Press, 1984), 44.

2. Marilyn Frye, *Willful Virgin: Essays in Feminism, 1976–1992* (Freedom, CA: Crossing Press, 1992), 22.

3. In classroom discussions I distinguish bisexuality from both homosexuality and heterosexuality, yet it's difficult to find bisexual-identified works to include in my syllabi. For personal narratives and theoretical essays on bisexuality, see Elizabeth

Reba Weise, *Closer to Home: Bisexuality and Feminism* (Seattle, WA: Seal Press, 1992), and Loraine Hutchins and Lani Kaahumanu, eds., *Bi Any Other Name: Bisexual People Speak Out* (Boston: Alyson Publishing, 1991).

4. Henry Giroux, "Democracy and the Discourse of Cultural Difference: Towards a Politics of Border Pedagogy," *British Journal of Sociology of Education* 12 (1991): 509.

5. Ana Castillo, *The Mixquiahuala Letters* (Tempe, AZ: Bilingual Press, 1986) and *Sapogonia* (Tempe, AZ: Bilingual Press, 1990); Cherry Muhanji, *Her* (San Francisco: Aunt Lute, 1990); Alice Walker, *The Color Purple* (New York: Washington Square Press, 1982).

6. I follow bell hooks in using the phrase "feminist movement," rather than *the* feminist movement. To my mind, the former term is less monolithic than the latter; also, it more fully captures both the unity and the diversity among contemporary feminists. See hooks, *Feminist Theory: From Margin to Center* (Boston: South End Press, 1984).

7. For stories by Sarah Orne Jewett, Alice Dunbar-Nelson, and Mary Wilkins Freeman, see Judith Fetterley and Marjorie Pryse, eds., *American Women Regionalists, 1850–1910* (New York: Norton, 1992). Gloria Anzaldúa, *"El Paisano* Is a Bird of Good Omen," in Alma Gomez, Cherríe Moraga, and Mariana Romo-Carmona, eds. *Cuentos: Stories by Latinas* (New York: Kitchen Table Press, 1983) and also in Anzaldúa, *Prieta* (San Francisco: Aunt Lute, 1994); Judy Grahn, *The Queen of Swords* (Boston: Beacon Press, 1987) and *The Work of a Common Woman* (Trumansburg, NY: Crossing Press, 1978); Rolando Hinojosa, *Klail City* (Houston, TX: Arte Público Press, 1987); Scott Momaday, *House Made of Dawn* (New York: Harper and Row, 1966).

8. Cherríe Moraga, "La Guëra," in Moraga and Gloria Anzaldúa, eds., *This Bridge Called My Back: Writings by Radical Women of Color* (New York: Kitchen Table Press, 1983), 29. Gloria Anzaldúa, *Borderlands/La Frontera: The New Mestiza* (San Francisco: Spinsters/Aunt Lute, 1987); Becky Birtha, *For Nights like This One: Stories of Loving Women* (San Francisco: Frog in the Well Press, 1983); Cherríe Moraga, *Loving in the War Years: Lo que nunca pasó por sus labios* (Boston: South End Press, 1983); Audre Lorde, *Zami: A New Spelling of My Name* (Freedom, CA: Crossing Press, 1982).

9. Throughout this paper I have put the word *white*, when used in reference to people assumed to be of European descent, in scare quotes because I believe that the term is inaccurate, misleading, and divisive. Many people who look "white" are only partially of European descent and prefer to identify themselves as "Native-American," "Chicana," "African-American," "biracial," and so on. Indeed, I would argue that all references to separate "races" are inaccurate, misleading, and divisive. As a number of social scientists and philosophers have persuasively demonstrated, "race" refers to socially constructed categories, not to biological groups. See, for example, Kwame Anthony Appiah, "The Conservation of 'Race,' " *Black American Literature Forum* 23 (1989): 37–60; Michael Omi and Howard Winant, *Racial Formation in the United States from the 1960s to the 1980s* (New York: Routledge, 1986); and Yehudi O. Webster, *The Racialization of America* (New York: St. Martin's Press, 1992).

10. Paula Rothenberg, "The Construction, Deconstruction, and Reconstruction of Difference," *Hypatia* 5 (1990): 43.

11. For an overview of various ways non-western cultures have viewed homosexuality, see David F. Greenberg, *The Construction of Homosexuality* (Chicago: University of Chicago Press, 1988), and Walter Williams, *The Spirit and the Flesh: Sexual Diversity in American Indian Culture* (Boston: Beacon Press, 1986). In *Sexual Dissidence: Augustine to Wilde, Freud to Foucault* (London: Oxford University Press, 1991), Jonathan Dollimore discusses some of the reasons contemporary westerners see homosexuality as so threatening.

12. Frye, *Willful Virgin,* 55.

13. Anzaldúa, *Borderlands/La Frontera,* 19; Moraga, *Loving in the War Years,* 52. In her review of *Borderlands/La Frontera,* Moraga reinterprets Anzaldúa's assertion and claims that it indicates her political decision to identify as lesbian, rather than her decision to become sexually involved with women. See Cherríe Moraga, "Algo secretamente amado," *Third Woman: The Sexuality of Latinas* 4 (1989): 151–56; for Anzaldúa's response, see AnnLouise Keating, "Writing, Politics, and *Las Lesberadas: Platicando con* Gloria Anzaldúa," *Frontiers* 14 (1993).

14. For a discussion of lesbian identities in Allen and other contemporary writers, see Bonnie Zimmerman, *The Safe Sea of Women: Lesbian Fiction, 1969–1989* (Boston: Beacon Press, 1990).

15. Teresa de Lauretis, "Queer Theory: Lesbian and Gay Sexualities/An Introduction," *differences* 3:2 (Summer 1991): iii–xviii; Gloria Anzaldúa, "To(o) Queer the Writer—*Loca, escritora y chicana,* in Betsy Warland, ed., *Inversions: Writing by Dykes, Queers, and Lesbians* (Vancouver, BC: Press Gang Publishers, 1991), 249–64.

16. Ruth Ginzberg, "Audre Lorde's (Nonessentialist) Lesbian Eros," *Hypatia* 7 (1992): 82; Sarah Lucia Hoagland, *Lesbian Ethics: Toward New Value* (Palo Alto, CA: Institute of Lesbian Studies, 1988); Marilyn Frye, *The Politics of Reality: Essays in Feminist Theory* (Freedom, CA: Crossing Press, 1983); Monique Wittig, *The Straight Mind and Other Essays* (Boston: Beacon Press, 1992); Adrienne Rich, "Compulsory Heterosexuality and Lesbian Existence" (1980), in Rich, *Blood, Bread, and Poetry: Selected Prose, 1979–1985* (New York: Norton, 1986), 23–75. Ginzberg and Phelan provide a useful overview of these debates on lesbian identities.

17. Anzaldúa, "To(o) Queer the Writer" and *Borderlands/La Frontera,* 17–21 and 194; Jane Caputi, "Interview with Paula Gunn Allen," *Trivia* 16 (1990): 56.

18. David Halperin, *One Hundred Years of Homosexuality and Other Essays on Greek Love* (New York: Routledge, 1990), 9.

19. Arnold Davidson, "Sex and the Emergence of Sexuality," *Critical Inquiry* 14 (1987): 18–21. A number of books and essays explore the social construction of sexuality. Michel Foucault's groundbreaking *The History of Sexuality* (New York: Random House, 1978) examines the development of sexual identities in western culture, and David Halperin's *One Hundred Years of Homosexuality* puts contemporary conceptions of sexuality into historical perspective by providing an overview of the various ways westerners have perceived gender and sexual identities.

20. Audre Lorde, "The Transformation of Silence into Language and Action" (1977), in Lorde, *Sister Outsider,* 43–44.

12

Breaking the Silence:
Sexual Preference
in the Composition Classroom

Allison Berg, Jean Kowaleski, Caroline Le Guin,
Ellen Weinauer, Eric A. Wolfe

In a session titled "Writing, Teaching, and the Politics of Sexual Preference" at the 1989 Conference on College Composition and Communication (CCCC) in Seattle, Paul Puccio argued for the importance of breaking the silence surrounding the issue of sexual preference. Though many composition classrooms are increasingly devoted to examining the ways social membership can shape and construct our identity, we as teachers tend to consider that membership as limited to questions of gender, race/ethnicity, and socioeconomic class. We overlook sexual preference and, in so doing, replicate a societal and institutional silence that is destructive to ourselves and our students. As Puccio indicated, this situation "will never change unless there is more of a 'coming out'—a coming out not only of lesbian and gay academics but also a coming out of the subject itself." Implicit in this statement is the suggestion that dealing with gay and lesbian issues, and confronting homophobia in the classroom, must be more than a lesbian or gay teacher's concern. This coming out must involve many voices—those of gay, lesbian, and straight academics, teachers, and students. But we must also recognize that each of us will face the responsibility for breaking the silence in different ways, confront different problems, and find different solutions. Our goal in this essay is to explore our own experiences as straight teachers introducing sexual preference into a first-year writing course at Indiana University. Through this exploration, we carry on a dialogue with other voices working to break the silence.

At the conference session mentioned above, we presented papers that grew out of our teaching experience; this panel was our first substantial entry into just such a dialogue. Our experience as the straight member of a mixed gay and straight panel addressing a largely lesbian and gay audience forced us to reexamine our teaching, to question the values and assumptions implicit in our classrooms, and to recognize the ramifications of the ways we had approached the topic of sexual preference as teachers. The papers we gave at the conference were largely scholarly; we examined excerpts from our students' writing and attempted to account for and categorize their responses, which ranged from expressions of disgust to calls for violence. With hindsight, it seems clear that in our conference papers we approached the issue first as scholars, and only secondarily as teachers. By describing the patterns we saw in our students' writing—in effect viewing our students' virulent homophobia as a phenomenon to analyze—we were distancing ourselves from what was perhaps too painfully obvious: we had raised an issue in the classroom that we were unprepared to deal with. Thus, our papers focused on how students responded to the topic of sexual preference, and omitted the ways in which we, as teachers, approached the topic. Significantly, the audience's response to our panel centered on the dynamics of our classrooms and not on our interpretation of student writing. This response forced us to reassess critically our practice as teachers addressing the topic of sexual preference. From this reassessment came the newfound understanding that as we teach we must not exempt ourselves from the process of learning about this issue, or fail to recognize that we are laboring under the same sorts of silences our students experience— silences that are directly reinforced by the profession in which we work.

During the 1987–88 academic year, six Indiana University graduate students—Allison Berg, Chris Iwanicki, Jean Kowaleski, Caroline Le Guin, Ellen Weinauer, and Eric Wolfe—taught with David Bleich. Bleich's course, Studying One's Own Language, was a two-semester, freshman-level composition course that met three times a week, once a week in general lectures that all 144 students attended, and twice a week in discussion sections led by us, the teaching assistants. During the first semester of the course both students and instructors wrote biweekly, in-class essays in which we described a remembered conversation dealing with the current topic of discussion: family, gender, education, class, race, or sexual preference. The second semester brought literature into the course, and the biweekly essays were written as responses to literary texts which corresponded to the same general topics that structured the first semester. Throughout the year, these "lecture essays," copied and distributed to class members, became the text for class discussion and the basis for further analytical writing. Ultimately, the aim of the course was to understand the ways in which our language situates us in terms of social group membership and reveals and perpetuates ideological values.

In conceiving of the course, we—David Bleich as well as the associate instructors—participated in the same kind of silencing that Paul Puccio argues against. We did not originally include sexual preference as a topic for the course; it came as a kind of afterthought. When the syllabus was put together in the fall, the final few weeks were left open. It was only as the semester moved toward its end and the necessity of settling on a sixth topic became pressing that we decided definitely to include sexual preference. Our decision was based in part on our observation that when students discussed the other topics of the course, they seemed to have no language with which to discuss sexuality. Our goal was to elicit concrete examples of how students talked about homosexuality; through discussion and analysis of students' everyday language, we hoped to begin unraveling the complex power dynamics inherent in sexual and social relations, and to explore the connections between sexual preference and the other topics of the course. Because the topic was not listed on the syllabus at the beginning of the course, however, students no doubt got the message that the issue was an afterthought, and inferred, therefore, that sexual preference was not a significant social issue, or, at least, that it was less significant than the earlier topics. This may have allowed our students to believe that homophobic attitudes would be sanctioned.

The lecture essay for the topic of sexual preference followed a format similar to all the previous assignments, and read: "Describe a conversation with someone either of your own or another sexual preference (lesbian, male homosexual, bisexual, asexual, heterosexual) on the issue of homosexuality. Give as many salient details as you can about this conversation, particularly how attitudes about homosexuality were expressed." We tried to design the assignment in such a way that no writers would need to risk identifying their own sexuality. Yet, despite this attempt to attend to the needs of gay and lesbian students, we realize in retrospect that our question was, first, speaking primarily to our heterosexual students and, second, allowing students to be homophobic. For gay and lesbian students, the question must have seemed horribly ironic, because the phrase "attitudes toward homosexuality" implies that the expected audience is clearly heterosexual; our question presents homosexuality as something "other," something that the writer should have an attitude "toward." For a gay or lesbian student to attempt seriously to answer the question in the terms we provided would call for a level of personal disconnection inimical to the goals of the course. Indeed, the one student who had already come out to his class could only comment that the question did not fit his perspective.

The phrasing of the question also allowed our heterosexual students to remain disengaged, uninvolved; because we asked them to discuss only homosexuality, our heterosexual students could treat sexual preference as an issue that applied only to others, not themselves. In other words, the question invited them to respond with no sense of personal stake because they were not asked to reflect on their own sexuality and the degree to which it represented a choice. In contrast, the essay question on the topic of race asked students to describe a time when they were made aware of their *own* race or ethnicity; thus, it tried to interrupt the common white tendency to think that only people of color have a racial identity. By asking students to focus on homosexuality, we supplied a means for our straight students to keep the topic on a level safely outside of themselves. From the beginning, then, we set terms that would allow for homophobic student responses: we brought the topic of sexual preference in too late, we spoke not to lesbian and gay but to straight students, and we let those straight students remain personally distanced from the topic itself.

Many of our students answered in kind. Their responses ranged from violence to disgust (often linked with violence) to "it's OK as long as they stay away from me" to "I never think about it and I don't want to." Coupled with this was an assumption of consensus; despite the fact that students knew they would share their writing with peers and teachers, many of them seemed to feel that it would be acceptable to advocate "shooting all the gays." This perceived consensus prevailed even in the responses of students who knew one of their classmates was gay. In part because we were not prepared for such responses, we allowed the students' homophobia—and our indignation—to dictate our teaching of the issue.

Since this topic came at the very end of the first semester, the first opportunity that we had to deal with our students' essays was in the first class meeting of the second semester, a general lecture. During this lecture, Professor Bleich, who has a rather confrontational teaching style, was able to use the lecture format and his own strong personality to give voice to his anger and, by extension, ours. In this extraordinary lecture, he confronted students directly with his feelings about the violent homophobia expressed in their writing and told them, essentially, that such expressions amounted to fascism, were unacceptable, and that those who voiced such attitudes must be responsible for the implications of what they chose to say.

All of us felt that Bleich's confrontation was important—indeed, imperative. In many ways, in fact, Bleich simply brought to the surface the tensions that our question and student responses to it had engendered. The expression of his—and our—anger and the overt confrontation of tensions came, however, at a price: the creation of a classroom atmosphere that was fraught with conflict and alienation. Students felt betrayed and angry toward Bleich, believing that he had asked for their honesty and then condemned them. Some students were angry at other students, feeling that they all had to suffer as a result of the more overtly homophobic members of the class. We were involved in these oppositional tensions as well: we were Bleich's surrogates, in part, and also the conduits through which student-student conflict could flow. Further, we were personally angry as well, disturbed by the students' homophobia. The classroom had thus become completely polarized: it was now a tangle of "us versus them" relationships.

The polarization of the classroom further deflected our attention away from the topic of sexual preference. Our students' emotional responses to Bleich's lecture became primary: was he being unfair? Was he taking away their right to express their opinion? We needed to attend to those responses to some degree; but in allowing them to dominate the classroom dialogue, we perhaps collaborated with our students' unwillingness to engage the topic itself. In addition, since many students felt that Bleich was taking away their right to express their "true" feelings, they responded by claiming their homophobia even more strongly. For many students, it became an issue of free speech and free thought. Ultimately, then, the polarized classroom dynamic perpetuated the already-developing focus on homophobia.

We seemed to be caught in a vicious circle. Our question engendered (or at least did not do enough to prevent) homophobic responses; our opposition to those responses only consolidated students in their position and kept us on the topic of homophobia. Clearly, teaching in terms of homophobia has problematic ramifications: it reinforces social sanctions against homosexuality by establishing heterosexuality as the standard from which homosexuality is "judged." Even more important, it silences gay and lesbian students. Paradoxically, by trying to break the silence surrounding issues of sexual preference, we were reinforcing it for our gay and lesbian students, rendering them voiceless, recreating their sense of invisibility, and heightening the risks of coming out. In addition, we were cutting ourselves off from the possibility of hearing them and learning from their perspectives.

We see now that only when we moved toward talking about sexual preference in concrete terms—resisting abstract and distanced statements about "homosexuality"—did we shift from this destructive focus on homophobia. We realized early on that our students had a propensity to objectify sexual preference in their lecture essays: few students talked about gay or lesbian people they knew personally; many students removed themselves completely from the issue by recounting conversations they had only "overheard"; few, if any, depicted heterosexuality itself as a choice. At the beginning, we added to this tendency toward abstraction by not talking about these essays in the same ways that we had discussed students' previous writing. While we usually selected a single essay to distribute to the students, so we could focus on specific language features and patterns, this time—in an attempt to impress students with the enormity of their own homophobia—we excerpted bits and pieces from several essays, thus taking them out of context and distancing the "language of homophobia" from the writers themselves.

Yet we did try several strategies that we hoped would make the issue more concrete. First, in an attempt to give students a context in which to explore emotionally authentic ways of talking about sexuality—whether homosexual, bisexual, or heterosexual—we distributed Audre Lorde's love poem "On a Night of the Full Moon" to our students. We did not, however, reveal the author. We assumed that most students would read the poem as a heterosexual love poem and that once we had discussed the issues it brought out—emotional need, intimacy, trust, as well as physical eroticism—we might reveal who the author was and talk about heterosexuality and homosexuality in their more concrete and human dimensions. Yet even before students learned that the poem was a lesbian love poem, many of them found its explicit eroticism disturbing and "disgusting," once again demonstrating the difficulty they had in finding an authentic language for sexual experience. The usefulness of our approach was further limited by the element of trickery implicit in our lesson plan, which now seems a clear reflection of our own discomfort. Using the poem anonymously allowed us to assume a kind of knowledge that set us apart from our students, rather than giving them the message that we too were engaged in the struggle to think about sexual preference in a social context, to deal with homophobia, and to find a more human language for sexuality.

Of course, the move to bring gay and lesbian literature into the classroom could have been very useful. Our experiences have taught us that we, as straight teachers, need to listen to different voices so that we can discuss gay and lesbian issues from as informed a perspective as possible; similarly, we need to provide our students with the opportunity to hear voices besides heterosexual ones. Ideally, we would hear from gay and lesbian students in the classroom; but while we must work to make our classrooms safer spaces for coming out, the number of gay and lesbian students who will come out to their classmates is most likely small, particularly when the teacher is straight and while the culture remains heterosexist. Texts by gay and lesbian writers can provide some new voices and new angles of vision. Yet the teaching potential of gay and lesbian writings will be limited as long as we read them only in relation to gay and lesbian issues; using texts in this way will only enhance our students' perception that gay and lesbian people are defined primarily in terms of their sexual preference and so can only speak on this, "their" issue.

The most successful approach we took in concretizing the topic was to invite a woman from the Gay and Lesbian Alliance's Speakers' Bureau to come to our classes. The speaker, a senior at IU, talked a little about homosexuality and homophobia in general, and then specifically about her own life experiences—coming out, dealing with her family, her relationships. She devoted the rest of the time to answering questions. The responses that we heard from our students following this session were uniformly positive. Our heterosexual students seemed relieved to meet, albeit in a controlled environment, a lesbian student, and to realize that a gay person could be a perfectly "ordinary" and likable human being. It was at this point that previously very homophobic students began saying "gays are people too." Though such a position is a long way from an understanding of the systematic and institutionalized oppression of gays and lesbians (not to mention a recognition of their unique life experiences and culture), it was an important and positive first step for many of our students, and our first step toward countering the abstraction that we, as well as our students, fell prey to. Perhaps, too, for our gay and lesbian students, this experience provided them with a positive role model—someone who was open about and proud of her sexual preference. Yet straight teachers who invite gay and lesbian speakers to their classes must do so not in order to foist responsibility onto the shoulders of gays and lesbians (i.e., it's your problem, not mine), but rather as a way of engaging other voices in their attempts to raise the issue of sexual preference.

Overall, we worked to counter the polarization and abstraction that we faced—and to a degree recreated—in our classrooms by searching for ways to bring in lesbian and gay voices and break the silence that surrounds them. The risk involved here is that focusing exclusively on gay and lesbian voices allows straight students and teachers to consider themselves exempt from the issue of sexual preference. It was perhaps all too easy for us as straight teachers to perpetuate the normative silence that surrounds heterosexuality, and thereby to protect it from critique and questioning. While we sought ways to encourage a concrete human understanding of "homosexuality" by inviting our students and ourselves to learn from our own language use, from gay and lesbian texts, and from a lesbian speaker, we missed one immediate and concrete means of understanding sexual preference—our own and the majority of our students' choice of heterosexuality. We never really put ourselves as teachers in the position where our own sexual preference would be subject to questioning, nor did we invite students to do the same for themselves.

In retrospect, it is possible to see what we might have done to begin problematizing heterosexuality. Certainly, the whole issue of coming out, of announcing one's sexual orientation, might be made a topic of class discussion. When students assume, as in our case they did, that their teacher is heterosexual, that teacher might ask students what it would mean to them if she were lesbian, and why heterosexuals in general tend to assume other people are straight until proven otherwise. We could attempt to explore the ways heterosexuality is made to seem inevitable, a given.

It is telling that this most immediate way of teaching about sexual preference—problematizing our own heterosexuality—didn't really become clear to us until we had the opportunity to enter into a dialogue with gay and lesbian teachers at the CCCC panel session. This was the first time any of us had been aware of being in a sexual minority in a professional setting, and the experience forced us to realize the importance of acknowledging our sexual preference when dealing with this issue. At the same time, the conference created opportunities for gay and straight teachers to talk with each other and exchange perspectives about their classrooms and teaching methods. Ultimately, this coming together was an important learning experience, without which our insights would have remained limited.

In spite of all the problems we faced, then, raising the issue of sexual preference provided an important learning experience for us as teachers as well as for our students. The slow process of unlearning heterosexist assumptions and fears is one in which we as teachers participated and in which we are still engaged. Our classroom experience was a first step, an initial breaking of the silence that surrounds sexual preference and perpetuates institutional and social homophobia. Our experience at CCCC was another step for us, one that made us talk about and ultimately reexamine our teaching. Now that we've started talking we need to keep talking, to straight teachers, to lesbian and gay teachers, above all to our students. We need to continue the dialogue into which we have entered, to continue making this issue speakable in our professional lives as well as in our classrooms.

Notes

An earlier version of this essay was published in *Feminist Teacher* 4:2/3 (Fall 1989).

13

"Type Normal like the Rest of Us": Writing, Power, and Homophobia in the Networked Composition Classroom

Alison Regan

During discussions about networked writing classrooms, I have heard promises of increased "social interaction and engagement, cooperative discourse, intellectual exchanges, and the formation of discourse communities that are student-centered rather than teacher-centered" (Hawisher and Selfe 10) and of "a means of liberation, particularly for those marginalized in American classrooms" (Faigley 291). At my university, students and instructors alike said they were finding ways of participating in conversations that exceed the limits of discourse in traditional classrooms. Moved by their enthusiasm, I came to a networked classroom in 1989, where I have been teaching and learning ever since.

A semester of teaching in the classroom attached to the English department computer research lab at the University of Texas made a convert out of me. Enough of those promises came true that I have been reluctant to return to a traditional setting. In significant ways, however, the networked classroom failed to fulfill the eulogistic claims I so often heard made for it. I find that instead of easing the problems of the traditional classroom, the computer medium exaggerates some disturbing and often ignored features of classroom dialogue.

Several researchers have explored negative aspects of electronic classroom conversation, noting that some students take advantage of the increased freedom of expression and engage in disruptive acts of what are known as "mutiny" and "wilding," acts which deviate from the instructor's focus and are characterized by vulgar language and insults (DiMatteo, George, Peyton, Kremers). I did not, however, observe such behavior in my classroom; what I want to address in this essay is another aspect of computer-assisted discussions. Using data from my Fall 1990 rhetoric and composition class, I want to explore the question of what kinds of exclusions can occur when nearly all students participate and when students are not "wilding" but attempting to follow the plan of the class. In particular, I want to focus on expressions of homophobia which may result in the exclusion of lesbian and gay participants from networked conversation.

Like most instructors, I am eager to hear from all of my students, especially those who usually remain silent while a few of their peers dominate class conversation. I found appealing the argument that electronic conversation was "enfranchising, open and egalitarian in emphasis" (Barker and Kemp 23). Central to this argument is the claim that when paralinguistic clues are removed, people who are not favored by the traditional social hierarchy (for example, women, people of color, nonnative English speakers, people with speech impediments) are more likely to join in class discussions. I am not contesting this claim; my experience and the experience of many other instructors show that such students are more likely to join in class discussions in the networked classroom than in the traditional classroom.

Many descriptions of computer conferences laud the possibility for anonymity (or a sense of anonymity) which comes with reduced access to social context clues. It is a mistake, however, to employ computer technology with the goal of making classrooms blind to color, class, gender, and nationality. Even if this were possible, it would not be desirable; a world where everyone can pass for a white, male, middle-class, heterosexual, native English speaker would be no utopia: It would be neither a more intellectually stimulating nor a more liberated place.

In any case, it is a mistake to employ such prescriptions for conversational liberation to lesbians and gays, for lesbians and gays are not necessarily marked by social context clues.[1] It seems that when it comes to issues of sexual preference, peer pressure is often exaggerated in the computer classroom. We imagine that once free from bodily constraints (beyond typing speed and facility with language), we and our students will find new freedom of expression. Yet instead of serving as a tool for liberation, the computer medium can become a tool of oppression. When students feel free to express their homophobia, the consequence for lesbian and gay participants is isolation, alienation, and marginalization.

Before moving to the networked classroom I imagined that rather than reducing difference, the networked classroom might be a place where difference can no longer be ignored, because the technology offers everyone equal access to conventional space. However, a short week of teaching in the networked classroom forced me to recognize the fact that merely providing access to conventional space and encouraging students to "speak freely" does not ensure that students will feel safe in taking that space. I believe that, instead of merely providing an open forum for discussions, we need to actively promote what the philosopher Iris Young has called a "politics of inclusion . . . in which persons stand forth with their differences acknowledged and respected, though perhaps not completely understood, by others" (119).

My class discussions were conducted on InterChange, the real-time conversation system designed by the Daedalus Instructional Group. InterChange was constructed to support and foster classroom conversation, and it fulfills the intentions of its creators. The use of InterChange for class discussion guarantees that a course which is described in the university catalogue as "writing intensive" will be just that. In addition to the normal series of essays, students produce pages and pages of text in every discussion. Transcripts for my fifty-minute class were regularly twenty to thirty single-spaced pages long.

In this kind of class discussion, the boundaries of student-teacher relations are altered in remarkable ways. Roles become more fluid than fixed; there is no podium or imposingly large desk to reify the instructor's power; the "blackboard" is the computer terminal, and it is only an arm's length away from everyone in the room. At first, it seems that everyone benefits from this kind of conversation. Students have more power to participate in and to direct the classroom discussions; we instructors have many more opportunities to see our students at work as they think and write through problems, form and reform opinions, alternately support or disagree with each other's positions. Yet the "open classroom" has its costs; at the same time that the networked classroom offers students opportunities to join in conversations, it also provides them with space to express themselves in ways that may close off communication. In my experience, the voices of gay and lesbian students and instructors are silenced as effectively in the networked classroom as in the traditional classroom, and may in fact be more silenced, because the electronic medium provides homophobic students with the space to express themselves in ways that serve to further suppress gay and lesbian voices.

In the traditional classroom, the life of student utterances is short; called forth by an instructor's question or the desire for further instructor clarification or explanation, they are soon lost. Such is the way with most conversation, inside and outside universities. Because all of the comments made in the networked classroom become part of our permanent classroom files, the networked classroom offers us the opportunity to capture and reflect on even the most ordinary comments.

As noted earlier, a number of researchers have remarked that the freedom students find in networked discussions sometimes results in vulgar and insulting language. These researchers have concentrated on off-task remarks that are racist, sexist, and often obscene. The students in my first-year writing class devoted a good deal of space to off-task conversations, but I cannot characterize those conversations as racist, vulgar, or obscene. None of my students cursed obsessively; in fact, none of them cursed at all. In between class assignments they discussed the football season and the gubernatorial battle between Ann Richards and Clayton Williams, complained about their physics teachers, and shared information about negotiating the university bureaucracy. Beyond a few snide remarks about the election candidates (no worse than the remarks the candidates made to each other) and a few jabs at their archrival Texas A&M, their side remarks were inoffensive. This is not to say that they kept their prejudices to themselves: the computerized medium freed students to express their hostilities during regular class discussions. The conversation I found most distressing occurred when the students were decidedly on-task.

Several researchers have advised intervening in situations of "mutiny" (Kremers 35) or "wilding" (George 50). This is sound advice, which I would follow if I observed such behavior in my class. It is less clear to me what my responsibilities are when students are following the plan of the course. The following series of remarks demonstrates the oppressive possibilities of computer-mediated class discussion, and forces me to consider when it is important for an instructor to intervene in class discussion, and when an instructor should wait for students to challenge one another's bigotry and (one hopes) to convince each other that there are more productive ways to encounter difference than with fear and hatred.

This conversation took place in the beginning of the semester, during the opening InterChange session. It was the first opportunity the class had to converse with each other on-line. During the previous class meeting, the students had been directed to review and consider a list of research topics. In the assignment for the day in question, I directed the students to share their possible research topic choices with their classmates, explaining why those topics interested them and exchanging information and advice about the project. It was my intention to serve as observer rather than as participant; however, eventually I joined in the conversation.

The focus of the following excerpt from the transcript of our class discussion is homosexuality, which was one of the research topic options. It was also a topic of great discussion on campus and in the university newspaper after the Gay and Lesbian Students' Association staged two demonstrations in the campus free-speech area during the first days of the semester. These fifteen messages, which were sent by eight people (seven of the twenty-two students and myself), represent only a small portion of the 181 messages generated in the fifty-minute class period. There were many other conversations competing for the attention of conference participants; the topics of euthanasia, smoking, and censorship received attention that was of comparable length, if not of comparable intensity.[2]

2 John: I WAS TOLD THAT I COULD SEND A MESSAGE TO ALL OF Y'ALL BY USING THIS PART OF INTERCHANGE. I HAVE NO IDEA WHAT TOPIC I AM GOING TO WRITE ABOUT, HOW ABOUT Y'ALL.

6 Judy: I am not sure what my topic is going to be. I have to write about something I think is interesting, and there are several subjects listed that are. Pornography and homosexuality are possibilities. Especially the latter because of all the exposure and controversy it has here.

7 John: JUDY—NOT JUST HERE, BUT EVERYWHERE IN THESE UNITED STATES.

22 Alison Regan: Your topic sounds promising, Judy. You will find ample information for your research. The University recently passed a non-discrimination clause which protects gays and lesbians from unfair treatment here on campus.

36 Gerald: To whoever was thinking about the topics of death and homosexuality, here's a thought, why not join together and do a project on the death of homosexuals? Not by AIDS.

43 Judy: Don't you think the paper may be slanted though, depending on how I personally feel?

46 Ed: way to go Gerald!!!

97 Matthew: GERALD You seem to have some hostile feelings about homosexuals. Is there a reason behind this we should know about?

121 Gerald: Matthew, I don't know about you, but a homosexual once made a move on me. I really didn't like it. I mean I really didn't like it!

127 Judy: Gerald and Matthew, My boyfriend had one make a move on him, and I really didn't like it. A girl is bad enough!!!!

137 Matthew: Gerald . . . Since this gay guy made a pass at you he should die? What if an ugly girl made a pass at you and you didn't like that? should she die too?

143 Michael, to Judy: Due to the obvious tension that has been aroused through this INTERCHANGE perhaps you could write about the affects of homosexuality in school.

153 Maria, to Gerald: I don't blame you for letting gays upset you. I know I'd be extremely upset. We're taught that homosexuality is a sin among other things, and can suffer great shock when actually approached with it in any way.

160 Gerald: Matthew, it depends on how ugly she would be. Seriously, there is one drawback about this computer, you can't here the tone of my voice. If I were to say it out loud you would notice sarcasm in my voice. I didn't say or mean they should die, I just want them to stay away from me.

161 Alison Regan: Has anyone thought about writing about homophobia?

170 Judy: Alison, What is homophobia? By the way, I like this InterChange. It is really stimulating alot of good communication and debate.

172 Matthew: Gerald . . . There exists no hostility in my voice. Only throwing the subject around. Can we still be friends?

180 Alison Regan: Judy—Homophobia is a term for irrational fear and hatred of homosexuals. It causes people to discriminate against gays and lesbians.

In many respects, this is a typical InterChange conversation. Judy is correct in her pronouncement that it "really stimulated . . . communication and debate"—the question of whether or not it stimulated "good" communication is another matter. There is much to be said for this exchange: it is rare that one student remark elicits responses from seven of her classmates, and also unusual that students are this communicative in the first discussion of the semester. Judy's classmates certainly followed the assignment, but while heeding my suggestion that they might "help each other to discover promising areas for research by discussing some of the issues associated with topic choices," several of them engaged in a kind of socially sanctioned classroom terrorism. No participant should have to endure such abusive comments.

I was distressed that the discussion of research topics became an opportunity for Gerald and others to articulate their fear and hatred of homosexuals in a way that would not have happened in the traditional classroom, where I would have served as moderator of the discussion. I can well imagine Judy posing her initial question in a traditional classroom, but I would be surprised to encounter a series of responses like those that followed in an educational forum where students wait to be recognized by their instructor before responding.

I do not want to suggest that the conversation would have been more open in a traditional classroom. I recall all too well my own silence in my first-semester English class when we were asked to discuss a lesbian novel that I had read as a high school student intent on finding representations of lesbians in literature, and then reread for the course. No one, including me, was willing to join the discussion. "It seems that none of you are prepared this week," our instructor admonished. I remember the cause of my silence very clearly: I felt that discussing the book would identify me as a lesbian. I trusted my instructor would be supportive of my reflections and sensitive to my lesbianism (after all, she assigned the text), but I did not feel I could express myself freely in front of my classmates. Reflecting on my experience in that class, I can see how in some situations the noncollaborative proscenium classroom might actually benefit lesbian and gay students. In that class, where we students never read or commented on each others' work, I turned in an essay comparing several lesbian novels. The production of that essay held great meaning for me; for the first time, I saw that it was possible to make connections between my academic life and my personal life. If the subject of my essay had been a matter of group discussion or if my peers had been called on to critique my work, I doubt I would have been able to write a paper that revealed an unusual level of familiarity with the lesbian canon.

I am certainly not arguing against the practices of having students read each other's texts, produce texts in a communal context, or turn texts in as public documents. As an instructor I value the effort to make education a collaborative enterprise, and I continue to require my students to share their work. Technology provides us with tools to turn our classrooms into places where student texts are central; it is important, however, that we recognize how the strategies we use to promote intellectual liberation may actually create additional stress for some students and may limit certain kinds of expression.

Almost a decade after being an uncomfortable lesbian student in a first-year college English class, I found myself in the position of the instructor "in charge" of a student-centered discussion in a comparable course. Filled with the rhetoric of the decentered networked classroom, I was reluctant to set an authoritarian tone so early in the semester. I was uncertain of my rights as an instructor and my responsibilities to my students, and uncertain of how to turn my classroom into a place where positive gay and lesbian rhetoric counters homophobia. In any case, I am not sure that a lecture on homophobia from me would have proved useful: on two other occasions I have confronted individual students who expressed homophobic attitudes in essays or in class, only to have them stop attending. I do not believe in tolerating homophobic behavior, but in this case it seemed best to avoid alienating students in the first week of class. The irony of this is that through the decision to not alienate certain students, I may have contributed to the alienation of the lesbian and gay students. It is important to remember that I had asked my students to discuss their research topics with their peers, not with me. Thus, instead of intervening in the discussion in a dramatic way, I suggested researching the topic of homophobia (which Judy did adopt as her project) and relied on the students to educate each other.

I appreciate InterChange because it allows for differences of opinion, but I also fear it because it can amplify the intellectual and social hegemony of the traditional classroom. In this situation, though Matthew's jibes serve to highlight some of Gerald's homophobia, no one in the class confronts Gerald directly. Even Matthew tempers his critique with his final comment that "there exists no hostility in [his] voice," and that he is "only throwing the subject around." There are many voices in this conversation, but there is no openly homosexual voice, not even my own. If there were homosexual students (and I believe there were), they had no room to speak.

In his initial remark, Gerald engages in the assumption of a community of people in the class who would welcome the death of homosexuals when he addresses his remark to "whoever was thinking about the topic of death and homosexuality." In point of fact, he was the first person to mention those two topics together. Yet instead of countering Gerald's hatred by refusing his gestures toward community building, the class (with the exception of Matthew) follows Gerald's remark with similar scenarios and even (in Maria's case) with a long explanation for the root of his dislike. Maria's remarks seal the conversation: her discussion of what "we" are taught and her argument that we "can suffer great shock when actually approached with it in any way" effectively removes the possibility of a dissenting perspective. This is not simply a matter of self-censoring (something with which gays and lesbians have a great deal of experience); it is a matter of group censoring. "We" are assumed to be heterosexual. Although the controversial campus demonstrations that served as the impetus for Judy's interest were conducted by gay and lesbian students, the students in my class still treat the subject of homosexuality as something safely outside their conference.

Teaching at the University of Michigan, D. K. Schriner and W. C. Rice also report instances of homophobia in their networked conferences. "On occasion," they note, "the expressive freedom of a community of writers nearly turned sour. The subject of homosexuality arose, and one male foreign student entered a response in which he advocated public execution of convicted 'offenders,' a practice common in his homeland." They report that the teacher "advised . . . that students who were offended by the discussion should feel free to ignore it and go on to other 'items'" (477). I wonder if it is that easy? Lesbian and gay students should not have to "ignore" homophobic remarks. Schriner and Rice clearly disapprove of the homophobia that threatened to ruin the expressive freedom in their class discussions, yet on one level, advice to ignore such comments serves as an exhortation to endure them.

Anthony DiMatteo has argued that the teacher in real-time networked classroom discussion "no longer [has] hegemony over classroom language; no longer select[s] who is to speak, what questions are to be answered, what style is used" (71). This kind of claim, which suggests that instructors might be divested of the institutional power that accompanies their position at the university, is misleading. Though the computer-assisted classroom is undeniably more democratic than the traditional classroom, the instructor keeps her institutional power outside of the classroom even as she sits at a terminal with her students for fifty minutes three times a week.

In any case, even if we wanted to relinquish our institutional power, our students might not let us. The title of this essay alludes to an incident that illustrates this point. "Type normal like the rest of us," one student ordered another in the final minutes of an InterChange discussion. The story behind the line is telling: the student who made the comment did not issue it from his or her own terminal; the message was sent from the terminal I had been using for the class period. The command was directed to a student who insisted on making all of his contributions to class discussions in full capital letters, a habit which annoyed many of his classmates. Though during an earlier InterChange a peer had suggested that he "Stop Shouting," he continued to assert his right to type as he pleased. When I left the room for a few minutes, the unknown student took advantage of the occasion to pirate my "signature" and send the heavy-handed typist a message. The result of the terminal switching was that the command looked as if it was issued to me. On the transcript it reads: "Alison Regan:/John—Push that little button on the keyboard marked 'CAPS LOCK' and type normal like the rest of us."

This exhortation serves as a reminder of two important points: first, even the instructor who shares authority remains identified with institutional power, and second, any person who is different disturbs the classroom environment. The command to "type normal" is nothing less than a command to *be* normal; John's remarks were never unreadable, they simply did not conform to the standards maintained by his classmates and instructor.

Thus, even within a space where expression appears most free, institutional and social forms of authority remain. Although I am as enthusiastic a user of networked classrooms as anyone, I believe we need to rethink our rhetoric of computer-mediated liberation and find new ways to ensure that we provide our students with an open and accessible forum—a forum in which differences are acknowledged and respected. We need to further explore the kinds of exclusions that can occur when our students are "on-task" and find ways to counter those kinds of exclusions. We need to recognize that lesbian and gay writers feel alienated in our classrooms, and that alienated students are less likely to be empowered to write, whether or not the subject matter covers lesbian or gay topics. We need to acknowledge the risks of self-disclosure at the same time we encourage all students to contribute to conversations. We need to turn our classrooms (networked or traditional) into places where we actively counter the vicious stereotypes about gay and lesbian people that college students (and others) so freely articulate.

Notes

This essay was originally published in slightly different form in *Computers and Composition* 10:4 (November 1993).

1. I make the argument that lesbians and gays are not marked by social context clues advisedly. Many lesbians and gays suffer harassment by strangers and many report

experiences of recognizing other lesbians or gays without their being explicitly identified as such. Clearly, some lesbians and gays are marked by social context clues in some situations.

2. I have not edited entries for correctness. I have changed the students' names. The number to the left of the writer's name signifies the location of the entry in the series of remarks made in the course of the InterChange. In this case there were 69 preceding and 111 succeeding entries made in the fifty-minute conference.

Works Cited

Barker, Thomas T., and Fred O. Kemp. "Network Theory: A Postmodern Pedagogy for the Writing Classroom," in Carolyn Handa, ed., *Computers and Community: Teaching Composition in the Twenty-First Century*. Portsmouth, NH: Boynton/Cook, 1990. 1–25.

Cooper, Marylyn, and Cynthia Selfe. "Computer Conferences and Learning: Authority, Resistance, and Internally Persuasive Discourse," *College English* 52:8 (December 1990): 847–69.

DiMatteo, Anthony. "Under Erasure: A Theory for Interactive Writing in Real Time," *Computers and Composition* 7 (April 1990): 71–83.

Faigley, Lester. "Subverting the Electronic Workbook: Teaching Writing Using Computers," in Donald A. Daiker and Max Morenberg, eds., *The Writing Teacher as Researcher: Essays in the Theory and Practice of Class-Based Research*. Portsmouth, NH: Boynton/Cook, 1990. 290–311.

George, Laurie. "Taking Women Professors Seriously," *Computers and Composition* 7 (April 1990): 45–52.

Hart, Ellen Louise. "Literacy and the Gay/Lesbian Learner," in Sarah Hope Parmeter and Irene Reti, eds., *The Lesbian in Front of the Classroom*. Santa Cruz, CA: HerBooks, 1988. 30–43.

Hawisher, Gail, and Cynthia Selfe. "Letter from the Editors," *Computers and Composition* 7 (April 1990): 5–13.

Kremers, Marshall. "Sharing Authority on a Synchronous Network: The Case for Riding the Beast," *Computers and Composition* 7 (April 1990): 33, 44.

Peyton, Joy Kreeft. "Technological Innovation Meets Institution: Birth and Creativity or Murder of a Great Idea," *Computers and Composition* 7 (April 1990): 45–52.

Schriner, D. K., and W. C. Rice. "Computer Conferencing and Collaborative Learning: A Discourse Community at Work," *College Composition and Communication* 40 (December 1989): 472–78.

Young, Iris. *Justice and the Politics of Difference*. Princeton: Princeton University Press, 1990.

Classrooms:
High School

14

Lesbian/Gay Role Models in the Classroom: Where Are They When You Need Them?

Janet Pollak

The nation's classrooms are staffed with more lesbian and gay teachers than any school board or superintendent imagines. You can see the female teachers, African-American teachers, Latina/Latino teachers, and Asian teachers. Women, and other-than-lesbian/gay minority teachers either make their presence obvious by their appearance or else freely reveal minority identity to students. Their motives and morality are seldom, if ever, questioned. But the lesbian/gay teacher who reveals her/his minority identity in an elementary, middle, or high school classroom is likely to be on the road to the unemployment line. Even the college or university classroom is not necessarily a safe haven. You can't count on academic freedom to save you from what the anthropologist Esther Newton has termed the "sneak" of homophobia in academe.[1] We therefore mark our lesbian/gay role models mostly absent at any level of the teaching profession. And so the answer to the question I pose in the title of this essay is, of course, "in the closet."

Growing up lesbian/gay in this society is either agony or a big surprise, because we are denied role models in the schools. The youngsters who recognize their same-sex identities early are, alternately, the most fortunate or least fortunate. Some find accepting friends or relatives. Some are lucky to run into a lesbian/gay youth group or Parents and Friends of Lesbians and Gays (P-FLAG). But some get pregnant or father babies in failed attempts to go straight. Some are taunted and/or beaten by their classmates or parents. Some run away from home and seek refuge in big cities, often with disastrous results. And, as reliable statistics demonstrate, some kill themselves. Lesbian and gay youngsters commit/attempt suicide at a far greater rate than youngsters in the population at large.[2] None of them is likely to know any out lesbian or gay teacher. There is no safety net.

Frequently we have no idea that gays and lesbians actually exist as real people in the world, so we emerge from twelve or more years of schooling only to realize that the vague uneasiness we experienced all through high school wasn't cafeteria food at all. We spring into the adult world as neophyte lesbians and gays. What a surprise! If only Miss X or Mr. Y could have had pictures of their same-sex partners on their desks we wouldn't have wasted those crucial "wonder years." Imagine, you wouldn't have to wait until you're eighteen or twenty-one to be lesbian or gay and go out on your first real date.

The same people who may be reluctant to have racism and sexism brought up in classrooms (never mind sex education) are the ones who want to keep gays and lesbians out of education or at least safely locked in their little closets. These misguided morality police are, to be blunt, ignorant, and they have made education much more expensive in terms of human costs. They think their logic is flawless. It goes something like this: sex education encourages sexual activity among students, therefore allowing openly lesbian and gay people to teach will mean that ordinarily heterosexual students will be influenced to be homosexual. Right. The same logic could be used to argue that African-American teachers will unduly encourage white students to seek a change in skin pigmentation or that female teachers will encourage male students to become transsexuals.

When Meg Christian's song "Ode to a Gym Teacher" appeared on Olivia Records' first album in 1974, *I Know You Know,* nearly every lesbian who heard it could name one or more whistle-toting women who had touched their lives in phys ed. The sad truth is that even our graduating college seniors today relate enthusiastically to the lyrics, while never knowing for sure if Miss X or even Mrs. Z is really "one." Although the tune is about role models (specifically in women's phys ed) it is not about being out. Somehow, by mannerisms, behaviors, a certain assertive style, or whatever, the young lesbian in gym class gets to "know" that her teacher is a lesbian, too. There seems to be a rather high concentration of lesbians in phys ed departments, thus the chance of seeing one in a gym class is quite good. So, let's say you see one there and you, too, want to become a teacher. What kind of teacher? Well, a phys ed teacher, of course. You've seen that Miss X can do it, so why not you? Besides, you can wear sporty outfits and comfortable shoes forever.

But a role model who is in the closet is not a role model at all. Some lesbian and gay educators say that they are able to effectively convey their identities to those students who really need to know without saying anything too specific. These teachers actually think that they are out and are serving as appropriate role models. What they are really saying is that you can be lesbian and gay in education provided that you hide your identity from all but a few lesbian or gay students who might hang around after class. This is not good news. There doesn't appear to be any alternative on the horizon just now in the K–12 classrooms, however. Almost without exception, lesbian and gay school teachers simply do not enjoy basic civil rights.

The college or university classroom does offer some degree of protection once a person is tenured. Coming out on campus may mean, though, that you won't get promoted, and you won't get the sabbatical, and you won't get the research grant you applied for, and so on. Bigots can be very creative. And, by the way, lesbians can't necessarily count on straight or closeted lesbian feminists. It's as if the out lesbian faculty member is contagious. She's covered with secret lavender paint pellets. Support her openly and splat—you're a lesbian, too. Then, of course, there's the closeted lesbian college or university administrator who will feel more frightened and threatened by her out sister than by the patriarchal bureaucracy employing her. Go figure.

My experience in being an out lesbian professor for over ten years in a New Jersey state college has been both rewarding and discouraging. For instance, a few years ago only two straight students registered for my archaeology course. Everybody else in that class was lesbian or gay. When I met the students for the first time I asked, "What is this? A convention?" None of them was particularly interested in archaeology, by the way. They were just hungry for a role model. Sometimes a lesbian or gay student will agonize endlessly before stopping by my office. They'll come in, close the door behind them, look at their shoes, and tell me that they want to speak to me about something that I'm supposed to know about. (I have a lavender "We Are Everywhere" sticker on my door, along with a tasteful Provincetown decal.) I ask "What?" over and over until they tell me the big news. Usually, it's whispered so you can hardly discern what it is they've said. So, I go right ahead and say it out loud: "You're GAY?" They give me a horrified look which disappears quickly when they notice that I'm neither surprised nor upset. A student coming out to an out professor is an occasion to celebrate. Something went right for a change.

I only wish that my male brothers on the faculty would join me in being the out role models our students need. All students need lesbian and gay role models in education, not just lesbian and gay students. Those heterosexual kids are the ones most likely to grow up and have children of their own, and 10 percent of those children will be gay and lesbian. And all students need both lesbian and gay role models. But, in many settings, the only out educators are the lesbians. This is discouraging but true at my college, where the gay male faculty are too afraid or unconcerned or too comfortable to come out and be role models. Gay male teachers are the most absent of the absent. Of course, for those who are white, the closet lets them hang on to their male privilege.

I wonder what it would be like today if out gay and lesbian teachers taught Jesse Helms, Sam Nunn, or any of the Concerned Women of America. Just imagine what the lives of Sharon Kowalski and Karen Thompson would be like if Sharon's parents had experienced out lesbian and gay educators as they were growing up. Would so many noted professional sports figures and entertainers still be in the closet today if the nation's schools welcomed out lesbian and gay teachers along with other minorities? The classrooms still stand vacant as arenas for change, with lesbian and gay teachers, the real catalysts of change, looking out the peepholes of their closet doors.

Notes

1. Esther Newton, "Academe's Homophobia: It Damages Careers and Ruins Lives," *Chronicle of Higher Education,* March 11, 1987: 104.

2. P. Gibson, "Gay and Lesbian Youth Suicide," National Institute of Mental Health Task Force on Youth Suicide's Conference on Prevention and Intervention in Youth Suicide, Oakland, CA, 1986.

15

Reading, Writing, and Rita Mae Brown: Lesbian Literature in High School

Nancy Boutilier

"Have you ever read *Rubyfruit Jungle*?" a senior colleague asked me my first year teaching. A year out of college, but not yet out as a lesbian, I was not eager to have my athletic walk, my feminist view of literature, my short hair or my reluctance to wear skirts seen as signs of lesbianism. I studied his face for clues of the motives behind his question.

"Uh, yeah, I read it a while ago. Why?" I stuttered cautiously.

"Do you think twelfth graders could handle it?" he asked.

I laughed, trying to appear only slightly interested in his question, "I dunno, but let me know how it goes if you do teach it."

He never did teach the novel, and it took me five more years at the school before I dared introduce Rita Mae Brown's classic to my twelfth graders. By that time, I had identified myself as a lesbian and was gradually becoming more actively out on campus. I had come out to many colleagues at the school and was serving as an adviser to the campus Gay/Straight Alliance, but my lesbianism was not what I'd call common knowledge on campus. I was teaching English at a New England boarding school, a prep school that prides itself on diversity and embraces the idea of multiculturalism. Teachers exercise a great deal of classroom autonomy, and I never felt saddled by my department chair or by the efforts of those who sought a more uniform curriculum. As an independent school, we enjoyed the freedom of working outside state-mandated frameworks.

Even in such an unrestricting environment, for a number of years I was content to address only issues of racism and sexism in literature, leaving heterosexism hidden under the blanket phrase "and the oppression of other minority groups." Despite the inattention of most main-

stream feminist criticism to homophobia, I could thank feminist thinkers for teaching me to attend to factors of race and class in addition
to gender. My own homophobia, reinforced by literary critics, kept
my curriculum in the closet. The irony of leaving out lesbians eventually
grew unbearable for me, its having been a betrayal of my own principles. By the time I took seriously ACT UP's "Silence = Death" motto
and taught lesbian and gay books, my students saw it as part of my
commitment to include women in my courses and to advocate for the
voiceless by focusing on the experience of outsiders.

Because I so often taught books focusing on the experiences of
outsiders, students perceived me as an advocate for the voiceless. They
saw my teaching of gay and lesbian literature as part of my commitment
to include women in my courses.

The first lesbian text I ever brought into the classroom was Alice
Walker's *The Color Purple*, in an American writers course. Students
found it far easier to focus on issues of racism and sexism than the
homosexual relationship between Shug and Celie. For all the words
that Celie learns to use throughout the course of the novel, lesbianism
remains unnamed. I waited for my students to initiate discussion regarding the sexual component of Celie's relationship with Shug, but
no one brought it up. Classroom examination of the process by which
Walker's novel was shaped into a Hollywood blockbuster challenged
students not only to reexamine the novel's attention to racism, sexism,
and violence, but also to witness heterosexism at work. I showed my
students Steven Speilberg's movie and assigned Kathi Maio's feminist
review of it, "*The Color Purple:* Fading to White." Awakened by
Maio's critique of the film, students analyzed Hollywood's ability to
distort Walker's novel. They discussed the accuracy of individual
scenes, editing decisions, and possible motives for distortions of the
novel, including what Maio calls "Spielberg's soft-pedaling of the lesbian love story at the center of *The Color Purple*" (42).

I also taught Larry Kramer's *The Normal Heart* to ninth graders in
a drama unit. Since it focuses on the outbreak of the AIDS pandemic
in New York's gay male community, the play facilitated plenty of
discussion about gay male culture, the range of masculinity in American
society, and the government's responsibility for and response to the
virus. Students asked important questions about safe sex, and I found
myself countering a great deal of misinformation.

A senior elective course called Images of Women allowed me to set
Brown's *Rubyfruit Jungle* and Gloria Naylor's *The Women of Brewster
Place* alongside Charlotte Brontë's *Jane Eyre* and the stories of D. H.

Lawrence and Ernest Hemingway. The emphasis these texts place on sexual awakening as a rite of passage, and on independence as a result of coming of age, makes them rich with relevance for high school seniors looking ahead to graduation. I prepared myself with a dissertation-length defense of each book's place on the reading list, knowing that Rita Mae Brown would more likely be called into question than Ernest Hemingway.

The personality traits I shared with Brown's protagonist, Molly Bolt, made me anxious about teaching *Rubyfruit*. Compared to the unschooled Southern dialect of Celie in *The Color Purple,* Molly sounds a lot like me: a tough-talking, athletic, I-can-do-anything, independent, educated white woman—and a lesbian. Each day I waited for a student to ask me directly, either in private or in front of the class, "Are you a lesbian too?" I had promised myself to be honest, thorough, and confident in explaining to the class what it means to me to be a lesbian. But no one ever asked, so I never had to make good on the promise.

At boarding schools, all information—fact and fiction—travels quickly. The rumor that I was a lesbian had traveled along the grapevine, to be sure. Individuals counted the rumor true or false, based on what they wanted to believe. The students (and faculty members) who disliked me probably believed it to be true. In their minds, it was another reason to dislike or dismiss me. The students who liked me and did not have any huge misconceptions about lesbians probably believed it without any sweat or tears. For some of the rebellious students, it made me even more appealing as a role model, because I was a living example of counterculture existing in a relatively traditional environment. Those students who liked me but carried some ugly myth about lesbians probably decided that the rumor was false and continued to like me, while blocking out the information that might discredit me in their minds.

As it turned out, the student who expressed the strongest negative response to homosexuality in *Rubyfruit Jungle* asked me to be her escort to the senior-faculty dinner at graduation. She had written long journal entries about her belief that gay people had a right to do what they wanted, but they were wrong in the eyes of the Lord. Despite all the censure I endured while reading her work, I was delighted to see her acknowledge that reading the book had been important because it had forced her to rethink her own beliefs.

Encouraging students to think critically, to question their own knowledge, is one of education's aims. I was confident from the start that the gay and lesbian texts that I introduced to the classroom would spark new thinking for most students. However, I also worried from the start that when it came time to discuss the books in class, everyone would fall into a self-conscious silence, waiting for someone else to speak. The day before we began discussion of *Rubyfruit Jungle*, six of the fifteen students in my class approached me to say what a fantastic character Molly Bolt is, how great the novel is: "It's so funny, I can't put it down." My anxiety level rose in proportion to my suspicion that they were telling me these things in private so they wouldn't have to admit them in class in front of their peers. I opened discussion by asking, "Where do you get your information and images of lesbians?" No answer. "How about gay men? How do you know what they are like?" After a long silence, one boy suggested he had no image of gay men or lesbians. I asked, "How do little kids know whom to call 'fag' or 'dyke' on the playground?" which prompted someone's recollection of rumors about a grade school gym teacher. With that, an animated discussion about images and stereotypes was well under way, and I resisted my urge to break into an impassioned rendition of Meg Christian's "Ode to a Gym Teacher."

Generally, students responded in one of two ways: either they thought hard about their classroom comments and spoke with a refreshing sense of honest uncertainty, or they alluded to information they had heard, a party line of some sort, and without further information or personal knowledge, they were unable to support their views. What information the most enlightened students lacked, I usually had. Many knew the 10-percent figure. Many more spoke of personal knowledge of gay people.

Thoughtful reflection, reexamination of beliefs, and lively discussions were not the only results of passionate, curious, and provocative thinking. Across the board, the writing generated by the gay and lesbian literature was superb. Whether individual students chose to distance themselves from the subject matter or attempted to integrate issues from the literature into the context of their own life experience, all wrote with a willingness to admit that their lack of information made them eager to know more, which in turn made them believe that what they had to write might make the issue more clear to someone else. Their writing had a refreshing degree of risk taking, matched by a readiness to rethink every thought if someone was prepared to offer an alternate perspective.

One senior boy's first journal entry about *Rubyfruit Jungle* began, "I keep asking myself to what extent Rita Mae Brown is trying to encourage women to experiment with members of the same sex." A week later, the same student wrote: "One thing this novel seeks to accomplish is dispelling the myths that go with lesbianism. Through [the characters of] Carolyn and Faye the book shows that lesbians can, in fact, be very feminine."

In his final paper, the same student compared Molly Bolt to Jane Eyre:

> While Jane reveals that a woman can make it on her own without a man, she has killed Bertha in the process and finds her happy ending with her return to Rochester. *Rubyfruit Jungle* should now serve as The Manuscript, if you will, for how women should treat one another in a new age. Molly, like Jane, follows her own path and her own dreams. She eventually perseveres and makes a movie of her mother. . . . Molly is independent. She makes it on her own, but she positively influences all the people in her life. She is constantly enlightening those she comes in contact with. She is tough, but also compassionate and loving at the same time. *Rubyfruit Jungle* should be the novel of today's women's movement.

Many students wrote about their own socialization and the ways heterosexism and homophobia had functioned in their lives. One girl wrote: "*Rubyfruit Jungle* shakes the ideas of homosexuality that have been implanted in my mind for years. These images come from every- thing and anything around me. They come from the second look I give to both men and women holding hands with individuals of the same sex. The images come from having family members always speak of how I'll grow up and have a husband a children, when in reality maybe I won't want that. *Rubyfruit Jungle* allows me to speak about a topic banned from conversation."

Salvaging homosexuality from banishment, this particular student concluded her journal with a poem of her own that reshaped Brown's image of the jungle:

> Covering it, hiding it, sharing it
> with words of friendship
> when down deep an itching, impatient
> sensation to touch
> bare skin to bare skin
> begins to awaken: the hunt
> to venture in jungles that are
> off limits.

Outbursts of poetry in a journal are not common fare. Inspired writing usually reflects the degree to which a student engages with the literature, and literature that strikes a student's heart is the best catalyst for an eruption of creativity. The writing my students created in response to lesbian literature stands as a powerful testimony to the quality of the texts. Even students who claimed to be uncomfortable with the idea of discussing sexuality in the classroom found themselves acknowledging the value of the experience in their final analysis. They often grew to realize the heterosexism in their earlier failure to recognize straight coming-of-age rites of passage as pertaining to sexual orientation.

In this age of Jesse Helms and obscenity trials, providing a safe place for students to speak up about a topic banned from conversation is the professional responsibility of classroom teachers. As the doors of academic freedom are being closed down by reactionaries who want to return to an exclusive golden era of elitism and "the classics," it is essential that educators extend the borders of inclusion. When students see that their own teachers are ready to connect literature with life, they are more willing to include the study of self in their study of literature. When students discover that literature can serve as a window for viewing life, the image they see is often a double image, of the world beyond the glass and of the self reflected back. They see themselves in others.

One student's writing illustrates how deftly a student can look inward and outward at the same time:

> Before reading *Rubyfruit Jungle*, I always considered myself a liberal in the "true" sense. What that is, I had no clue prior to this semester. I have never been a racist and certainly had nothing against "progressive" women, but I just knew, when it all came down to it, the men called the shots. I guess this course has changed my thinking in a lot of ways. Reading *Rubyfruit Jungle* made me think about my sister, who is three years older than I am. She has always been a better student, athlete and whatever else than I have. She is also very attractive and great around people. The reason why Molly Bolt evoked so many memories of my sister is that I could only imagine my surprise if my sister happened to announce that she was a lesbian. I guess I'd respond much like how many people took to Molly after she opened up and showed people the great things in her closet.
>
> I guess you really had to know me in earlier stages in my life because for me to address Molly's homosexuality as being "a great thing" is truly incredible. Before, when I was asked about lesbians, I simply would say that they made me sick. But Molly evoked these

romantic images about it. When I finished section two, she was just beginning to reach me. I really can't remember where section two left off. Anyway, there was something so natural about these woman-to-woman relationships.

I have found that the process of bringing lesbian and gay literature into the classroom, like coming out, leaves no room for turning back. The experience has reaffirmed my personal commitment to challenging myself to face the worst of my fears. Because my school had a strong commitment to multicultural education, I was able to use the descriptions of the course I taught to introduce students to gay and lesbian literature. I do not assume that all teachers are in such a happy circumstance, but everywhere there is some boundary that needs exploring, some limit that needs to be pushed. The motivating force behind this essay is my hope that I will encourage someone, somewhere, to take whatever next step will lead to an educational system that more accurately reflects the breadth and depth of human experience—from the mainstream to the margins and everywhere between.

Works Cited

Brontë, Charlotte. *Jane Eyre*. 1847. London: Virago, 1990.

Brown, Rita Mae. *Rubyfruit Jungle*. 1973. New York: Bantam, 1980.

Kramer, Larry. *The Normal Heart*. New York: New American Library, 1985.

Maio, Kathi. "*The Color Purple:* Fading to White," in Maio, *Feminist in the Dark: Reviewing the Movies*. Freedom, CA: Crossing Press, 1988. 35–44.

Naylor, Gloria. *The Women of Brewster Place*. 1980. New York: Viking Penguin, 1987.

Walker, Alice. *The Color Purple*. New York and London: Harcourt, 1982.

16

Out in the Curriculum, Out in the Classroom: Teaching History and Organizing for Change

Barbara Blinick

I carefully prepared myself the day I was going to come out to a classroom full of high school students for the first time. The day before, my students had been griping about having to study about gay people in the Holocaust. With the audacity only a teenager can have, one student had tried to question me about my own sexuality, but I dodged the question. I knew it would come up again the next day, and I was ready. In order to challenge students' stereotypical ideals of what a lesbian is, I donned my frilliest dress with a lace collar, put on my pearls, and let my hair fall around my shoulders. When the question came, "Are you straight?" I calmly replied, "Why, no!" Conversation tumbled ahead, until my response had sunk in. Once the class grasped what I was talking about, I stood up on my stool and asked them, "So tell me, what does a lesbian look like?"

Recently while discussing my personal strategy for being out in my classroom, a fellow gay teacher remarked, "You're being a superteacher—having to be extra good, extra dedicated to prove how wonderful lesbian teachers are." I was a bit taken aback, until I thought about it. He was right. My strategy is clearly related to my political work with the Bay Area Network of Gay and Lesbian Educators (BANGLE), my involvement with my union and its gay and lesbian committee, Gay and Lesbian United Educators (GLUE), and my attempts to make myself as indispensable as possible at my school. Although I know it may not be necessary to be superteacher in order to be safely out (especially in San Francisco, where I work), becoming politically involved has been a way for me to make sure that if I ever need help, it will be there for me.

I have been a public high school teacher for ten years and have been out to my students for the last six years. For the first nine years I worked in a technical school; now I work in a college-preparatory magnet school. I am the kind of teacher who shares parts of my personal life with students, and I previously had felt angry and frustrated when I lied to them to cover up my lesbianism. However, my fear of being harassed and disliked by my students and my administration kept me quietly in the closet.

After teaching for four years and receiving tenure, I began to feel that it was my responsibility to come out. I realized that most of my fears were internal; there was already one out lesbian on campus who was voted favorite teacher every year by the graduating seniors. I was well liked by both the students and the administration and had a very strong support system consisting of my friends, BANGLE members, and my union (at the time the San Francisco Federation of Teachers/ AFT). More important, I felt it was crucial for young people—especially those who were questioning their sexual orientation or who already knew that they were lesbian, gay, or bisexual—to see another healthy, happy, and productive lesbian.

I also felt privileged. I lived and taught in San Francisco and was protected by antidiscrimination language in both a city ordinance and my contract. In many ways I was safer being out. Having identified myself as lesbian to the administration meant that any homophobic actions would be easier to fight. If I had never told them, the administration could always feign ignorance about my lesbianism and claim other motives for any punitive actions against me. I was also lucky because there were other out teachers in my district, however few, paving the way for me. If we couldn't be out in San Francisco, where could we be out?

Throughout the years I have had very few negative reactions from students and coworkers, and only two responses from parents. My contact with parents specifically about my lesbianism has consisted of one parent who praised me for being out to the students and another who challenged me about my work with her daughter in the Gay-Straight Alliance, a group that I cosponsor with a straight faculty member. The parent was concerned about her daughter's bisexuality, and feared that the Gay-Straight Alliance could be some kind of "recruiting" group. We spoke for an hour, and I was able to convince her that the group existed as a support group for the students who are lesbian, gay, bisexual, or questioning their sexuality, as well as for their straight friends and for straight students who had lesbian, gay, or bisexual family members. I also emphasized the importance of creating a safe place for students who might potentially feel very isolated and are at high risk for self-destructive behavior. After an hour we still did not see eye to eye, but I felt that the student's mother left respecting me, though still wrestling with her own biphobia and homophobia. A couple of weeks later I mailed her two books to read and learn from on her own: *Beyond Acceptance: Parents of Lesbians and Gays Talk about Their Experiences* and *Loving Someone Gay.*[1]

Although confronting an angry and distraught parent was difficult, as the co-coordinator of the Gay-Straight Alliance and the only out lesbian on campus I feel it is essential for me to be an effective go between with students and parents, when necessary. It is not a role I enjoy; rather, one that I feel is necessary.

I am lucky that my administration and the school district have supported me as an out lesbian teacher; as someone who teaches lesbian, gay, and bisexual history; and as a cosponsor of the Gay-Straight Alliance. This support is a result of intensive work done by the lesbian and gay community, including BANGLE, which led to the creation of Support Services for Gay and Lesbian Youth (SSGLY). SSGLY is a program created by the San Francisco Unified School District in 1989 to support lesbian, gay, bisexual, and questioning young people and their families as well as to educate the staff of the schools so that they can better serve sexual minority youth. Specific activities of Support Services include one-on-one counseling with students and their families; in-service training about sexual orientation, at-risk behavior, etc., for teachers, support staff, counselors, health workers, and administrators; training of designated lesbian/gay-sensitive adults at each high school and middle school; talking with groups/classes of students about name-calling, sexual orientation, and lesbian and gay families; funneling information about activities for lesbian, gay, and bisexual youth to the school sites; and writing and disseminating curricula. I was able to work part-time with SSGLY director Kevin Gogin from 1990 to 1992, doing outreach, trainings, and creating curricular materials. I credit the program with creating a greater sensitivity and awareness of lesbian, gay, and bisexual youth issues, as well as with making the school district a safer place for all youth.

For the students, having an out teacher has been educational and overall very positive. How I come out varies each year. Sometimes it is in response to homophobic name-calling, in which case I am always careful to point out that not only are students breaking district rules against name-calling, but as a lesbian I am personally offended by the slur. Or, as happened last year, I was interviewed for an article in the school newspaper about lesbian and gay youth suicide and was going to be quoted as the chairperson of the Bay Area Network of Gay and Lesbian Educators. I told my students about the forthcoming article and that I wanted them to hear from me that I am a lesbian. Usually I ask if they know any lesbians, gay men, or bisexuals. The number of hands that go up often surprises me, and I know these are students who will usually be my allies from the start. My self-revelation is followed by a question and answer period in which I respond to all respectful and appropriate questions. Very few students have the gall to ask a question that is specifically disrespectful (usually of a sexual nature); however, such questions present another opportunity for learning because they often lead to discussion about why lesbians and gay men are so often thought of in exclusively sexual terms. Typically the nature of the questions students ask shows that even if they know someone who is lesbian, gay, or bisexual, it is not often a topic that is discussed openly.

Even the negative reactions have been educational for students; although I do not tolerate disrespect, I will discuss homophobic students' opinions about homosexuality and why they hold them. I imagine that what these students feel is cognitive dissonance; they like me, but they don't like my lesbianism. Those who have the hardest time with me ultimately learn to live with the contradiction, and I believe I've made a crack in their armor. Students who are less entrenched in their homophobia process their contradictory feelings and almost always decide by the end of the semester that lesbians aren't so bad after all. Of course, I am always flattered.

Overall, being out in the classroom is a liberating experience. I am not fooled into thinking that it is easy—although it is easier in San Francisco than elsewhere—but it is preferable to lying about who I am, and thereby perpetuating the invisibility of all lesbians, gay men, and bisexuals.

Coming out is only part of the battle against homophobia, and of course is only an option for those of us who are lesbian, gay, or bisexual. It is also vital to create allies in the workplace to make sure there are people who will back us up and work toward a nonhomophobic environment for staff and students alike. Sometimes it is just too hard for us to deal with homophobia on campus, or it is necessary for a group of people to work together to try and achieve changes.

This is when heterosexuals can show their support and work to create a better working and learning environment for all.

Allies are straight faculty members who are willing to be openly supportive of lesbian and gay concerns, from putting an end to homophobic slurs during a faculty meeting to pushing for the teaching of a novel with lesbian themes. Creating allies is a result of being open and honest about who we are; as friendship and trust develop with straight faculty and staff, it becomes possible to ask them to take on issues of significance to the lesbian and gay community. A key role of allies is to broaden the issues at hand. No longer are they merely lesbian and gay issues; their importance to all people becomes clear.

Another critical part of the struggle is to make ourselves visible throughout the curriculum. The inclusion of lesbian, gay, and bisexual material is crucial in letting our students know that there were others before us, and there will be others after us; we have always been in their lives. Right now is a critical time to push for the inclusion of lesbian, gay, and bisexual content, as a variety of racial, ethnic, and religious groups successfully demand that history books be inclusive of the wide variety of people who actually participate in creating history. As a member of the San Francisco Unified School District's US history textbook selection committee, I reviewed more than fifteen US history textbooks submitted for adoption by the school district. None mentioned lesbians, some mentioned gay men via the AIDS epidemic and the Names Quilt, and only one mentioned the lesbian and gay March on Washington in 1987. In the literature textbook adopted by the district the homosexuality of James Baldwin and Gertrude Stein is not mentioned, despite the fact that both were openly gay people whose sexual orientation strongly influenced their work. The textbook merely labels Stein "eccentric."

When I began looking for material to use in my US and world history classes I found very little. Mostly there existed antihomophobia curriculum and one or two lessons on famous lesbian, gay, and bisexual people throughout history. This led me to write curriculum reinserting lesbians, gays, and bisexuals into the history of the Harlem Renaissance, the Holocaust, and the ongoing civil rights struggle.[2]

The three United States history lessons I've authored come with an introductory lesson, "Homophobia and Heterosexism." Whether or not a teacher needs to use it will depend on personal preference, the tenor of the classroom, and whether homophobia and heterosexism have already been discussed in class. Since it may be the first time that students have discussed these concepts, it is helpful to deal with some typical misconceptions before diving into historical material with lesbian, gay, and bisexual content. The introductory lesson requires students to begin by identifying examples of homophobia, heterosexism, and other types of oppression. (Examples of homophobia and heterosexism are provided in case students don't come up with any.) Students then discuss characteristics common to different types of oppression, what can be done to put an end to oppression, and how to become allies to each other. A role-play exercise, two ideas for writing assignments, and an extensive vocabulary list are also included.

"In the Life: Lesbians, Gay Men, and Bisexuals in the Harlem Renaissance" focuses primarily on singers and writers. After a background history highlighting the blossoming of lesbian, gay, and bisexual culture in Harlem, the activities in the unit focus on the blues of Gladys Bentley and Ma Rainey, and the poetry of Langston Hughes. Students discuss lyrics and poetry that exemplify the coded language of lesbian, gay, and bisexual people in history and draw parallels to contemporary popular culture.

"The Holocaust" includes an extensive history of homosexuals during the Holocaust, filling out part of the picture of who was tortured and murdered in Nazi death camps along with 6,000,000 Jews (non-Germans, politically active Catholics, Gypsies, and homosexuals). The background history traces Nazi ideology as it wove together sexism, racism, homophobia, anti-intellectualism and anti-Semitism. Students are asked to read and respond in writing to an excerpt from Heinz Heger's *The Men with the Pink Triangle,* a gay man's first-person account of the concentration camps.[3]

"Lesbian and Gay Organizing in the 1960s and 1970s" discusses lesbian and gay civil rights within the context of the larger civil rights movement. Instead of looking at lesbians and gay men as a separate interest group (which is also helpful, but which is neither my goal nor consonant with the ultimate goal of inclusion), the post-Stonewall push for civil rights is integrated into a broader discussion about African-American civil rights and the women's movement. Of course other movements could be added to expand this curriculum; I specifically limit the scope in order to more fully show the diversity within the movements discussed. After a background history, the student activity section includes material carefully excerpted from Martin Luther King, Jr.'s "The Social Organization of Non-Violence"; Stokely Carmichael's "What We Want"; Huey Newton and Bobby Seale's "The Founding of the Black Panther Party" and "Patrolling"; "The Redstockings Manifesto"; "The National Organization for Women

Bill of Rights"; Carl Wittman's "A Gay Manifesto"; Radicalesbians' "The Woman-Identified Woman"; and "The Combahee River Collective Statement."[4] The readings are intended to be used in a longer jigsaw activity, where small groups of students become experts on one reading and then share what they learn with another small group, or in a small-group activity where students read and compare three of the excerpts.

Student response to all four units has been positive. I have found that once homosexuality is normalized within the context of the classroom, students adapt fairly easily. Because I am comfortable discussing the contributions of lesbians, gay men, and bisexuals to history, students learn to be comfortable including us. It is amazing and empowering to be visible in a US history class: to have my students write essay exams explaining how the civil rights movement affected the lesbian and gay rights movement, or to hear a student exclaim, "This stuff is amazing!" in a small-group discussion of "The Woman-Identified Woman." By organizing lesbian and gay educators, meeting with school district officials, and demanding that we be included, it becomes possible to write lesbians, gay men, and bisexuals back into history.

Notes

1. Carolyn Welch Griffin, Marian J. Wirth, and Arthur G. Wirth, *Beyond Acceptance: Parents of Lesbians and Gays Talk about Their Experiences* (Englewood Cliffs, NJ: Prentice-Hall, 1986); Donald Clark, *Loving Someone Gay* (1977, reprint, Berkeley, CA: Celestial Arts, 1993).

2. To order the four curriculum units described in this essay, send request and $5 for copying and postage to BANGLE, P.O. Box 460545, San Francisco, CA 94146.
   Other sources of teaching material incorporating lesbian/gay material include:
   Gay and Lesbian Alliance Against Defamation-Los Angeles (GLAAD-LA), 7033 Sunset Blvd. #304, Hollywood, CA 90028, (213) 463-3632, curriculum: $12.50;
   GLAAD-San Francisco, 514 Castro St., Ste. B, San Francisco, CA 94114, (415) 861-4588, 2' × 3' multicolor poster of lesbian, gay, and bisexual history with 57 figures and 7 historical events, with key and bibliography, $15; and
   Arthur Lipkin, 210 Longfellow Hall, Cambridge, MA 02138, (617) 495-5301 various curricula.
   For curriculum materials and a video specifically aimed at stemming homophobic name-calling within the larger context of racism and sexism, contact Equity Institute, 6400 Hollis St., Suite 15, Emeryville, CA 94608, (510) 658-4577, video and curriculum materials: $325; curriculum materials only (in English and Spanish): $20.

3. Heinz Heger, *The Men with the Pink Triangle* (Boston, MA: Alyson Publishers, 1980).

4. Stokely Carmichael, "What We Want" (1966), in Clayborne Carson et al., eds., *The Eyes on the Prize Civil Rights Reader* (New York: Viking Penguin, 1991);

"The Combahee River Collective Statement" (1977), in Barbara Smith, ed., *Home Girls: A Black Feminist Anthology* (New York: Kitchen Table Press, 1983); Martin Luther King, Jr., "The Social Organization of Non-Violence," (1959), in Carson et al., *The Eyes on the Prize Civil Rights Reader;* Huey P. Newton and Bobby Seale, "The Founding of the Black Panther Party" and "Patrolling" (1973), in Carson et al., ibid.; "The National Organization for Women Bill of Rights" (1967), in Robin Morgan, ed., *Sisterhood Is Powerful* (New York: Random House, 1970); Radicalesbians, "The Woman-Identified Woman" (1970), in Anne Koedt et al., eds., *Radical Feminism* (New York: Times Books, 1973); "The Redstockings Manifesto" (1970), in Morgan, *Sisterhood Is Powerful;* Carl Wittman, "A Gay Manifesto" (1970), in Karla Jay and Allen Young, eds., *Out of the Closets: Voices of Gay Liberation* (New York: New York University Press, 1992, 2d ed.).

17

Working with Queer Young People on Oppression Issues and Alliance Building

Donna Keiko Ozawa

I came out in San Francisco in 1980, when I was sixteen years old, and at that time lesbian-of-color role models were hard to find. In high school I organized multi-issue political student groups and wrote letters to the editor of the school paper, who was a right-wing reactionary. I even got called a "commie" by one of my social studies teachers, which made me realize that I was having some impact even if I felt alone in my campaign to wake up the campus. I wrote in my journal about my feelings for women, and I made it through high school with the help of my well-hidden women's music records. When I finally escaped to a women's college, I realized that there were even more issues to face about my identity as a woman, a lesbian, a young adult, and an Asian American from a family struggling to send me to college. No one had ever explained to me how just being me would be so difficult. Once in a while a family member would tell me stories of government internment camps or a neighbor's betrayal during "the War." But no one ever told me anything about how I was to live in the present. After college, I could not maintain the energy to keep my sexuality a secret, so little by little I came out.

I have been working with lesbian, gay, and bisexual youth and young adults since 1987, when I cofounded a recreational and social program in San Francisco which is now the Lavender Youth Recreation and Information Center (LYRIC). Most of my experience working with young people on oppression issues comes from my work with New Bridges (now called Todos) and the Lambda Youth and Family Empowerment Program (LYFE).[1] During the last few years I also have spoken to thousands of young people and adults in school and community groups about hate crimes, sexuality, and oppression.

As a twenty-seven-year-old Sansei lesbian and one of very few lesbians of color in the San Francisco Bay Area organizing with queer youth, I came to lesbian, gay, and bisexual youth advocacy with urgency about making life better for young people and wanting to maintain some hope about my adult peers and my own adulthood.[2] I felt a huge amount of responsibility toward queer young people and especially young people of color, who make up about 80 percent of the San Francisco school district. I had a lot to remember and to learn about young people's resilience and wisdom.

In the substance abuse prevention/health education field, it is common to talk about factors that can help reduce the risks of young people participating in drug use or unsafe sex, such as self-esteem, strong family foundation, and healthy relationships with peers. But it is difficult for anyone to maintain these when most of one's experience of self, family, and friends is shaped by systematic and pervasive mistreatment and negative reinforcement, otherwise known as oppression. Lesbian, gay, and bisexual young people are fighting struggles on many social and political fronts.

One of the most important tools to offer young people is a framework through which they can look at their experiences of oppression and develop methods with which to resist it and assist each other. Most of the young people I have worked with were between ages sixteen and twenty-three, and all personally identified as bisexual, lesbian, or gay. The suggestions outlined in this essay are based on the work I have done with peer educators, youth facilitators, and other program participants in workshops and ongoing trainings which met as infrequently as three days a year or as often as twice a week. Youth staff receive the most intensive training; they cofacilitate discussion and tailor their presentations to their own styles.

It is vital to use oppression education as a means to prevent unhealthy behaviors among youth participants who, although they may be organized for their leadership abilities, are also members of targeted groups who exhibit a high occurrence of risk in their lives.[3] Many queer youth are familiar with poverty, homelessness, abuse, substance abuse, hate-motivated violence, nonsupportive and otherwise unhealthy families, and so forth. At the same time, through discussion of their experiences, young people can develop communication and analytical skills that will help them work with other young people.

My version of alliance-building work includes the teaching of an oppression theory, the use of role playing and exercises to illustrate real-life encounters with unjust circumstances, and the use of a variety of exercises to emphasize analytical and communication skills and cultural history and identity. There are many approaches to this work.[4] Teachers and other youth advocates are constantly looking for materials and methods to teach "multiculturalism." I avoid using the term "multiculturalism," the overused buzzword of the '90s, because it conjures up images of "America" as a "melting pot," images which I think are misleading and do not describe the realities of being a culturally identified person in a US context. Instead, I talk about "alliance building" or learning how to be an advocate for oneself and other people with whom one does not necessarily identify.[5]

Working Assumptions

1. Young people and adults can make the connections between their personal experiences of injustice and systematic injustice. Experiences of oppression can be used as a constructive reference point for acting to interrupt oppression when it happens.
2. Young people can use a framework of oppression/liberation to better advocate for other young people without allowing their own feelings of hurt and despair to block their clarity or prevent positive action.
3. Oppression and internalized oppression are two of the primary factors leading to self-destructive, unhealthy behaviors that put other young people at risk. Young people who can understand this can strategize to reduce stresses on themselves and others and can develop a stronger sense of personal pride.
4. Young people can use their understanding of oppression eloquently as leaders in our communities and can encourage attitudinal and behavioral change among their peers and older people. As adult allies, we can encourage opportunities for young people to develop their leadership skills.
5. Most of all, if given the opportunity, young people can see that they are the experts on their own lives,[6] and that they have the power to change the system.

Pretraining Preparation

Alliance-building work introduces ways of thinking, feeling, and communicating that may be unfamiliar to young people in a program.

Fortunately, there are peer education curricula that can help prepare trainers and staff for the more intense parts of the workshops.[7] Some things to do before beginning discussion about oppression issues:

1. Establish discussion guidelines, for example: say what's on your mind, no put-downs, maintain confidentiality, feelings are okay.
2. Begin building group rapport and group identity through games, outings, projects, and the like.
3. Review and train staff on basic communication skills. Two areas I emphasize are Active Listening (listening with interest and empathy) and Agenda Breaks (suspension of discussion by a group member to clarify feelings about a comment or dynamic in the group).
4. Introduce the concept of a personal toolbox: each person identifies their skills and experiences that would be useful in the workshop. Talk about feelings—how they affect the person who is having them and how they affect a group; how to cope with stressful situations; warning signals (changes in group dynamics that need to be addressed as soon as possible); and group agreements (that is, rules of conduct for staff and group members).

Oppression Theory in Action: One Model

After doing the prep work—which can take up nearly a third of an entire training program—I try to lay a theoretical and practical foundation by providing a contextual explanation of mistreatment and discrimination that the young people already have experienced or witnessed, consciously or not. First, I share a particular point of view about human nature: that all human beings are born inherently good, and no one is born bad or evil. The point of this is to talk about adultism, a starting point for discussing power and alliance building. Adultism is the institutionalized, routinized, systematic oppression of young people by adults/older people, which predisposes young people to think and act in specific ways with regard to being on the power and nonpower sides of institutional adultism in society. I have found that a consciousness about the conditioning to be adults is an excellent way to examine how oppression (including adultism, sexism, heterosexism, racism, etc.) operates in the queer adult community and the rest of society. Young people then can make the connections between a form of injustice they experience as a group and other forms of oppression that they have encountered. This introduction to oppression is fortified with brainstorming, role playing, and other short exercises that examine a particular oppression (in this case, adultism) and how it is enforced and reinforced.

After introducing the concept of adultism, I focus on how we internalize it and how it affects our attitudes and behaviors. Yes, oppression sucks, but half of our work to end oppression involves kicking out our internalized oppression, the psychic digestion of societal wrongs. We examine internalized oppression with a magnifying glass, do a lot of check-ins about how we feel, listen to each other, and remind each other about our strengths and resourcefulness.

When it feels right, we move on to alliance building, discussing what are important qualities for an ally, how we act as allies (to ourselves and others), and how we find allies. An ally is often, though not necessarily, a person not targeted by the oppression at hand, who acts on behalf of a person who is. For example a European-American straight male who respectfully interrupts racism against an Asian lesbian is an ally. Further exercises and role playing using actual situations the group comes up with are useful to this discussion. It has also been a good place for me to hear what the young people need from me as an adult colleague and ally.

In each of these sections, I integrate relevant information/discussion about the dynamics of multiple oppressions and how an oppression relates to other aspects of the health education curriculum, cultural identity, and current events. Young people look for role models in the community on different issues; sometimes individuals have pursued research on identity topics of interest to them outside of group, including interviewing queer people of their cultural background, taking ethnic studies classes, and going to non-queer-identified cultural events. These experiences can have a profound impact on youth of color in the queer community, who otherwise might not have a connection to their cultural heritage.

Here are some other tips to keep in mind:

Time. The main focus of each session is to give participants enough time not only to soak up information, but also to talk about their experiences and be heard. Make sure to check the amount of time you are presenting, and allow for large- and small-group/pair-off time.

Focus. If you start feeling group attention wandering, take a break, play a game, or move on to another section. Sometimes, a group fade-out means participants need to pair off and do a check-in. This will give you time to refocus with your facilitators or make the transition into a different part of the program. Sometimes, if the discussion drags, stop and continue another day. Dragging could be a sign that participants are overwhelmed.

Right to pass. Not everyone has to talk about their personal experiences every time. What is important is that everyone has agreed to the training at the get-go.

Crisis intervention plans. For most people, working on oppression brings up painful memories. Some youth may need more assistance with certain issues than you realize ahead of time. For example, I ran a sexism workshop with a large group of teen women where 75 percent of them shared personal experiences with sexual abuse or rape. This was overwhelming for facilitators as well as participants, but we had a plan for dealing with abuse, and the young people had support outside the workshop.

Staff support. Make sure that you and your staff have support when things get heavy. Urgency and the emotional impact these issues have on you as a facilitator can be a hindrance if you don't have a check on them.

Perspective. Remember that doing oppression/liberation work isn't about saving the world from injustice. It is about creating a safe forum to explore societal issues on an emotional level. The work dips into our feelings so we can think clearly about our actions to change the world.

Reflections on the Process

Doing work on oppression issues and alliance building with any group is emotional. It requires that you as a facilitator have some clear insight into your own history and current relationship to oppression. It requires that peer staff have training in basic communication skills and be willing to develop a group identity. It is also important that youth and adult staff find emotional support outside the program.

Doing work on oppression means taking risks. If you really want your program to transform unhealthy attitudes and behaviors into revolutionary power, youth and adult staff need to consciously decide that they are willing to get under their own skin (so to speak) and try to trust each other in the process.

Doing work on oppression is always multifaceted. It is a given that discussion about the impact of heterosexism and homophobia is critical in a queer youth program. But doing work on oppression with queer youth is not just about being queer. Queer youth who have a vision about their role as peer educators/leaders for other young people can be very exuberant and proud about being queer. Finding the fun in queerness is often quite easy and natural for them; this is one of our strengths as a group which can be utilized throughout the program. Young people who are less comfortable with their sexual orientation can often benefit from exposure to other youth who share the same feelings. Adults need not be insistent that they feel comfortable about their sexual orientation right away.

Sometimes being queer consumes most of a young person's energy with regard to developing his or her personal identity, and sometimes it doesn't. Being gay is not the only aspect of a gay youth's identity, although it often may appear that way. The struggle that comes with being queer in US society may not always be the biggest issue young gays and lesbians face. Depending on your relationship to them, young people will often tell you what is important to them. At the same time, peer and adult staff can encourage each other and other youth to explore different aspects of their identity in addition to their sexuality.

If you can create ways to bolster queer young people's self-esteem with regard to their cultural heritage, you are giving them a great gift. However, there seems to be a tendency for queer youth programs to ignore issues of color, to emphasize "multiculturalism" and maintain a pretense that our unity is in our queerness. This does a great disservice to young people and essentially reinforces the status quo in the queer community at large.

When an awareness of cultural history is instilled in young people—especially those who have grown up in ethnically identified communities—they can begin to integrate the sense of belonging at an even deeper level. Those young people who have had little identification with their ethnic heritage, especially Euro-American youth, often find that a feeling of cultural connectedness bolsters their ability to act when oppression happens to themselves and to others.

Notes for Allies: Institutional Issues

Why is it that in San Francisco, one of the most ethnically diverse cities in the US, there are so few lesbians of color (people of color, in general) working with queer youth? This is part of a much larger question: Why are there so few people of color in upper-management positions in queer-identified organizations? Like every community in the US, the lesbian, gay, and bisexual community has its own brand of institutionalized racism. White people get hired and hire each other. For middle-class Euro-Americans, the queer community is a safe place. For queer people of color, little changes in our everyday struggle against racism in the gay community. There is the same racism and white liberalism/racist politeness veiling systematically repressive working environments, exclusive political networks, and unethical and/or illegal business procedures. And how many stories have you heard about so-and-so, a lesbian of color, at the Whatchamacallit Center, leaving because of racial harassment—but she didn't sue because she couldn't prove it, or couldn't afford an attorney, or the organization folded anyway? Unfortunately, sometimes lessons are learned only after some brave front-line fighter wins a big, fat lawsuit.

Do young people really have the power to change the system? Do people of color have the power to change the system? I am assuming that both groups do, but I do not know the answer to these questions for sure. Queer young people (and young people in general) who are the core of any youth program deserve to be treated as full-fledged employees—not as tokens or hourly wage employees who get no benefits and are never integrated into other aspects of an organization's operations.

As a woman of color I have seen few and/or inconsistent changes in queer organizations with regard to affirmative action, equal treatment among staff, office culture, and ethics over politics. How can I hold up hope for young people when I myself feel the contradictions in the system? It is currently in vogue to do "multicultural" work, but agencies and institutions must evolve to competently carry it out. This means:

1. ensuring affirmative action in hiring of staff in community agencies, in all aspects of the organization (not just program staff), and hiring people of color who know the local community;
2. creating meaningful, appropriately salaried positions for young people's programs;

3. preparing for what it means to have young people as employees, volunteers, and/or participants in the agency;
4. confronting oppression issues before they happen, through staff trainings;
5. periodically evaluating office culture and dynamics;
6. recognizing that youth work is difficult and all staff need to have specific rest time;
7. asking yourself (individually and institutionally) how committed you are to the project—young people deserve consistency in program and staff contact;
8. having clear guidelines for adult and youth behavior in the program—regarding weapons, drugs, sexual behavior, etc.—and specific methods for dealing with any violations.

Conclusion: The Rewards of Doing Work on Oppression with Queer Youth

Teaching about oppression has benefits that go beyond the relationships queer young people develop with each other. It is an opportunity to see themselves as people on both sides of oppression, and to develop strategies to confront and change their situation. In addition to building a sense of belonging in a program, oppression/liberation work is critical to the leadership development of our communities. I have seen young people I have known in queer youth programs take charge of meetings, head committees, plan events, and make themselves visible. The world benefits from their strength to be themselves.

Notes

1. Todos is a week-long resident camp for young people to examine oppression and to build friendships, based in Oakland, California. The LYFE program of Lyon-Martin Women's Health Services of San Francisco is the first federally funded substance abuse prevention demonstration project for lesbian, gay, and bisexual young people and their families.
2. "Sansei" means third-generation Japanese-American. I use the word "queer" to mean "lesbian, gay, and bisexual." Transgendered, transsexual, and cross-dressing individuals are often included in the term "queer"; however, I did not knowingly work with young people with these identities.
3. A targeted group is one that is denied power institutionally and culturally. For example, people of color are targeted consciously and unconsciously for emotional, physical, and economic violence through racist oppression.

4. I have been fortunate to meet and work with people who have dedicated their lives to teaching others about deconstructing oppressive individual and institutional patterns, especially Allen Creighton, Cameron Hubbe, Josefa Molina, Pata Suyemoto, Alina Ever, Diana Phillips, Vincent Fuqua, Tho Vong, Yvette Gomez, Barbara Blinick, Kevin Gogin, Kosta Bagakis, Harrison Simms, Ricky Sherover-Marcuse, New Bridges, and Equity Institute. Much of my training with young people involves a lot of cutting and pasting of existing alliance-building, peer-education, and health curricula with my own.

5. For the purposes of this article, I focus on working with queer youth specifically. For information about doing peer-education work in general, much of which is relevant to working with queer youth, see Allen Creighton and Paul Kivel, *Helping Teens Stop Violence* (Alameda, CA: Hunter House, 1992) and "Grab Hold: Peer Counseling Training Manual," available from Ira Sachnoff, c/o San Francisco Unified School District, 1512 Golden Gate, San Francisco, CA 94116.

6. The late Ricky Sherover-Marcuse, whose life work was dedicated to teaching others about oppression, said this often.

7. For example, see "Grab Hold."

Institutions

18

Forging the Future, Remembering Our Roots: Building Multicultural, Feminist Lesbian and Gay Studies

Merle Woo

What I'd like to talk about today[1] is constructing a successful lesbian and gay studies that will survive with integrity. My remarks will be made from the context of my own experience. I would like to address what the content of lesbian and gay studies should be, whom it should represent, and some strategies for survival.

I am a beneficiary of the 1968–69 Third World Student Strikes at San Francisco State University. I was getting my Master's in English literature and was a witness to the strikes. What I saw students, community activists, radicals, staff, faculty, and unionists doing—that radicalized me. They put their lives and careers on the line, and because of that, I saw the establishment of ethnic studies, affirmative action, and the Educational Opportunity Program. I got my first offer to teach because of those gains. Campus activism and other movements for social change have not only given me a chance to affirm who I am, as a lesbian of color and a socialist feminist, they have also given me work. I'm very, very grateful to them.

When I saw the success of the Third World student movement, that radicalized me faster than dropping Catholicism, faster than becoming a lesbian. That fast! What changed me was becoming conscious in a lightning flash that my education had been full of lies and censorship. I realized I had never read anything by people of color. I had never read very much by women—except for maybe Emily Dickinson, the Brontës, always in a certain kind of marginal context, with a certain derision. I had never read anything by lesbians, never read anything

163

about the American labor movement, or what Asian Pacific Americans contributed to the history of this country, or to the world, and it infuriated me. That's what turned me into a radical right away, and it was with this anger, this consciousness, that I started teaching.

In time, however, I learned an important lesson: ethnic studies was by and large single-issue. Race was primary. Accompanying the Black, Yellow, Red, and Brown Power movements was a cultural nationalism that was sexist and heterosexist to the core. It took me another five years before I came to women of color activism and feminism and started teaching in women's studies. So then I came out as a feminist. And then I came out as a lesbian and became interested in lesbian and gay studies. And now I'm thinking, why did I have to come out in stages? Why can't we have an education where everything is there for me all at once, that gives me a chance to affirm who I am, as a lesbian of color, as someone who has something to contribute? And I also realized that all of these different studies—ethnic studies, women's studies, and what I hope will be a truly multicultural, multi-issue lesbian and gay studies—are based on theories of liberation.

In other words, we have established ourselves to confront university administrations, which have tried to inculcate and perpetuate through education a white, straight, patriarchal, elitist, and capitalist perspective, where students emerge as cooperative cogs in a multinational corporate machine. This training to be passive is what Paolo Freire calls the "banking concept of education." To this, we say No! Ethnic studies, women's studies, lesbian and gay studies should not cooperate. They should give us tools to change society. And that's why we have to survive. That is absolutely why we have to survive.

Students have always been in the leadership as far as I've been concerned, and they have taught me so much. It was the students at UC Berkeley in Peace and Conflict Studies who began multicultural lesbian and gay studies, and the curriculum was already multi-issue and multicultural when they asked me to be their faculty supervisor. That's when I started thinking about what an ideal—or rather a really great—lesbian and gay studies could be.

From the history of student movements, and especially from the Third World Student Strikes, I learned that there are three components to a successful alternative academic movement:

Number one is student participation in decision making—student democracy—students taking responsibility for the curriculum, for the hiring of faculty, for all of it. Students know exactly what they want because they know what it means to be powerless, especially in these times of soaring fees and diminishing class offerings.

The second necessity is community-related courses, taught by people from the community. What is the point of studying the history of lesbians and gays, or the history of racism or sexism, if you don't tie it up with the community today? Understanding history gives us the tools to go out there and change things for the better. I think education should be relevant to people's lives now and should teach students to be critical thinkers. Education must be made accessible to everybody.

The danger to the status quo by offering community-related courses is just this: that students of the 1990s will credit ethnic studies to radicals and students of the 1960s, who themselves were influenced by liberation struggles in the Third World and the anti-Vietnam War movement; they will credit women's studies to a burgeoning second wave of the women's movement—especially the prochoice movement when female and male activists and doctors, many of whom continued to provide illegal, safe abortions, took to the streets and won Roe v. Wade; they will credit lesbian and gay studies to the Stonewall rebellion in 1969, when Puerto Rican and Black drag queens, lesbians, and street people rioted for three days and said No! to all forms of repression. Students will learn the *truth* that no significant gains for themselves or the working class were ever gotten by a beneficent ruling class. Pressure was always brought to bear by the grass roots demonstrating, protesting, marching. This truth will encourage student activism and confidence in their ability to change society—the status quo.

The third component that San Francisco State University students demanded in 1969 was to eventually establish an autonomous Third World college, to grant degrees, create curricula, and hire faculty with total independence from traditional academia. Well, that's never happened, right? Because, of course, in 1969, as soon as we got what we wanted, the take-backs began right away. But the concept of autonomy and maintaining our integrity is absolutely key. It's always a struggle. Can we achieve independence under the system? True equality? It's always a struggle, and always the same question arises for any oppressed group, the one Rosa Luxemburg asked so long ago: reform or revolution? Freedom, equality, and democracy for all demand revolution.

Other questions are still relevant: Is our program going to be an extension of the community that put us here? Or is it going to be an extension of academia? Are we going to cuddle up to right-wing administrations, which are leaning further and further right every year, in a hypocritical and ineffectual attempt to preserve ourselves? Or are we going to be an extension of the communities that enabled lesbian and gay studies to exist and represent all the students, activists, faculty, radicals, and everybody else? We've got to consider these questions all the time. I want to see a lesbian and gay studies that is international and not solely Eurocentric, that truly represents lesbians and gays of color.

A few of us lesbians and gays of color have been talking together today, about the conference this weekend. We've been looking around, after hearing estimates of the number of people of color in attendance. People have been talking about Essex Hemphill and the leadership he showed through his speech by making visible and concrete the fight against racism, and bringing in economic and class issues and what that means in terms of AIDS, and who are the ones who are hit hardest by AIDS. And if we look at the conference program and look at who's really represented, and then count how many people of color we see, and how economically inaccessible this conference is, I have to say that I don't want to see a lesbian and gay studies like this! I don't want to see an elitist movement. I don't want to see us just focusing on craft or form, or publishing, although they are important. I want us honestly looking at the issues that most affect us: racism, sexism, heterosexism, class exploitation. I want us thinking about what education should and can be: liberating, sharing between faculty and students; students developing skills of critical analysis. Having students grow up to be able to choose from many, many perspectives, and not just one. It is diversity—of races, sexualities—all of those things that have been denied us for all this time.

Frankly, I think the future is in lesbian and gay studies, because lesbians and gays are now the cutting edge in the '90s. The right wing is going to come down on women, and the right wing is going to come down on lesbians and gays, and we are going to be on the front line. But who is going to stand up for us on the campuses and in the community if we don't ourselves become multi-issue? If we don't ourselves address race and sex as they connect up with heterosexism and class? I want to see us survive on the basis of real coalition building, not just using the phony term "outreach." I want to see us addressing every single issue that pertains to every single lesbian and gay person. There are lesbian and gay immigrants, there are lesbian and gay people of color, there are lesbians who are being sterilized because they're Puerto Rican, or Asian, or Black. All of these issues are lesbian and gay issues, and I want to see them discussed in the classroom.

I want to see the classroom connected up with the campus, and the campus connected up with the community, and the community connected up with the world, so that what we have is something viable, and strong, and unbeatable—absolutely unbeatable—without selling out to any of the university administrations. I want us to keep intact the concepts of liberation that were the foundation of the Third World Student Strikes. We must look around the world today and see what imperialism has done in Southeast Asia, Latin America, Africa, globally. Look to the youth, the women, the lesbians and gays. See what we can do as a plurality and as a majority, right here in this country.

Notes

1. This article is an edited version of a talk originally delivered as part of the "Scholarship and Community: Constructing Gay and Lesbian Studies" panel at Out Write '90: The First National Lesbian and Gay Writers' Conference, March 3, 1990, in San Francisco.

19

Humanity Is Not a Luxury:
Some Thoughts on a Recent Passing

Sharon P. Holland

In the late fall of 1992, Audre Lorde passed. I received the news from an old friend in Ann Arbor and it took awhile for the shock to subside and the quiet weeping to begin. Since my last years in college, when my discovery of *Sister Outsider* and *Zami* saved my life, taught me that I was one among millions—other sisters loving women—I have both admired and feared Lorde's power.[1] So many times, I longed to write her a letter or a bit of fan mail; but at the risk of appearing naive, or at worst stupid, I declined and dreamt from a distant place. I missed two opportunities to hear Lorde speak; each came in the midst of some other academic commitment or family emergency, the importance of which I can't even remember. The first time I did hear Lorde speak was on a hot April afternoon, while on the Mall during the 1993 March on Washington. In the company of at least a million other queer people I watched Audre Lorde on film as part of a commemorative piece—an excerpt from a paper delivered at the Copeland Colloquium at Amherst College in April of 1990. Her voice, her words, her face were finally together for me, but so very different from the other discourses on the platform that afternoon. She spoke to a place that we have yet to even contemplate as a political force, let alone as an academic movement. She spoke to a place in me that was shamed by my own silence, my fear of communicating, my lost opportunity.

My tears were hot and angry on the lawn that day, as I wondered if any of the folk around me were really hearing what Lorde had to say. I began to feel enshrouded with the silences that surround us as queer people. I remember walking in and around Dupont Circle in awe of the sheer numbers of us, and I also remember feeling constantly isolated, battling with myself to relax and enjoy the celebration. I saw antiracist agendas on placards and buttons, but I wondered how many of us held them closely enough that these plans would actually travel back home with us instead of being tossed in the heap of rally posters piled up near Mall trash cans. I feel very ambivalent about my experience on the Mall in April, perhaps because I believe that, despite the election of Bill Clinton, things will not positively change for people of color in this country. Things are getting worse for us, plain and simple.

In my ruminations about silence, agendas, and Audre Lorde, I recalled a letter she had written to Mary Daly in the spring of 1979. Lorde's particular critique focused on Daly's lack of and/or distortions in attention to the presence of African goddesses in her work; having received no reply after four months, Lorde opened her critique of Daly's book *Gyn/Ecology* to what she termed "the community of women."[2] At that point, Lorde's private observations became public, and the responsibility for dialogue and response became that of the community, as opposed to the named individuals. I have two questions, one private, the other public: Did Mary Daly ever understand what Lorde was trying to say? Do we stand the risk of sliding down the slippery slope of denial—to mirror the shameful silence Daly created by failing to respond, or better yet, to understand? I write this piece now and on this issue because I have a fundamental belief as a teacher and a scholar that we must recognize and understand Lorde's work and life if we are to become a viable political and academic force—a force not acknowledged for its qualitative difference, but for its absolute adherence to a belief that, as Lorde once declared, "it is not those differences between us that are separating us. It is rather our refusal to *recognize* those differences, and to examine the distortions which result from our misnaming them and their effects upon human behavior and expectation" (115). Mary Daly still exists in that spatial silence and Audre Lorde is dead, killed by a cancer we all know probably began in the bowels of Keystone Electronics where as a young woman she had to work to survive. What was Daly doing while Lorde was working and dying at Keystone? Did they pass one another at one of the "gay-girl" bars in the '50s and speak then, silence only imposed much later in their relationship? These questions might seem negligible, but I have to return to them because they help to bring some order to my own grief, and my own fears. Reexamining this old silence makes more sense to me than any other exploration I've undertaken during this past year because as a movement that wants to become institutionalized on campuses across this country we need to return to that letter that Lorde sent to Daly and to that clip on the screen from April 1993.

It occurs to me that if we are going to teach our students about racism, then we ought, as lesbians, to teach it where it hits home—not as something exterior to lesbian/gay movements but as integral to their (trans)formation. If our fear is truly in the recognition of difference, and not difference itself, then the project of antiracist discourse must renew itself and take a look at the subject within, as opposed to the happenings without. Perhaps this is the primary stumbling block for folks with respect to Lorde's philosophy, especially for academics who are brought up with the incredible notion that those projects which are the most sophisticated always begin and end with reference to and critique of someone else's work, but rarely (except in novel form) concern the soulwork of the author. This objectivity has created a lovely crop of intellectually ambitious but emotionally unhealthy academics, and I do include myself in this infamous group. This might be the source of my discomfort on the Mall in April—that Lorde's theory of the "self" as the "other" was somehow lost on the millions of people who had gathered to turn their sights on the behaviors of others, particularly those in power. But we have learned that self-scrutiny and in particular, the request that others begin that same journey, can often be not only a painful process, but also that it is not required in the postmodern schema where anything that represents hybridity is in and of itself considered a declaration of self-examination, even in its noisiest state.

Maybe it was the shock of opening up, of self-exploration implied by Lorde's letter that caused Daly to retreat into silence. Of course, we will never know, but we can learn from the incident. What appears most striking about this particular call and response is its similarity to an ongoing struggle in the era of the New Age. Many people of color have protested the wide use of religious materials and nomenclature in the rituals proposed and utilized by New Age sages, practitioners, and bookstore owners. These protests have been met primarily with silence, and this stillness extends itself in many directions. Traditional academic feminism seems reluctant about, if not hostile to, any serious critique of the new "culture," apparently denying any relationship to this new spirituality that has so captivated the intellects and purse strings of women; present logic dictates that if we ignore it and its problematic, it might somehow fade or pass on. This pattern of relating is dysfunctional on several levels. The adoption of women's studies as an integral facet of the university curriculum was seen by those advocating more mainstream discourses as a fleeting event, one that would and could pass as a trend. As feminists we should then realize that this same logic does not work when applied to our own community. We have to understand as well that the forces within often mirror the forces without. As white women in the consciousness-raising groups of the '70s realized, racism and homophobia are equally pervasive as forms of institutionalized and internalized sexism. Therefore, it is unproductive to recreate hierarchies of oppression or categories of inside/outside when we relate with one another. This pattern of exchange prevents us from entering into challenging contemporary debates. For example, as I witnessed at a women's studies conference at the University of Connecticut in October, critiques of the selling of native religion, specifically, often extend the same blanket incrimination to both native and white sellers. However, there are very specific and important historical and socioeconomic distinctions to be made between the motivations of whites to sell native religion and of native peoples to market what they might already own. The problematic of access is intimately tied to the issue of purchasing and marketing. We have to ask ourselves who's buying these products, what percentage of the profits even reaches those responsible for their creation, and do those folks actually have access to the plethora of merchandise available in western markets? More important, we need to ask about the institution's role in fostering and developing new discourses; we need to ask ourselves these questions constantly.

Recently, I studied meditation techniques with an excellent teacher who went to a friend's pipe ceremony at a local center for the arts. The ceremony was led by a white woman and was advertised throughout the community as a sacred celebration of a Lakota ritual. Native peoples in the vicinity came to the event to protest against the marketing of sacred ritual. Shocked by this news, my Yoga teacher expressed a commitment not to participate in events geared toward the exploitation of sacred Native traditions. I wondered how someone who worked in a cooperative atmosphere and had daily access to the local New Age bookstore could view the protest as surprising. I learned that any intellectual project, even when disguised by the "spirit," can be largely self-motivating if we don't check ourselves. In the context of these other misunderstandings and silences it is quite possible to see a reasoning and a context for not only Daly's silence, but also our own. Much of New Age spirituality is devoted to the intensity of self-exploration through ritual techniques. On the surface this appears to be very much needed in postmodernity. I believe that my argument, and perhaps Lorde's as well, is not with the intent, but with the practice.

The call to examine our practices in alignment with our good intentions is quite possibly the most difficult form of self-critique, because our mistakes so often mirror the larger patterns which we define as racism, sexism, or homophobia—usually propagated by a dominant group whose practices we, as lesbian feminists, so often separate ourselves from. In her letter to Daly, Lorde scrutinizes the positing of the "myth of white women" as the "legitimate and sole herstory and myth of all women." She continues: "I ask that you be aware of the effect that this dismissal has upon the community of Black women and other women of Color, and how it devalues your own words. This dismissal does not essentially differ from the specialized devaluations that make Black women prey, for instance, to the murders even now happening in your own city.[3] When patriarchy dismisses us, it encourages our murders. *When radical lesbian feminist theory dismisses us, it encourages its own demise*" (69, emphasis mine). The project Lorde encourages Daly to undertake involves much more than a tacit inclusion of difference. It calls for a recognition that difference is the essence of the self, the unique blend of past and present that informs each of us; that to dismiss it is to dismiss ourselves. A denial of the force of difference allows us to adhere to the master's plan and encourage our own destruction.

Feeling the power of this analogy—when the self becomes so like the dominant other—is both shaming and enlightening. I remember having a conversation with a fellow female graduate student, in which I referred to her as a white woman, and then tried to correct myself by saying, "Jewish." She immediately cut me short and said, "Don't try to categorize me!" I was ashamed, embarrassed, and struck dumb. I apologized, and we continued our highly charged conversation. The next time we saw one another, I was still ashamed, but the burning redness faded after time and gave way to a deep sense of mutual respect. Out of that brief encounter I learned a lot about community and the individual, and a lot about myself. I would have preferred to hide from my friend and pretend that her correction was the mistake, and not my behavior. But we forced ourselves to move beyond that moment, and part of our journey was always to remember the crack in our discourse with one another, to utilize it as a bond rather than as a roadblock.

Part of the motivating logic behind the New Age women's movement is a recognition that Sisterhood transcends. But beyond this inherent belief, Lorde reminds us, "is still racism" (70). The permanence of racism, to borrow a phrase from legal scholar Derek Bell, is an undeniable and constant fact of life for myself and other sisters out there.

Often the undeniable is somehow mutated and transformed under the New Age discourse, so that Black women who express the reality of their lives are somehow made to feel shallow in this new and strangely deep pool of the spirit which recognizes all difference by allowing none. It is a complex landscape where difference is camouflaged and replaced by something else more homogeneous, where an individual's experience must reflect some preelected universal sampling—a sample in which racism is often missing. Acknowledging the reality of Black female experience, Lorde writes that Daly "fails to recognize that [difference] expose[s] all women to various forms and degrees of patriarchal oppression, some of which we share and some of which we do not. For instance, surely you know that for nonwhite women in this country, there is an 80 percent fatality rate from breast cancer; three times the number of unnecessary eventrations, hysterectomies and sterilizations as for white women; three times as many chances of being raped, murdered, or assaulted as exist for white women. These are statistical facts, not coincidences nor paranoid fantasies" (70). The reality of these statistics has not changed, and Lorde's passing is representative of the power of fact in the lives of Black women. However, in this society where seeing is believing and spectacle is preferred, happenings must be accompanied by proof and, if at all possible, entertaining proof. Very often the feeling of racism is less tenable than the witnessed fact. We will find it very difficult as lesbian teachers and academics to underscore the feeling of racism rather than its evidence in an institution that relies on proof as the primary representative of fact. Moreover, it will be near impossible to relay this sentiment to students and colleagues who are used to a society that exists without mutual trust and respect. The process of naming and unfolding racism is very much dependent upon respect and trust; we have the dual responsibility of fostering this in the classroom and in the workplace by challenging those spaces where it is not felt.

Beyond the problematic of naming racism is owning it, and with ownership comes responsibility. One key to owning racism is a recognition of its consistency. Before the colloquium at Amherst, Lorde observed, "For us [as women of Color], increasingly, violence weaves through the daily tissues of our living—in the supermarket, in the classroom, in the elevator, in the clinic and the schoolyard, from the plumber, the baker, the saleswoman, the bus driver, the bank teller, the waitress who does not serve us . . . You fear your children will grow up to join the patriarchy and testify against you, we fear our children will be dragged from a car and shot down in the street, and you will turn your backs upon the reasons they are dying" (119). I do not doubt that there are countless white lesbian feminists out there who have an intellectual and emotional understanding of racism; what I am suspicious of is how present this realization is during their daily encounters. And my suspicion grows into distrust when I know that, as Lorde points out, we are still dying—bloodied on the streets, removed from classrooms, silenced in mainstream politics—and that forms of institutionalized racism still continue to multiply, demonstrating that there are not enough white feminists acknowledging the consistency of racism in the positions of power that they hold. Because of this, the process of institutionalizing any radical thought not only frightens me, but also appears as antithetical to itself. Adhering to radical philosophy is understanding that the institution also exists within the individual and that it can also become, and change, accordingly. But it cannot evolve if we do not recognize as lesbians and feminists that it exists because we contribute to its making.

We have to be universally vigilant and brave in both the classroom and the workplace. During my tenure as a graduate student at the University of Michigan, I had the misfortune to witness the demise of the collective structure in the women's studies program. As the structure was being replaced with a more efficient hierarchy, our concern as women of color was the maintenance of visibility and voice in the program. We asked that the new "leadership" grant at least two positions in the new structure to women of color over a three-year period. Our proposal was vehemently opposed, most particularly by white lesbians in the program who felt it important to remind us that quotas were against the law. (I remembered that it was once illegal for Black people to drink from a fountain marked "white"; it was also still against the law in Michigan to commit sodomy, in public or private.) They reduced our request to mere advocacy of a bankrupt system, rather than recognizing it as a legitimate demand for permanence as opposed to mere presence within the institution. Stunned and outraged, we argued with one another until we were all tired and resentful. The agenda that we all had felt we had in common under collectivity was greatly compromised in the face of a very white and very male structural model. Moreover, our ability as a political force to institute change, to unmake the dominant structure, gave way to its strengthening. I have not forgotten the experience, and I learned that our agendas for radical change must be carried close to us, must not become rhetoric or lip service. If our words and actions help to promote the status quo, then we have served the institution well; we have preserved the patriarchy, and we have promoted heterosexism. If we uphold the law of the land rather than attempt to dismantle it, then we promote institutionalized forms of racism, sexism, and heterosexism. These are the results, plain and simple.

At times the project of change seems monumental and overwhelming; it is. But at the same time, it can be quite simple. I want to use a bit of logic from Toni Morrison here, because what she unfolds is pertinent to this discussion, and what concerns her has specific impact for theorizing and practicing the project of change. In "Unspeakable Things Unspoken: The Afro-American Presence in American Literature," Morrison argues: "Looking at the scope of American literature, I can't help thinking that the question should never have been 'Why am I, an Afro-American, absent from it?' It is not a particularly interesting query anyway. The spectacularly interesting question is 'What intellectual feats had to be performed by the author or his critic to erase me from a society seething with my presence, and what effect has that performance had on the work?' What are the strategies of escape from knowledge? Of willful oblivion?"[4] Morrison's query helps to define the project at hand. It is not useful for us to ask "why" anymore, but "how." To ask why would be denying the power of the knowledge that we as teachers and scholars have accessed and shared. As writer and critic Toni Cade Bambara has expressed it in the form of her grandmother's admonition, "What are we pretending not to know today?" Asking why blurs the power of the work to be done, because it takes the focus off of us as participants and places it in the hands of the nebulous few in power. We might be able to exit ourselves from the creation of systems of oppression (the "why" of the question), but we can't often escape how we fit into these very present and very real systems. Inquiring about how our presence, as women of color, as lesbians, has been erased is a much more revealing endeavor. In asking how, we discover the power of numbers as well as the force behind hegemony and the key to its dismantling. This "how" project serves a dual purpose—to remind us that indeed we are many, and to call attention to our own sense of agency, both negative and positive, in the making of history and its institutions. As we continue to ask "how," we call attention to questions and answers that have relevance to our own work; the project of change is, after all, deeply personal and deeply felt.

These explorations and probings don't always reveal aspects of ourselves that place us in the most honorable light. More often than not these encounters in the classroom and with our colleagues and friends can be very threatening and isolating. In her closing remarks to Daly, Lorde reminds herself: "I had decided never again to speak to white women about racism. I felt it was wasted energy because of destructive guilt and defensiveness, and because whatever I had to say might better be said by white women to one another at far less emotional cost to the speaker, and probably with a better hearing"(70). Mary Daly's silence proved a sad manifestation of Lorde's initial fear. However, as the community of women, we can unmake the damage, engaging first with ourselves and our own agendas, and doing so very honestly. Professor Nesha Haniff asks her African-American studies students at the University of Michigan: "Do we, as people of color, need white people in antiracist struggle?" The answer for her, and for me, is yes, but it is an affirmation that each of us utters reluctantly. The hesitancy is due to a shared understanding that this answer implies a continued struggle on our part to undergo the emotional cost of making our feelings known; the affirmation stems from a belief that it is crucial to our survival on this planet that we stop the madness by any means necessary.[5] We cannot stop the madness unless we recognize it in ourselves.

I am still unsettled and exhilarated by my experience on the Mall some months ago. I will never forget the feeling of power in sheer numbers, and the fear of having my concerns as a Black lesbian take a backseat to other considerations. I move forward with this dual memory and share it with those in the institution around me, and I take with me an understanding that I gleaned from Lorde's work and life: that forging connections across differences is our only hope out of our present crisis. And if you're asking yourself what the particular "crisis" is, then I ask in response, "What are you pretending not to know today?"

Notes

1. Audre Lorde, *Sister Outsider: Essays and Speeches* (Freedom, CA: Crossing Press, 1984) and *Zami: A New Spelling of My Name* (Freedom, CA: Crossing Press, 1982).
2. Audre Lorde, "An Open Letter to Mary Daly" (1979), in *Sister Outsider*, 66–71. Reference to this essay will subsequently be made parenthetically in the text. Mary Daly, *Gyn/Ecology: The Metaethics of Radical Feminism* (Boston: Beacon Press, 1978).
3. Lorde refers here to the serial murder of twelve black women in the Boston area in the spring of 1979.
4. Toni Morrison, "Unspeakable Things Unspoken: The Afro-American Presence in American Literature," *Michigan Quarterly Review* (Winter 1989): 11–12.
5. Personal conversation with Nesha Haniff, March 1992.

20

"The Very House of Difference": Toward a More Queerly Defined Multiculturalism

Polly Pagenhart

> Being women together was not enough. We were different. Being gay girls together was not enough. We were different. Being Black together was not enough. We were different. Being Black women together was not enough. We were different. Being Black dykes together was not enough. We were different. ... It was a while before we came to realize that our place was the very house of difference rather than the security of any one particular difference.
> —Audre Lorde, *Zami: A New Spelling of My Name*[1]

I invoke Audre Lorde's decade-old words to begin a discussion of strategies: how might we advocate for queer studies in academic institutions?[2] One arena is opened by the current debates concerning multiculturalism as an antioppressionist educational reform movement. But to till this field is to unearth larger, more fundamental problems: when we try to enact a pedagogy based on the kind of multiple subjectivity from which Lorde and others write, we bump up against—and need to strategize around—the binarized, segmented structure of Western thought and modern academic institutions.

Why use multiculturalist reform as an inroad into queering up the academy? Partially because the rhetoric of cultural pluralism—deeply flawed though it may be—is, as Jacquelyn Zita argues, cunning; so far it has been the the most effective means of placing large endeavors to study oppression into mainstream institutions.[3] For this reason, examining the language and logic of multiculturalism, in order to revise and extend it, is fruitful. Further, a critique of multiculturalism leads us inevitably into a critique of the epistemology of identity upon which it is based. It is the false notion of a unitary subject—and the institutions and language which reinforce it—that is at the root of the conflict.

The term multiculturalism is slippery. Mostly it seems to be employed as a euphemism, helping those who use it to avoid naming the power relations that distinguish and stratify the multiple cultures constituting US society. In academic institutions the word multiculturalism is invoked as a panacea, to promote a colorizing of US history and culture without fundamentally questioning its structural underpinnings. This superficial type of multiculturalism sees US society as a colorful tossed salad rather than as a tasteless and monolithic WASP melting pot. Either way, the language does not challenge us to go beyond the cultural tourist/minority-du-jour level of analysis.[4] The culinary metaphor allows for only limited revision; the tossed salad of United States cultures is not constituted of equally positioned ingredients, and hegemonic power relations dress the whole thing. Such dreary-sounding concepts threaten to wilt the perky mood that multiculturalism attempts to convey.

David Mura charts these semantic vicissitudes in his review of the anthology *Out There: Marginalization and Contemporary Cultures.* He writes: "As its title tells us, this collection focuses not on multiculturalism but on marginalization. . . . The editors' choice not to use the word multiculturalism is telling. Multiculturalism is too easily depoliticized. Marginalization, on the other hand, views culture as a battleground for economic and social power."[5] Mura's juxtaposing the term "multiculturalism" with "marginalization" foregrounds a key distinction. "Multiculturalism" draws attention to the various constituent groups that make up US culture and which have thus far been edged out of the master narrative of history. "Marginalization," on the other hand, draws attention to the construction of that master narrative, and in so doing foregrounds questions of how and why such groups have been written out.

Whether we use multiculturalism or marginalization as a defining tool, the subjects at the center of inquiry are those who have been heretofore at or near the margin: individuals and groups who, to varying degrees, differ from what Audre Lorde calls "the mythical norm": "white, thin, male, young, heterosexual, christian, and financially secure."[6] The multiculturalist movement, at its broadest, redresses gaps in public knowledge regarding the cultures and lives of those who reside, varyingly, outside this mythical norm. Cultural pluralist or American cultures requirements on college campuses—where we would find institutional definitions of multiculturalism—are designed to focus most essentially on comparative studies of race and ethnicity in US society, sometimes including European Americans or so-called white ethnics, sometimes not. (This matter itself is no small debate.) Often as subsequent or secondary considerations, the study of gender and class are also suggested for inclusion in the courses which would meet such a requirement. The net of multiculturalism is cast out wider in other contexts. In their book *Multicultural Education: Issues and Perspectives*, James Banks and Cherry McGee Banks provide chapters on social class and religion, gender, ethnicity and language, and exceptionality.[7]

Discussion of sexuality or sexual minorities crops up in some contexts. *Unequal Sisters: A Multicultural Reader in U.S. Women's History* includes an essay specifically on lesbian culture.[8] Another recent anthology, *Out There*—which reprints the essay in which Audre Lorde introduces her discussion of the mythical norm—includes an essay by Monique Wittig titled "The Straight Mind," one by Martha Gever on the politics of inclusion and exclusion in lesbian identity, and one by Richard Dyer on gay male pornographic cinema.[9] For the Minority Discourse Initiative of the University of California Humanities Research Institute, one of the faculty research fellows is writing an essay called "the queering of America."[10]

These inclusive anthologies show that a growing awareness and inclusion of sexuality as a power-laden signifier in US society are finding their way intermittently into the literature on multiculturalism and minority issues. But it is difficult to distinguish the contexts in which sexual minorities are central or peripheral to discussions of multiculturalism and marginalization. When the literature of multiculturalism is silent about sexuality, the silence is not accompanied by cogent arguments against including an analysis of the hegemony of heterosexism. Without clarity on the terms of exclusion, we are left to conclude that heterosexist biases and ignorance, rather than conscious analysis, generate the silences.

How then, would we strategize fillings those gaps? What would be the most useful and the wisest means with which to queer up the dialogues around multiculturalism and power relations within the academic institution? I want to explore two paths here, each based upon a different conception of identity. The first, what we might call the "single pie" approach, capitulates to the fragmented, sorted, and ranked organization of identity which the current structure of the academy reinforces. This route, focusing on adding another constituent group to the panoply of those in US culture, supports the segmented ways of thinking that the logic of "multiculturalism" presupposes. The second route focuses on the forces that construct individual subjects in US culture, and is better supported by the language of "marginalization." This path pursues a supple, polysemic understanding of identity which is more responsible to the ways people understand themselves, and which challenges the traditional structure of disciplines and the epistemology of identity in the academy. This is the path illuminated by the work of Audre Lorde, Cherríe Moraga, and Trinh T. Minh-ha, to name just a few.[11]

The single pie approach conceives of identity as fixed and limited, a sum of individuated parts, some essentially privileged over others. This perspective is powered by Enlightenment individualism, which recognizes a single, unitary subject. Using this model, to acknowledge each new slice of identity would be to necessarily diminish the amount of space remaining for the other slices. So one would either lobby for consideration of sexual minorities by incorporating them into already existent categories, or by demanding space for a new one.

One could make the case, as Stephen Epstein does, that gayness in North American cultures functions in much the same ways as ethnicity.[12] While "queer ethnicity" is not nurtured from within the family, as ethnicity is with other groups, the community with which lesbians, gay men, and bisexuals can choose to identify contains most elements that characterize ethnicity: a common culture, a sense of shared history, rituals or signs of initiation into the community, a sense of solidarity formed by sustaining threats from without. In short, queer ethnicity would represent a sense of group identity, something which lesbians, gay men, and bisexuals have developed fiercely since the medicalizing, pathologizing, and codifying of so-called deviant sexualities in Western cultures dating from the end of the last century.[13] There's an obvious shortcoming with this argument, though: it does not account for the degree to which sexual minorities are always already embedded in another ethnicity.[14]

Another problematic approach to queering up the multicultural curriculum, still using the single pie model, would be to carve out a whole new slice in the pie. The reform here, in the analysis of identity, would be to tack sexuality onto the trilogy of race, class, and gender, a familiar and unsatisfying tactic. For instance, an introductory class called, say, Literature of American Subcultures, would now contain a unit on Lesbian, Gay, and Bisexual literature, ostensibly diminishing the time students would spend studying (heterosexual) African-American, Chicano, Native-American and Asian-American works. Within this rubric, how does one decide where to place the writings of Jewelle Gomez, or Kitty Tsui, or Chrystos?

The futility of such an organizational structure points up that we are utterly derailed when we regard such facets of identity as separable from one another. But current institutional structures cloud our vision of a synthetic approach to understanding the dynamic, coimplicated nature of subjectivity and oppression. Given the fractured, departmentalized structure of the university, it is a challenge to think outside these divisions and an even greater challenge not to reinforce them as we work within them. Further, the sites in the academy where identity politics and the politics of oppression are by definition made central are places that are ostensibly organized around one unitary facet of identity. Ethnic studies programs have foregrounded the study of race and ethnicity as they interact with power in society. Women's studies programs have privileged gender.

For all the problems this fractured conception inevitably entails, people tend to organize around their first emergency—the facet of their identity that they feel plunges them most deeply into social crisis. For those who are multiply minoritized, with more than one emergency, this recalls the familiar sorting and ranking of identity, that no-win "oppression derby."[15] But we need to understand the first emergency as always in flux, dependent upon conditions which themselves are always shifting—a contingent emergency, changing both vividly and subtly with our movement between differing social spaces, some of which foreground one dimension of identity, others of which foreground others.

Hate-crimes statistics throw the complexity of identity into striking relief. Not surprisingly, in the gay community it is white men who most often report hate crimes perpetrated against them. Because the number of their emergencies is smaller than that of many white lesbians, gay men of color, and lesbians of color, they can be more certain that they are being bashed for being queer.[16] Those who collect such statistics and organize lesbian and gay community responses to hate crimes, such as San Francisco's Community United Against Violence, find this dynamic borne out.[17]

Whatever lens we use—the complexity of hate-crimes reporting for the multiple minoritized, or the language of multiculturalism as it's spoken within the structures of the academy—it's clear that we need to insist on analytic structures that account for the multiplicity and simultaneity of identity. We know that many writers have been articulating this conception of identity with eloquence and power for a long time now. But how, then, do we visualize and apply this analysis in the institutional structures within which we are working, especially if those structures are identity-based, such as ethnic studies, women's studies, and lesbian or queer studies?

I am imagining a three-dimensional graphic field in which to plot identity, one whose horizontal base axis is replaced by another when the analytic context is shifted. For example, if a study or a course were based on late twentieth-century lesbian literature, one would plot that dimension of identity along a horizontal axis provisionally, merely as a means to provide a consistent basis for analysis. That axis—in this illustration, writers who are lesbian—could not be conceived of as one-dimensional. It would by definition be intersected with other axes: of class, of race, of ethnicity, of ability, of age, of region, and so forth. But for the purposes of the class—to study writing by lesbians—the position of lesbianism, yet to be intersected by other axes of identity, is plotted as the consistent horizontal axis. Using the same structure, a course on the Harlem Renaissance would plot African-American cultural workers in Jazz Age Harlem as the base axis, through which multiple axes of gender, of sexuality, and perhaps other power-laden facets of identity such as skin color could be intersected.

The analytic subtleties following from this multidimensional conception of identity are known to us. Clearly, when we regard identity and oppressive dynamics with the complexity they warrant, we strengthen our ability to understand each in isolation. Anti-Semitism, racism, sexism, classism, and homophobia are all in differing ways coimplicated, and in fact through their definitions and mythologies buttress one another.

To actively employ this fluid analysis not only does justice to the material we study, but broadens the impact of our work as we advocate for queer studies in the academy. It's not simply that we cannot talk of the oppression of sexual minorities in Western history outside of a recognition of their multiply identified status as, among other things, gendered, raced, and classed subjects, though the strength of this argument alone argues for such an approach. The fact is there are too many illuminating historical parallels to draw between the reception and rejection of Jews and other minorities, and the reception and rejection of homosexuals. For example, when anti-Semitism is on the rise, racist and homophobic intolerance and violence consistently increase apace. To overlook this would weaken our analysis and deprive us and our students of more sophisticated analytic tools with which to construct queer studies and queer theories. Further, the advent of queer studies in the academy at this historical moment—after ethnic studies and women's studies—provides a rare opportunity for this new antioppressionist field to learn from the exclusionary mistakes made by its predecessors. Their early underpinnings have been based on an un- or underinterrogated sexism or racism (and for both, hetero-sexism), reinforced by inadequate constructions of identity.

At the root of these constructions is Aristotelian logic, positing identity around binarisms—you are either A or Not-A; Me or Not-me. We know that the "me" who has theorized himself at the center of this order is he who occupies Lorde's "mythical norm." So as we reconstruct a conception of identity that is multiple and simultaneous, we need to come up with a system more useful than an Aristotelian dualism, or even a one-dimensional, finite pie in which sections of identity are comprehended individually and sequentially, in which one portion robs space from another.

In *Woman, Native, Other*, Trinh T. Minh-ha describes "multiple presence": " 'I' is, therefore, not a unified subject, a fixed identity, or that solid mass covered with layers of superficialities one has gradually to peel off before one can see its true face. 'I' is, itself, infinite layers."[18] The best visual image I have to contain such a notion of identity is the house of difference of which Lorde speaks. I don't know what shape this house will take—or, actually, if this conception would even be served by something resembling a fixed blueprint. I do know that we who wish to construct it, inside and outside the academy, are best served if we discard notions of identity built around Aristotelian logic and Enlightenment individualism, the most powerful of "the master's tools."[19]

Notes

For their diverse contributions to this essay, I thank Jenifer Fennell, Kitty Millet, Rebecca Ramirez, and Jacquelyn Zita.

1. Audre Lorde, *Zami: A New Spelling of My Name* (Freedom, CA: Crossing Press, 1982), 226.

2. I employ the term "queer studies" advisedly. While I recognize the significant political debates regarding the implications of the term—especially regarding its potential elision of lesbians—they must be bracketed here; I use the term as a shorthand to refer to work which could include lesbian, gay male, bisexual, and transgender studies.

3. Jacquelyn Zita, personal interview, October 29, 1991.

4. Tomás Almaguer speaks of "articles on third world issues written by white queers who have ventured into our communities ('tourist' literature I call it)," in "Race and Its Discontents at Out/Look," *Out/Look* 12 (Spring 1991): 4.

5. David Mura, "Multiculturalism and Marginalization," *Hungry Mind Review* 17 (Spring 1991): 13.

6. Audre Lorde, "Age, Race, Class and Sex: Women Redefining Difference," in *Sister Outsider: Essays and Speeches* (Freedom, CA: Crossing Press, 1984), 116.

7. James A. Banks and Cherry A. McGee Banks, eds., *Multicultural Education: Issues and Perspectives* (Boston: Allyn and Bacon, 1993).

8. Madeline D. Davis and Elizabeth Lapovsky Kennedy, "Oral History and the Study of Sexuality in the Lesbian Community: Buffalo, New York, 1940–1960," in Ellen Carol DuBois and Vicki L. Ruiz, eds., *Unequal Sisters: A Multicultural Reader in U.S. Women's History* (New York: Routledge, 1990). Davis and Kennedy's groundbreaking study of working-class lesbian life has since been published as *Boots of Leather, Slippers of Gold: The History of a Lesbian Community* (New York: Routledge, 1993).

9. Russell Ferguson et al., eds., *Out There: Marginalization and Contemporary Cultures* (New York: New Museum of Contemporary Art; Cambridge, MA: MIT Press, 1990).

10. As of this printing, work from the first year of the Initiative was being gathered together for publication.

11. I refer here to Lorde's collection of essays, *Sister Outsider*, Moraga's *Loving in the War Years: Lo que nunca pasó por sus labios* (Boston: South End Press, 1983), and Trinh's *Woman, Native, Other: Writing Postcoloniality and Feminism* (Bloomington: Indiana University Press, 1989).

12. Stephen Epstein, "Gay Politics, Ethnic Identity: The Limits of Social Constructionism," *Socialist Review* 17:3–4 (May–August 1987): 9–54.

13. Michel Foucault's *The History of Sexuality* (New York: Pantheon Books, 1978) and David Halperin's *One Hundred Years of Homosexuality* (New York: Routledge, 1990) are two influential works that have pursued this notion as it has played out in western culture. See also Jonathan Ned Katz, "The Invention of the Homosexual, 1880–1950," *Gay/Lesbian Almanac* (New York: Harper and Row, 1983), 137–74, and Lillian Faderman, *Odd Girls and Twilight Lovers: A History of Lesbian Life in Twentieth Century America* (New York: Penguin, 1991) for her discussion of the development of lesbian identities and communities.

14. Teresa de Lauretis points this out in "Queer Theory: Lesbian and Gay Sexualities/ An Introduction," *differences* 3:2 (Summer 1991).

15. For this term I am indebted to Ian Barnard.

16. Jacquelyn Zita also points out that white men tend to have a greater sense of ownership over the public domain, and thus turn more often to public institutions to redress infringements on their movement there (personal interview, October 29, 1991).

17. Ming-Yeung Lu, Community United Against Violence, personal interview, April 17, 1991.

18. Trinh, *Woman, Native, Other*, 94.

19. Audre Lorde, "The Master's Tools Will Never Dismantle the Master's House," *Sister Outsider*, 112.

21

Moving the Pink Agenda into the Ivory Tower: The "Berkeley Guide" to Institutionalizing Lesbian, Gay, and Bisexual Studies

Alisa Klinger

Despite our history of being treated as unwanted guests in our own institutional homes, large numbers of lesbians, gays, and bisexuals—among "others"—continue to choose to build our futures in the academy. While "survival is not an academic skill" (Lorde 112), activism and advocacy are our most powerful, yet least used, tools for making the academic environment more hospitable to lesbian, gay, bisexual, and transgender students, staff, and faculty.

While serving as coordinator of the Task Force for a Multicultural Bisexual, Lesbian, and Gay Studies Center at the University of California at Berkeley, I discovered that the most effective way to overcome the difficulties endemic to campus activism was to engage with lesbian, gay, and bisexual activists at other universities and colleges throughout North America. By sharing our strategies and publicizing our experiences, we can bypass the exceedingly time-consuming, costly, and self-defeating task of recreating the wheel each time we seek institutional recognition and material support. Although the provost of the College of Letters and Science finally approved funding for the development of the academic component of the Berkeley Bisexual, Lesbian, and Gay Center in March 1992, the painstaking history of lesbian, gay, and bisexual organizing on my campus reveals that even at a large public school, renowned for its "liberalism," the road to institutional recognition is not paved with yellow bricks.[1]

The University of California at Berkeley is situated in the heart of what is often affectionately referred to as "Queer Mecca." Nestled between San Francisco and the East Bay Hills, UC Berkeley quite likely has the largest population of lesbian, bisexual, and gay students, staff, alumni, and faculty of any American university. Despite the optimal geographic and demographic conditions, neither the laws of supply and demand nor the city's reputation for radicalism ensured the creation of a single, permanent lesbian/gay/bisexual studies course or program at UC Berkeley until 1993. Even with UC Berkeley's sizable lesbian, gay, and bisexual student population, courses treating issues of sexual diversity have been offered only occasionally by faculty in such departments as English, women's studies, ethnic studies, and sociology. The continuity of such courses, or even the availability of qualified faculty to teach them, has not been guaranteed from semester to semester (or from year to year). In this respect, the University of California at Berkeley is much like the overwhelming majority of universities and colleges in much less congenial locales.

Besides the sporadic faculty-inspired lesbian and gay studies courses, there have been several courses concerned with lesbian, gay, and bisexual issues initiated and taught by Berkeley students themselves. These Democratic Education at Cal classes, or DE-Cal courses as they are now called, have created the misleading impression of an institutional commitment to l/g/b studies. DE-Cal courses, however, receive no direct university funding whatsoever. Rather, students' service fees pay for the DE-Cal program, and students volunteer to design and facilitate courses. Although the student instructors should be entirely commended for their efforts (and for their uncompensated labor), it is unconscionable that UC Berkeley, a public institution, historically has cast off its responsibility to educate all students—straight and queer— onto the lesbian, gay, and bisexual students themselves.

In my work as a student advocate and campus activist over the past ten years, I have noticed that the initial impetus to create new social services and academic programs responsive to students' sexual diversity has invariably come from students themselves.[2] Surely, l/g/b studies would have been institutionalized at Berkeley and throughout this country years ago if tenured faculty—who may well have the least to lose professionally by coming out—had steadfastly included lesbian, gay, and bisexual topics and materials in their course offerings. In the last decade, it has also become clear that women's studies programs cannot be relied upon to represent satisfactorily the specificities of queer studies—a field that by definition ought to focus on the experience of both women and men. In all too many women's studies classes, as Adrienne Rich points out, "the basis for dialogue and discussion remains heterosexual, while perhaps a section of a reading list or a single class period is supposed to 'include' lesbian experience and thought" (200). Women's studies programs, nonetheless, have "often created a safe place for lesbians to come out and familiarize themselves with lesbian culture," as Jeffrey Escoffier notes. However, "in the eighties, as these programs came under attack from conservatives and budget cutbacks, the lesbian content of the courses was downplayed or eliminated" (Escoffier 42). When the UC Berkeley women's studies department refused recently to retain the only faculty member teaching and doing research in the field of lesbian and gay studies, it once again became glaringly apparent that the educational interests of innumerable students and scholars would not be served until an independent lesbian, gay, and bisexual studies program was established.

The first student effort to legitimize lesbian and gay studies at UC Berkeley in fact began in the early 1980s. At the time Berkeley was the leading institution for lesbian and gay studies in this country. By the end of the decade, the fledgling Multicultural Lesbian and Gay Studies Program (MLGS) had ceased operation, and the beleaguered students and scholars involved had disbanded. Over the past five years, Paula Gunn Allen, Tomás Almaguer, David Miller, Valerie Miner, Cherríe Moraga, Kathryn Roe, and Merle Woo have joined the steady exodus of eminent lesbian and gay scholars and writers from UC Berkeley.[3] Ironically, most of the instructors and professors who had contributed to UC Berkeley's international reputation as a leader in the field of lesbian and gay scholarship left the campus to accept positions at universities and colleges more willing to accommodate their teaching and research interests.

The administration's neglect of lesbian and gay studies from the mid-1980s until quite recently has been a great source of contention for many students.[4] In 1989, incensed by the systemic homophobia and heterosexism on campus, the Multicultural Bisexual Lesbian Gay Alliance (MBLGA) joined other student groups in the United Front Strike for gender, racial, ethnic, and sexual diversity. As a result of the strike, one of the United Front's six demands—the appeal for a permanent bisexual/lesbian/gay studies program—received the approval of the provost of the College of Letters and Science, albeit with many strings attached. In the years since the United Front Strike and the provost's provisional commitment, there has been a concerted effort by the Task Force—a group of lesbian, gay, and bisexual students, staff, and alumni—to create a working coalition of interested constituencies, to generate faculty support, and to appoint a director for our center.[5]

Although the onus has been largely on students to make campus culture more responsive to issues of sexual diversity, students do not generally come to university with much prior training in or experience with organizational work. Neither do they arrive on campus with an understanding of the labyrinthine administrative procedures and protocols they must observe to garner institutional attention. Besides attending classes and working part-time, many students are also acknowledging publicly their sexual orientation for the first time and dealing with the familial reprisals that all too frequently accompany the coming out process. Given the intense combination of personal and bureaucratic factors lesbian, gay, and bisexual student organizers have to contend with, it is no wonder that they routinely burn out, drop out, or graduate long before institutional commitments to lesbian, gay, and bisexual programs and services are secured.

The efforts of the student-initiated Task Force that formed to pick up the pieces from the MLGS Program and the United Front Strike would have been immeasurably simpler if our predecessors had left some record of their intellectual mission and of their organizational activities. With very little information about and almost no institutional memory of previous endeavors to develop lesbian, gay, and bisexual studies, the Task Force spent enormous amounts of energy at minimal levels of the bureaucracy unable to shake the smug complacency of administrators well accustomed to the sight of angry, but ineffectual student organizers. To compensate for our lack of experience with program development, members of the Task Force searched for what little printed information was available about the dozen or so institutionally funded lesbian and gay studies programs or clusters already operating across the United States and Canada—at places like CUNY, City College of San Francisco, Yale, MIT, Harvard, Princeton, Cornell, Chicago, Concordia, and Toronto.[6] By connecting the l/g/b studies initiative on our campus to other similar efforts, we hoped to spare ourselves some time-consuming and costly trial and error, as well as to demonstrate to conservative faculty members and administrators the national and international significance of lesbian, gay, and bisexual studies.

I believe that the ultimate success of the Task Force's campaign for university funding for the development of an l/g/b studies program can be replicated at other educational institutions. The level of knowledge and the degree of continuity required to affect permanent institutional changes, however, necessitate that campus activists form groups that cross gender, race, ethnic, and class lines. Doing otherwise is not only morally reprehensible, but completely self-defeating. Simply stated, community action by a monolithic group of people unrepresentative of the "community"—all white, or male, or financially secure—is a form of colonialism. Since institutional practices of exclusion have left innumerable identity groups under- or unrepresented on our campuses, activist groups must not simply reflect the diversity of the immediate campus communities. Campus activists must be diligent in their commitment to inclusivity by also working with members of neighboring communities. The most significant advances can be made in institutionalizing l/g/b studies when, as Nancy Stoller urges, we "celebrate difference and . . . understand that everyone can be a victim or a perpetrator of oppression" (199).

While maximizing an organization's longevity, a multiculturalist approach also often promotes lesbian and gay causes in completely unexpected ways. For example, North Dakota University serves a large Native-American community whose domestic situations do not conform to traditional, narrow definitions of what constitutes a family. When drafting their institution's employee benefits program, North Dakota University administrators agreed to the Native-American community's demands for a broad definition of family that included domestic partners. Consequently, lesbian and gay families now also qualify for coverage under the university's benefits program.[7] At UC Berkeley, the United Front Strike had demonstrated the significant programmatic impact that students could have by participating in broad coalitions with other liberation groups seeking mutually advantageous political goals. As it turned out, most members of the Task Force were also involved simultaneously with several other identity groups (for women, for people of color, for Jews, and so forth). Our recognition of our own multiple subjectivities made us strive continuously to make the Task Force responsive to the concerns of other advocacy groups, while permitting us to learn from activists who had been struggling to legitimize ethnic studies and women's studies well before we began to campaign for a lesbian, gay, and bisexual studies program.

In addition to connecting with other progressive groups, lesbian, gay, and bisexual advocates must also make strong alliances with less migratory and often more bureaucratically savvy members of the campus community, such as staff and alumni. At UC Berkeley, we were very fortunate to have the support of LeGaSee and UCGALA—the gay and lesbian staff and alumni associations, respectively. Not only were the staff and alumni well acquainted with institutional structures and procedures, in many cases they had insiders' information about administrators' soft spots and sore points. Additionally, the alumni had the financial resources to cosponsor events, to provide scholarship support to lesbian, gay, and bisexual students, and to command the attention of high-level university administrators.[8] For instance, after UCGALA raised more than $10,000 for a lesbian, gay, and bisexual student scholarship fund, the chancellor, for the first time in the university's history, agreed to meet with lesbian, gay, and bisexual alumni to discuss their concerns about campus services and programs. Whether or not the lesbian, gay, and bisexual staff and alumni at your school are well organized, the success of your efforts to institutionalize lesbian, gay, and bisexual studies will nonetheless depend largely on the degree to which you are able to involve them in your efforts.

For a multiconstitutive activist group to survive long enough to accomplish its mission, however, it must from the onset develop and codify an equitable system of distributing responsibilities. Many people on the Task Force resented the fact that faculty members, accustomed to having secretarial support and research assistance, tacitly expected staff people and students to perform the more tedious tasks of posting flyers, typing agendas, maintaining mailing lists, and stuffing envelopes. Because even the most unintentional acts of elitism and subtle imbalances of power can spawn a debilitating level of enmity between group members, it is essential that all members of an activist group have an equal opportunity for leadership (to chair meetings, plan strategies, make decisions, conduct negotiations, and so forth) regardless of their race, ethnicity, gender, or institutional position.

Since each constituency brings different, but potentially beneficial, knowledge and experience to an activist group, it is in a group's best interest not to unwittingly replicate the institutional hierarchy when devising its own organizational structure. In the stratified campus setting, tenured faculty members are held in higher esteem and considered to be more knowledgeable than students, lecturers, and staff people. At UC Berkeley, the provost reinforced this by stipulating that institutional funding would only be available if a tenured faculty person directed the l/g/b program and, in consultation with other faculty people, defined its intellectual core. However many of the staff and student members of the Task Force had more experience with and greater insight about l/g/b scholarship, organizing, and political action.[9] Despite how tremendously difficult it is to negotiate the legitimate conflicts of interest that arise when students, staff, alumni, community workers, and faculty people work together, the development of a new, controversial campus unit requires both tenured faculty members' cred-

ibility and professional connections and activists' experience and audacity. Serious attention therefore needs to be given to the potentially
divisive issues of position and privilege, if a multiconstitutive campus
activist group is to accomplish its goals without alienating individual
participants in the process.[10] To improve their group dynamics, board
members of the Toronto Centre for Lesbian and Gay Studies worked
with a professional consultant ("Vision Statement" 2), and board
members of CLAGS had to "go to a retreat facilitated by an outside
person" (Farley 159). It is unlikely that any group will be able to
attract, train, and retain the very people necessary to maintain a viable
lesbian, gay, and bisexual studies program without some kind of similar
forum to study principles of equal opportunity, gender parity, and
multiculturalism.

While group dynamics play a vital role in the survival of any coalition, the actual campaign for the development of a new academic
program consists primarily of raising awareness about the program's
intellectual mission. Student groups have been very successful at publicizing lesbian, gay, and bisexual existence through awareness weeks,
nights out, kiss-ins, and shock posters. The news, entertainment, and
fashion industries routinely publicize our presence as well, though with
little sense of discretion or accountability. To create a receptive campus
environment for lesbian, gay, and bisexual academic programming
and research facilities, however, the enormous amount of creative
work and scholarship being done by writers, scholars, and artists in
diverse disciplines must be publicized widely as well. Three years ago,
the Lesbian, Gay, and Bisexual group in the Graduate Department of
English at Berkeley began several effective visibility projects, emphasizing l/g/b research, writing, and publishing. We hosted a weekly, interdisciplinary colloquium for students and scholars to share their research, and we started a study group for people interested in lesbian
and gay theory. We routinely sent letters to the chair, asking for the
department to hire someone in the field, to offer lesbian and gay
literature and theory courses, and to invite such scholars as Eve Kosofsky Sedgwick, Alan Sinfield, Judith Butler, and Terry Castle to give
lectures. Recently, the Berkeley Bisexual, Lesbian, and Gay Center put
together a "pink course catalogue" listing all the courses being offered
throughout the university that treat some aspect of lesbian and gay
life.

In a similar effort to increase l/g/b visibility, I began publishing a
newsletter, *The Pink Agenda*, two years ago. The shocking pink, dou-
ble-sided page publicizes calls for papers, lecture announcements, fel-

lowship opportunities, and recent publications, and includes a calendar of events and a list of local groups and resources. Copies of the newsletter were distributed not only to people who asked to be on the mailing list, but also to hundreds of professors across the campus regardless of their sexual orientation or area of academic specialization. For an entire year, l/g/b student activists endeavored to line mailboxes at least once a week with our queer direct mail. Since newsletters are relatively simple and inexpensive to produce, they are ideal for generating widespread interest in lesbian, gay, and bisexual studies. Our aggressive visibility campaign and academic organizing ultimately inspired faculty from a variety of disciplines to write letters of support to the provost and prompted the English department to advertise its first tenure-track position in lesbian and gay studies in fall 1992.

Since the wheels of change turn so slowly in higher education, it is absolutely imperative that lesbian, gay, and bisexual campus activists create a formidable paper trail to guide their successors and to inspire l/g/b activism on other campuses. Information about the work being done on any campus can be disseminated readily through the increasing number of lesbian, gay, and bisexual newspapers, newsletters, electronic bulletin boards, journals, and conferences.[11] Without some kind of institutional record or printed documentation, the stability and survival of a program will be threatened severely each time members of the coordinating group move on.

Although this discussion focuses primarily on strategies for academic program development, a lesbian, gay, and bisexual studies program will not satisfy all our institutional needs. While seeking academic legitimation, lesbian, gay, and bisexual campus activists must also endeavor to secure benefits for domestic partners, to improve AIDS and HIV information and outreach, and to eliminate discriminatory ROTC programs. At UC Berkeley, we continue to seek the appointment of a lesbian/gay/bisexual administrator for advocacy and bias intervention. Without a compliance officer of some sort, we feel that the systemwide statement of nondiscrimination, including sexual orientation, provides little real protection to members of our campus community who are verbally harassed or physically assaulted, or who are denied housing or tenure. As lesbian, gay, and bisexual students, scholars, staff people, and alumni, it is imperative that we create a vision of institutional inclusion that addresses our full range of social and legislative needs, not simply our academic predilections.

The first generation of students born since the liberation movements of the mid-1960s and since Stonewall are now attending college. In-

creasingly these students—heterosexual, homosexual, and bisexual—
are challenging the conservatism of the institutions they attend. Academic administrators and educators, fearful of ceding academic legitimacy to "special-interest" groups, must begin to reckon with the fact
that lesbian, gay, and bisexual history and culture are not only relevant
to the estimated 10 percent of the population who are same-sex identified, but also to the siblings, relatives, friends, neighbors, coworkers,
and children of lesbians, gays, and bisexuals.[12] At this unique historic
moment, we must take advantage of the heightened social interest in
lesbian, gay, and bisexual rights to make our university and college
campuses more responsive to all of our educational needs and interests.

Notes

1. William Norris documents the paradoxical coexistence of "extensive attitudinal
   support and widespread victimization" of lesbians, gay men, and bisexuals even at
   well-known, seemingly progressive liberal arts colleges (81).

2. Although the efforts of lesbian, gay, and bisexual student activists are rarely re-
   warded or even recognized by faculty members and administrators, Roland Hunt
   acknowledges the instrumental role that students have had in the development of
   lesbian and gay studies: "Ten years passed before the idea of creating a course on
   the politics of the gay and lesbian rights movement dawned on me as a possibility.
   It was not until I was approached by a group of students active in the Gay and
   Lesbian Association in Athens, Ohio, that I began to consider teaching a class on
   the subject. They proposed a readings course on the subject of homosexuality and
   politics, and it was this readings course that first exposed me to the burgeoning
   literature on sexual orientation and to the politics of the gay and lesbian rights
   movement" (220).

3. The deaths of Dr. James Brown, the director of the Student Health Service, Professor
   John Walsh, a specialist on homosexuality in contemporary Spanish literature, and
   Professor Len Marasciulo, a member of the Multicultural Lesbian and Gay Studies
   Program (MLGS) board in the early 1980s, as well as the early retirements of
   Professor Simon Karlinsky, a noted gay studies scholar in the Department of Slavic
   Language and Literature, and Professor Warren Winkelstein, Jr., a specialist in the
   epidemiology of AIDS, contributed to the rapidly diminishing lesbian and gay
   presence at UC Berkeley during the 1980s (Task Force 3–4).

4. I am grateful to Colette Patt both for giving me a firsthand account of campus
   affairs during the 1980s and for providing me with a copy of her unpublished essay.

5. Professor Carolyn Dinshaw was named the director of the Berkeley Bisexual, Lesbian, and Gay Center late last spring, and she is now working with the Academic
   Planning Subcommittee to develop an undergraduate minor and major in l/g/b
   studies under the aegis of Undergraduate Interdisciplinary Studies.

6. For discussions of l/g/b affairs at other colleges and universities, including Rutgers,
   the City University of New York, and the University of California at Santa Cruz,
   see Bolonik; Farley; and Stoller. Lesbian, gay, and bisexual educational issues and

    social needs are also addressed by Gammon; Segrest; and Tierney. For an extensive treatment of campus leadership issues pertaining to women, but also, for the most part, applicable to queer students, see Sagaria; and Wine.

7.   Maria Gil de Lamadrid discussed the example of North Dakota University in her lecture on lesbian and gay organizing.

8.   UCGALA established a permanent, named endowment, the UC Gay and Lesbian Alumni Association Scholarship, with the California Alumni Association (CAA) in 1991. In addition to providing scholarship support to lesbian, gay, and bisexual students, UCGALA also sponsors the annual Martin F. Stow Leadership Awards and has established the Gay/Lesbian/Bisexual Mentorship Program. The potential economic incentive alumni can provide for the establishment of l/g/b programs is also exemplified by Michael Dively, a gay alumnus of Williams College, who donated $75,000 to his alma mater. The Michael Dively '61 Lecture Fund for Human Sexuality and Diversity "supports performances and lectures focusing on gay and lesbian topics" ("Give and Take" A29). A $250,000 gift to the University of Southern California Law Center, in the memory of Alan Holoch, a USC Law Center graduate and former faculty member, on the other hand, "will fund scholarships to support lesbian/gay/bisexual law students and students who plan to use their legal skills to support equal rights for queers" (Mecca 17).

9.   It was also the case at UC Berkeley that the students and staff people, many of whom had experience working in ACT UP, GLAAD, and Queer Nation, envisioned an l/g/b center that included both academic and social services. Faculty members, however, tended to emphasize the research and teaching components at the expense of the social service dimension of the center. To date, the Berkeley Bisexual, Lesbian, and Gay Center has only secured funding to develop the academic branch.

10.   From her years of experience as a community activist and an observer of the development of women's studies, Dorothy Allison has noticed that it is an unfortunate fact of academic program development that "the alienated activists who do all the groundwork are driven out by the most conservative few who end up in control of the new programs and departments." The power imbalances between the various groups with a stake in the development of l/g/b studies, moreover, are reinforced because faculty people gain institutional and professional recognition by developing new academic programs, whereas students, staff, alumni, and community people rarely receive any appreciable rewards or career benefits for their campus service. According to Allison, the fact that "academics are in a position now to get hired to teach gay/lesbian/bisexual studies without having done their dissertations in the field" has only exacerbated the rifts between segments of the lesbian, gay, and bisexual community inside and outside of the academy.

11.   There are several national conferences, including the annual National Lesbian Conference, the annual Graduate Student Conference on Lesbian and Gay Studies, and the roughly annual North American Conference on Lesbian, Gay, and Bisexual Studies. There are also many more discipline-specific colloquia and conferences organized throughout the year. Information about a variety of l/g/b newsletters, calendar notes, publications, and events appears in the *Lesbian and Gay Studies Newsletter*, published by the Gay and Lesbian Caucus for the Modern Languages. Editorial correspondence should be directed to Margaret Morrison, Editor, *LGSN*, Department of English, P.O. Box 3721, North Carolina Wesleyan College, Rocky

Mount, NC 27804; subscription inquiries should be directed to Shelton Waldrep, *LGSN* Managing Editor, *LGSN*, Box 90021, Duke University, Durham, NC 27708-0021. The Electronic Directory of Lesbigay Scholars is another source of information. For details, contact Professor Louie Crew, Academic Foundations Department, Rutgers University, University Heights, 175 University Avenue, Newark, NJ 07102, or send E-mail to lcrew@andromeda.rutgers.edu.

12.   As Eve Kosofsky Sedgwick reminds us, "for the last century or so, many of the institutions of culture—law, medicine, psychiatry, aesthetics—have been erected around maintaining and consolidating the separation between the 10 per cent and the 90 per cent. That's been a constant and increasing preoccupation" (qtd. in Heller A6).

Works Cited

Allison, Dorothy. Address. Working Out: A Lesbian/Gay/Bisexual Studies Curriculum Colloquium. Berkeley Bisexual, Lesbian, and Gay Studies Center. Berkeley, 1 Oct 1992.

Bolonik, Kera. "Rutgers." *Deneuve* 2:3(1992): 50–52.

Escoffier, Jeffrey. "Inside the Ivory Closet: The Challenges Facing Lesbian and Gay Studies." *Out/Look* 10 (Fall 1990): 40–48.

Farley, Tucker Pamella. "A Center for Lesbian and Gay Studies at the City University of New York." *NWSA Journal* 1:1 (1988): 157–60.

Gammon, Carolyn et al. "Organizing Lesbian Studies at Concordia." *Lesbians in Canada*. Ed. Sharon Dale Stone. Toronto: Between the Lines, 1990. 209–20.

"Give and Take." *Chronicle of Higher Education*, 3 Feb. 1993: A29.

Heller, Scott. "Influential yet Controversial among Literary Scholars, Duke U. Professor Uses Sexuality in Analyzing Culture." *Chronicle of Higher Education*, 24 Oct. 1990: A6+.

Hunt, Roland J. "Gay and Lesbian Politics." *PS: Political Science & Politics* 25:2 (1992): 220–24.

Lamadrid, Maria Gil de. Lecture. Alternative Lifestyles? Alternative to What? "Family Values" and Lesbian and Gay Legal Issues. Boalt Hall Civil Rights Speakers Series. Berkeley, 15 Oct. 1992.

Lorde, Audre. "The Master's Tools Will Never Dismantle the Master's House." *Sister Outsider: Essays and Speeches*. Freedom, CA: Crossing Press, 1984. 110–13.

Mecca, Tommi Avicolli. "News Briefs." *San Francisco Bay Times*, 6 May 1993: 17.

Norris, William P. "Liberal Attitudes and Homophobic Acts: The Paradoxes of Homosexual Experience in a Liberal Institution." *Coming Out of the Classroom Closet: Gay and Lesbian Students, Teachers, and Curricula*. Ed. Karen M. Harbeck. New York: Haworth Press, 1992. 81–120.

Patt, Colette. "Ideas for the Development of the Multicultural Bisexual, Lesbian, and Gay Studies Program at UC Berkeley." Unpublished essay, 1990.

Rich, Adrienne. "Invisibility in Academe" (1984). *Blood, Bread, and Poetry: Selected Prose, 1979–1985*. New York: Norton, 1986. 198–201.

Sagaria, Mary Ann Danowitz, ed. *Empowering Women: Leadership Development Strategies on Campus.* San Francisco: Jossey-Bass, 1988.

Segrest, Mab. "Homophobia and the University Community." *IRIS: A Journal about Women* 21 (Spring/Summer 1989): 60–62.

Stoller, Nancy. "Creating a Non-Homophobic Atmosphere on a College Campus." *Empathy* 3 (1992); reprinted in *Tilting the Tower,* 198–207.

Task Force for an MBLGS Center at UC Berkeley. "Preliminary Proposal for the Establishment of a Multicultural, Bisexual, Lesbian, and Gay Studies Center at Berkeley." Unpublished report submitted to Carol Christ, provost and dean of the College of Letters and Science, 1992.

Tierney, William G. "Building Academic Communities of Difference: Gays, Lesbians, and Bisexuals on Campus." *Change* 24:2 (March/April 1992): 41–46.

"Vision Statement." *CENTRE/FOLD: The Newsletter of the Toronto Centre for Lesbian and Gay Studies* 2 (1992).

Wine, Jeri Dawn. "Outsiders on the Inside: Lesbians in Canadian Academe." *Lesbians in Canada.* Ed. Sharon Dale Stone. Toronto: Between the Lines, 1990. 157–70.

22

Creating a Nonhomophobic Atmosphere on a College Campus

Nancy Stoller

In 1990, *Out/Look* magazine published a survey article on gay and lesbian studies which implied that there is little contact between the old and the new gay scholars, that abstract theory has triumphed in the university, and that the new intellectuals of gay life are as cut off from gay community issues as the intellectuals of the left are from labor activists. This is far from the truth, at least in the university where I work.[1] While these divisions do exist, they are more appropriately seen as part of an abstract typology than as a photograph of the diverse population of people who call themselves both gay and scholarly.

At the University of California at Santa Cruz, these presumably separate spheres (activism and intellectualizing; literary analysis and social science documentation; research and teaching; white male scholarship networks and multiracial feminist analysis; teachers and students) exist together, sometimes within the same person. Perhaps this is because our campus is unusually diverse in the forms through which openly gay, lesbian, or bisexual sensibility, scholarship, and activism are expressed. But we think it is more because our condition as gays, lesbians, and bisexuals—simultaneously oppressed and politically emergent—demands and encourages this mix. It is also because we have created some structures which support diversity and connectedness.

At Santa Cruz, in addition to a wide range of courses in the social sciences and humanities and a university-funded faculty research group focused on our issues, we also have a residential college (one of eight) whose new academic and cultural theme is the exploration of the cultural intersections of sexuality, race, class, and gender. As of 1991, of the twenty-eight permanent faculty located at Kresge College, thirteen were either gay or doing research about some aspect of homosexuality. A new curriculum and extracurricular programs support the college theme, which includes explicit recognition of gay sexuality along with that of others. The college theme acknowledges diversity within the lesbian and gay community in terms of race, gender, and class simultaneously.

To our knowledge, our gay studies office cluster at the college is the first in the UC system and perhaps a first elsewhere as well. While the cluster is not a full-fledged department with a major, the faculty collectively offer a variety of undergraduate and graduate courses. For faculty and students across the campus, it also provides an institutional locus for events, collaborative research, and supportive contact. Gay, lesbian, and bisexual students at Santa Cruz are also open and active both on campus and off. On campus, they insist on relevant courses, support faculty who are out, and, by creating a positive institutional atmosphere for themselves, have produced an environment that makes survival possible and enjoyable even for the most out faculty. This all works in a mutually reinforcing way: faculty and students support each other, so do the intellectuals and the activists, and the university and the community. As a result, we seem to survive and appreciate each other.

But how did it develop and how does it work? We used strategies that build on coalitions and alliances. My use of terms is drawn from concepts developed by Papusa Molina.[2] A *coalition* is an organization where compromises are made between *groups* for a political goal that is mutually advantageous. *Alliances* are connections based on individual love, commitment, and responsibility, incorporating a *shared vision* of a better society. Effective alliances celebrate difference and help us understand that everyone can be a victim or a perpetrator of oppression. Sometimes we need coalitions, but what we want is coalitions based on alliances—they are much stronger and infinitely more satisfying. At Santa Cruz, gay politics, especially as practiced by students, has increasingly focused on building alliances. These alliances inevitably do and must cross gender, race, ethnic, and class lines. They take work and they are worthwhile. Alliance strategies are based on the notion that one can acknowledge and celebrate one's own socially constructed identity as well as other individual and group constructions. The idea is that we use our different strengths to defend, support, and encourage each other.

In an academic institution people can build alliances and coalitions by using the institution's three major structural components: students, faculty, and staff. Our analysis includes the top administrators in the staff because their power is also limited—by presidents, chancellors, and boards of trustees. An awareness of administrators' constraints is a key to preventing self-intimidation. The belief that administrators can retain and increase their power even if they don't satisfy students, faculty, and lower-level staff leads to self-censorship and inaction. At Santa Cruz, when we have refused to be intimidated or fatalistic, we generally have been successful in achieving our goals by developing alliances among students, faculty, and staff.

Each of these groups has its own needs and strengths. Students' needs include visibility, relevant courses and cultural support, physical and social safety, improved campus atmosphere, and faculty support in their fight against internalized oppression and homophobia. Their strengths are first of all in their numbers as students and as members of the high proportion of US citizens, especially young ones, who see their sexuality as different from the prescriptive norm; additionally, their strength is in the fact that they are in an independent phase in their life cycle and in their courage, principles, and imagination. Faculty need an intellectually supportive atmosphere, employment security (especially regarding tenure), and domestic partner recognition and benefits. Their strengths are the authority and respect they command within the institution; job security (for those who are tenured); the institution's basic dependence on them as teachers; their research skills, which can be applied to specific challenges associated with homophobia; and their national connections with other scholars. Staff needs include employment security, domestic partner benefits, and, as with students, visibility and recognition. Gay staff tend to be invisible to both faculty and students. Factors such as a lack of staff organization, general staff invisibility, and more overt homophobia contribute to this situation. On the other hand, staff know the institution and how to work it to the benefit of lesbian and gay members; moreover, no university can function without its staff.

The Santa Cruz strategy, developed and pursued between 1986 and 1991, involved cooperative work between staff, faculty, and students, drawing on their respective strengths and resources. What follows, an overview of campus changes, demonstrates the cooperative strategy.

Background. The University of California at Santa Cruz, founded in 1964, is a cluster of decentralized, small residential colleges in the tradition of Oxford or Yale. Currently the colleges' primary activities are in the areas of residential life, student events, and academic advising and counseling. The colleges also sponsor a few basic courses required of all new students.

Always liberal, the campus has been home to feminist, leftist, and critical scholarship as well as nontraditional teaching techniques. A strong women's studies program, as well as one or two other graduate and undergraduate programs, has provided a sympathetic home to lesbian and gay-male scholarship for the past ten years. Additionally, a well-publicized and successful tenure case involving this author further encouraged more faculty to come out and legitimized the gay and lesbian presence on campus. The combined effect of these factors has been to make Santa Cruz a campus that is hospitable to institutional change in the direction of the greater "normalization" and acceptance of lesbian and gay existence.

The first two years. In 1986, following several homophobic incidents, students demanded an investigation of conditions for gay, lesbian, and bisexual students on campus. During 1987–88, a Task Force appointed by the vice chancellor for Student Services, chaired by a heterosexual woman and including both gay and straight members, conducted an investigation. Its research included well-attended public forums to hear from gay, lesbian, and bisexual students. The primary focus of the investigation and the Task Force report was on student life. In spring 1988, the Task Force report recommended changes in campus life and a permanent committee of faculty/staff/students. In fall 1988, the chancellor established a permanent committee, with financial and staff support from the Student Services Division, to implement the Task Force findings.

The third year. The Gay, Lesbian, Bisexual Community Concerns Committee (GLBCCC) included eight students, four faculty, and three staff, with ethnic and gender diversity. Committee cochairs were a lesbian associate professor and a gay male undergraduate. The committee met eleven times during the year. On the strength of the stories told by gay, lesbian, and bisexual students to the Task Force, the new committee received funding and technical support to conduct a systematic survey of the student population. It administered two surveys. One used a large random sample of the total student population, heterosexual and gay, lesbian, or bisexual (g/l/b), to document heterosexual students' attitudes about g/l/b issues and to get better estimates of the numbers of students who are g/l/b. A smaller survey, distributed through g/l/b student organizations, allowed the committee to get in-depth information about the experiences of g/l/b students on campus.

Introduced by a cover letter from the student body president and other campus figures, both surveys yielded decent response rates and produced valuable information:[3]

- UCSC students identified themselves as 9 percent gay, 8 percent lesbian, and 6 percent bisexual. The committee was able to point out to the university that probably about 1500 of its students were g/l/b. (Visualize 1500 gay students marching on the chancellor's office!);
- Only 40 percent of the students were aware that UCSC has an antidiscrimination policy for sexual orientation;
- When discussing their classroom experience, many students said that professors and teaching assistants made homophobic and heterosexist remarks and frequently ignored issues concerning sexuality that were appropriate to include;
- In terms of campus housing, g/l/b students reported incidents ranging from discomfort to outright harassment, pointing to a clear need for education of housing staff and reexamination of housing policies;
- Students reported difficulty finding appropriate psychological counseling on campus (at that time no counselors identified themselves as g/l/b). Armed with these data, the committee convinced counseling services to offer groups specifically aimed at g/l/b and "questioning" students;
- Gay, lesbian, and bisexual students felt a strong need for a place to talk and feel comfortable with other g/l/b students. Shortly after these data were publicized, one of the colleges volunteered space for a G/L/B Resource Center;
- Homophobic feelings were most intense among our newest students, and were least prevalent in students who had attended educational sessions about g/l/b issues and who knew out g/l/b students. The survey identified a core of "severely homophobic" students, about 6 percent, who seemed immune to education efforts;
- Perhaps the greatest surprise of the survey was discovering how loosely students' sexual identities were connected to their actual sexual experiences. A small but significant number of students who said they were heterosexual had had sex with a person of the same gender—10–15 percent at least once and 4 percent within

the last year. Four out of ten students who identified themselves as lesbian had had sex with a man within the last year, and two-thirds of gay male students reported having sex with a woman within the last year. Yet, these students did not identify themselves as bisexual. About 30 percent of both gay- and lesbian-identified students had never had sex with a same-sex partner.

The committee also sponsored several workshops. For example, a gay psychologist from the local community conducted homophobia workshops for each college for resident assistants and other housing staff. Also, an all-day training session was held for sexual harassment advisers, complaint resolution officers, Sexual Harassment Education Committee members, counselors from Counseling and Psychological Services, and members of the GLBCCC. Presentations included videos, a segment on sexual assault of lesbians by the Rape Prevention Education Coordinator, and a presentation on sexual harassment by a lesbian officer from the University Police Department.

Three staff members (not on the committee) and the faculty committee chair developed a draft policy and procedures on sexual orientation harassment/discrimination in November 1988. It was distributed to the committee for comment and to General Counsel for review and was approved in final form by the chancellor in April. The committee began work on development of a domestic partnership policy to assure equal access to family student housing on campus. During the next three years, the committee and individuals on it continued to pursue these rights. The committee also began work to amend the definition of "family" in the staff personnel policy on sick leave, since the present definition excluded gay partners. By 1990, it was clear that supervisors had the option of granting sick leave for family matters to lesbian and gay staff. A brochure, based on a Rutgers model, "Straight Talk about Homosexuality," was drafted, to provide information on homosexuality, g/l/b groups, and the recently approved Sexual Orientation Harassment/Discrimination Procedures. The brochure was distributed in fall 1989. Faculty members on the committee took the lead in supporting the long-range goal of establishing gay/lesbian studies on campus. Vito Russo, a well-known film critic, author, and activist, taught two classes during the academic year.

Armed with data from the survey showing that gay, lesbian, and bisexual students had trouble finding appropriate counseling, the committee expressed a strong desire for a gay counselor to be hired or designated and requested expanded counseling groups for g/l/b people.

As a result of the meeting, Counseling Services offered to develop a homophobia component for fall orientation of college personnel, to be presented by staff counselors. Additional counselor training included an all-day workshop by an outside consultant on effective therapy with g/l/b people, sponsored by Counseling and Psychological Services, and a Coalition for Learning about and Undermining Homophobia (CLUH) workshop presented to the counselors by two students.

The fourth year. In 1989–90, organizing and innovation continued on campus. Student organizations and faculty were especially active throughout the year. In the fall, we completed our brochure and distributed it to all students on campus. This process was heavily supported by student services staff. A new organization of Lesbians, Bisexuals, and Gays of Color (LBGOC) was founded. A Lesbian and Gay Faculty Research Group applied for and received social sciences and humanities division funding, similar to that accorded other faculty research clusters. During winter quarter, faculty held a "Queer Theory" conference with out-of-town speakers, graduate and undergraduate involvement, and community activist audience critique.

Several courses on gay themes were offered, including The Celluloid Closet, Sexual Politics, Documenting Gay Activism, Male Homoerotic Desire, and Gay and Lesbian Studies. Students in one course organized a rally to protest homophobic graffiti. They worked with ethnic and general student organizations to develop a broad agenda. The rally turned into a sit-in about ethnic studies and resulted in a new (ad hoc) student organization, Coalition for Democratic Education (CODE), which was explicitly multiracial, multisexual, and mutually supportive concerning racism and homophobia. The organization, built on principles of both coalition and alliance, established a "homophobia hotline" for reporting incidents of graffiti and harassment. It also forced top administrators to agree to attend CLUH workshops during the next year and argued publicly for more classes on lesbian and gay themes, along with courses about ethnic and religious (especially Jewish) issues.

The fifth year. In 1990–91, more changes occurred at UCSC. The GLBCCC had a quieter year, but the rest of the campus saw greater institutionalization of trends begun during the previous two years of organizing. In the faculty area, three major developments occurred. The Research Group continued with a new year of financing. In addition to its study group activities it also sponsored a conference, "Querying/Queering the Academy," about gay life within universities. Secondly, one of the colleges was academically reorganized to support the theme of "cultural intersections," focused on the study of the forms of cultural contact in contemporary society, with explicit attention to race, gender, class, and sexuality. Part of the reorganization included the development of a lesbian and gay faculty cluster of offices at the college. A lesbian was appointed acting provost of the college and a variety of programming for staff, faculty, and students initiated. A peer adviser (a gay Latino student) was appointed; additionally, by the end of the year, several staff and residential preceptors who were gay or lesbian were working or living at the college.

Finally, with the support of two faculty senate committees, the Academic Senate (the faculty's governing body) unanimously supported a domestic partners resolution urging full partner coverage for g/l/b faculty, staff, and students for all benefits currently available to married couples. Research for this resolution uncovered a much wider range of benefits and more material discrimination than most people had realized. For example, there were significant differences in retirement and death benefits because an employee could not designate a partner as a "survivor" unless they were married. Implementation of the resolution will require a UC system-wide strategy, which some people began to plan simultaneously with the passage of the resolution.

In fall 1990, UCSC students and staff established the first gay and lesbian theme housing at one of the colleges. This unit, a series of apartments, is intentionally for both straight and gay students. In spring 1991, the housing unit was permanently dedicated to the late gay professor and activist Vito Russo. UCSC students continued to take major leadership roles in state and national organizations associated with lesbian and gay issues. On campus, they continued to fight for more courses and more Third World perspectives in those courses. G/L/B staff focused their attention in 1990–91 on visibility, networking, and benefits by holding several social events, providing communication linkages, and supporting domestic partners policy through research, publicity, and organizing within the administrative segment of the institution. In addition, the affirmative action office conducted three staff workshops on sexual orientation. Meanwhile, new lesbian and gay faculty have been hired and many are teaching with explicit attention to sexual diversity; and the campus continues to normalize its treatment of lesbians, gays, and bisexuals by dealing with homophobia in the same way that racism or sexism are handled and by treating sexual cultures as analogous to ethnic cultures.

The limitations of progress.   What have we accomplished? For students, we've created more safety, more visibility, more courses, more social support. But there is still no institutional recognition of their personal lives (family housing, other benefits). For faculty, we've created an intellectually supportive atmosphere with some research and teaching legitimation. We have not been able to provide enough muscle at the top to overcome systems of racism, sexism, and homophobia. And there is still no institutional recognition of faculty members' personal lives. For staff, more visibility and a little more employment security have been provided. But again, there is no official recognition of staff members' personal lives. Currently, most major universities and colleges forbid discrimination based on sexual orientation. However, few in academia work for or attend a college that gives the same benefits and acknowledgment to its gay members as it does to its straight members. *We have the policy but not the practice.*

In addition to the limited successes with this basic issue (recognition that gay relationships are real), many campuses, including UCSC, are experiencing attacks on their existing gay and lesbian programs. In 1990–91, UC reaffirmed its exclusion of gay families from family housing; numerous verbal attacks occurred on gay courses, faculty, students, housing, and Kresge College. The motivating forces behind these attacks are homophobia and a right-wing agenda. Homophobic forces view our institutional changes as part of broad social changes associated with economic restructuring and the emergence of new vocal groupings based on identity, ethnicity, class, and sexuality. Viewed positively, the increase in resistance can be seen as a reflection of just how successful we have been in creating real change.

Five years after the first task force at UCSC, we have a well-established community of students, staff, and faculty with a tradition, no matter how young, of working together successfully. A number of changes we initiated have now become institutionalized—places for students to meet and live, processes for educating new students and staff, courses and research clusters on issues of sexuality. Making these changes a continuing part of daily life has freed up our energy to concentrate on the issues we still have to win. We think that we were able to accomplish all of this because we didn't settle for *coalition* but insisted on *alliance*. Perhaps there are forces in the university that tend to separate intellectuals from community life, but our experience is that it doesn't have to be that way.

Notes

Reprinted by permission of *Empathy*© GLARP, 1992. The author gratefully acknowledges the editorial assistance of Valerie Simmons and Zoe Sodja.

1. Jeffrey Escoffier, "Inside the Ivory Closet: The Challenges Facing Lesbian and Gay Studies," *Out/Look* 10 (Fall 1990): 40–48.

2. Papusa Molina, "Recognizing, Accepting, and Celebrating Our Differences," in *Making Face, Making Soul/Haciendo Caras, Creative and Critical Perspectives by Women of Color*, ed. Gloria Anzaldúa (San Francisco: Aunt Lute, 1990), 326–31.

3. Copies of the survey and results are available from the Office of Analysis, UC Santa Cruz, Santa Cruz, CA 95064.

23

Tau(gh)t Connections:
Experiences of a "Mixed-Blood, Disabled, Lesbian Student"

Anneliese Truame

> Do we, in fact, have the guts to say: "You may not like it, but here I am."
>
> —Susan Krieger

> Once I realized it was going to be a fight, I decided to make it a beautiful fight.
>
> —Townsend Carr[1]

At the risk of being charged with false advertising, I'd like to admit right up front that the title of this essay is a misnomer; I misname myself as a mixed-blood, disabled, lesbian student. It is true that I am of Anglo/Native-American/Mexican heritage. I do have a chronic muscle condition that causes me pain, fatigue, and limited mobility. I do have sexual, intimate relationships with women, and only women. I am, in fact, a middle-class graduate student in English Literature. But when I identify myself in these ways, I feel as if I had taken truth serum in my morning tea, and I am forced to add: These identifications are contingent, partial, appalling. It would be more accurate simply to say that I am a lot of trouble. However, if I had subtitled the piece, "Experiences of Trouble," instead of using the effective but limiting shorthand of those clumsy adjectives, I would be choosing accuracy over intelligibility. In the context of this essay it is more valuable to me to concede that point and highlight the process, my struggle to be true to my desires within the social texts of academia.

My desires are to represent the specifics of my experiences and insights in all their ambiguities and to respond actively to coercive efforts to modify or codify my representations. The difficulty of embodying my desires in this paper began with the title, with confronting the problems that particular categories are more easily recognizable than others, that particular points of view are associated with particular subject positions, that expectations are sutured to these associations. I am sensitive to these issues in part because I wear my ethnicity, my sexual orientation, and my physical limitations as primarily unmarked categories. Which is to say that most people looking at me would not instantaneously describe me as a mixed-blood, disabled lesbian. Thus, it is not surprising that I see verbalizing my identities as a way to make aspects of my experience visible at particular moments. I experience myself as shifting surfaces, rising out of the water in different forms, draped in different kinds of debris, depending on the current and location. I suspect that my experience is different in degree, not kind, from other people's experiences.

I see these moments of surfacing and creating visibility as useful in a continuing series of acts of struggle, not as end points in themselves or static representations that I must embody. This is an important distinction for me to make because my ambivalence about identifying as a "mixed-blood, disabled lesbian" stems from pressure to do so. I am wary of what happens once I am identified with a particular subject position, such as a lesbian one. A lesbian identification can take on meaning for others that does not reflect my experience; it can become ascendant in the representation which people recognize as me in ways that elide not just other parts of me, such as my ethnic background, but fundamentally who I am as a composite of changing interests. For me, it is not my particular subject position at any given moment that is most crucial. I am more concerned with my positioning, with the negotiated process of representing myself, for example, as a lesbian in a classroom.

If my representation of myself is figured by others, not as a ground for movement, but as a place I am expected to consistently occupy, and occupy in a particular way, it is easy for me to become frozen by the look that sees me in stasis. I am thinking here of the fixing nature of the gaze evident in the way that some of my heterosexual peers turn to look at me whenever they raise queer issues in class. That turning of the head is not an act of true recognition. On the contrary, it tends to mark the partial nature of someone's recognition of me. I am asked to validate this partial acknowledgment by filling in the established and circumscribed place for my participation as a lesbian by talking on cue. This act of recognition is partial because it suggests that I will no longer be recognizable if I move out of the specific lesbian space with which I have been identified. This interaction also warns me that if I contest the construction of the space that has been designated as lesbian, and if I point out that it has been established by the unmarked power of the individual heterosexual student backed by a heterosexist institution and not formed according to my queer interests, then I risk losing the space. By risking this verbal space, I jeopardize the possibilities of discussion and of relating myself intelligibly to other people within the academic community.

I am not saying that those risks should not be run. I am recognizing where the power lies, and the ways in which it is deployed to induce particular modes of interaction. The coercive nature of this dynamic is exemplified by the specter of scholars who are said to be so unassimilable into the available categories and to have developed their work so much according to their own desires, that they/their work became almost unspeakable, almost unfundable. It is their purported failure to assimilate that is frequently pointed out, not the academic community's practices of nonaccommodation. I am concerned with what there is in each of us that is not representable, with creating a space for what is currently unintelligible. I believe the untranslatable is always rearing its head from the water. Aiding its surfacing is a matter of recognizing that I am seeing only a portion of what is present, of not erasing what I do not yet recognize, of exercising my near vision and far sight until I can glimpse a shadowy shape.

Lack of recognition of ambiguity is a prominent feature of the coercive, petrifying nature of categories. It is this characteristic, combined with the lack of control the identified has once the identity is in circulation, that not only keeps people participating in the categories of the academic community, but participating in specific ways, which may involve nonparticipation. For example, the desire to resist the negative effects of stigmatized categorization leads some women who are concerned about gender issues to insist on their nonidentification with feminists. I too am wary of the lack of recognition, or misrecognition that can follow identification of the self, the gap between what I make visible and what is seen. Categorizations as forms of visibility become clearly unsatisfactory to me when it comes down to the issue of filling that space with a body, how it feels when it is my body that fills that space.

I feel torn when the need is raised for a disabled voice, or a lesbian voice, or the voice of someone of color, and here I am, all three. What a bargain. So my response has to be to give people more than they reckoned on. This is partially due to the fact that recognizing aspects of who I am is not merely an additive process; my identities are exponentially interactive properties. In other words, it is not just a matter of taking into account my mixed-blood background in addition to my sexual orientation. Mapping who I am requires acknowledging multiple, interrelated axes that create a field of simultaneous activity, rather than isolated, parallel binaries that the eye can only focus on one at a time, like channels on the television. Instead of being placed on this side or that side of the gay/straight line, I am placed temporarily at the nexus of multiple lines, divergent trajectories. What it comes down to for me is that I am not willing to give up the visibility that categories afford, but I want to work them, question their relationships to each other, figure out what is being blocked out and reclaim it, figure out what is being valorized and level it. I am trying to learn how to flirt with these words, how to have long-term affairs with them, but never move into any or all of their houses.

It is due to my desire to represent myself specifically and comprehensively that my relationship to the academic community and its discourses is one of continuous struggle. A friend of mine once said, when I mentioned that in one of my classes I was dealing with racist and heterosexist tensions, as well as insensitivity toward people with disabilities: "You need to choose your battles." At first I thought this was a great concept; then I realized that choosing among them still means I am fighting all the time. My visualization of my academic participation in these terms is partly due to my heritage. On one side of my family tree, I have the Pima, a warlike tribe that has a documented history of insurrection against European invaders dating back to 1633. On the other side, I am related to General Tecumseh Sherman, the man who ransacked the South and who coined the phrase "War is hell." My people have never known peace. I am no exception. The particular form of my participation in this centuries-old battle is merely dictated by its present incarnation as a war of words and representations. I arm myself with academic vocabulary and my stubborn counterimages. I am a double agent with the urgent desire to teach the spiritual mechanics of individual survival. Pursuing my graduate degree is my means to that end, my cover.

The war is going to go on for some time. I need to discover how best to outfit myself for the long haul; I have tried futilely to fit in for too long. I need to ask specific questions about the war: How can I short-circuit my internalized fear, which keeps me from speaking my truths, the way I see written texts and lived texts? How much of my desire can I get out of my mouth and put on the map? How long can I hold out under siege? How many partners in crime can I find? The final question, of the size of the army I am fighting with, is the most important one to me. It is the people who remind me to keep reloading my bow, who encourage me to aim for the most difficult targets, who insist I strike with resolution, that make my fight possible.

I'm looking, not specifically for people who are queer in their sexual orientation, or who identify with other oppressed communities, but for people who are queer in the head, who have queer minds. By "queer-minded," I mean people who are unconventional in their suspicion of the coercive nature of the academic institution, who think what's just not thought and try to do what's just not done. I use the term advisedly. I do not wish to create a dualism between the sexually queer and the mentally queer. They may be the same people. I would go so far as to say that many times they are. Whatever the origin of their insights and whichever itinerary led them to meet me here on this battlefield, I am looking for them, the queer-minded veterans who still grace the war zone with their passion and persistence.

The first queer-minded person I met in academia happened to be the first lesbian professor from whom I took a class. She unnerved me by taking what I thought at the time were unnecessary risks. In a class of all straight women, except for me, she announced at one point that she felt like she had been given honorary straight status, reminding us that she was a lesbian. In a classroom where lesbian issues were treated by most as a threat of divisiveness to the feminist community we were trying to create, I was awed by the way the professor risked jeopardizing the tenuous acceptance of the class to assert the self she felt being erased. She encouraged us all, whether we were gay or straight, to come out, to think about the losses we and our communities suffered by hiding aspects of ourselves due to the fear that we would not be accepted if we spoke of them. She acknowledged that support was essential to staying out, but that one couldn't find the support until one took the initial step.

My struggles echo her words; keeping my queer mind is linked to asserting my authentic experience in the face of pressures to dissolve it and is maintained through the recognition of others. It is a twofold struggle. The initial difficulty is finding the courage to fumble around in front of my peers and my professors while I try to create questions that the discourse of the moment doesn't accommodate very well. Fear makes me feel inarticulate, dumb. I think of it as a cost-effective silencing tool of the academic community, perhaps most communities.

It makes the act of silencing a remarkably quiet act. The costs, to the self and to the community, may be severe, but like so many other crucial parts of my experience, those costs are not necessarily visible. Once I have spoken, however, recognition is not easy to elicit. Even when I share an ethnic background or sexual orientation with a teacher, it is no guarantee that s/he will be able to hear me. As a result, I am learning to respond to efforts to undermine my sense of truth as if I were performing physical self-defense; when someone tries to take me down, they are going to have to do it while my volume is calmly turned all the way up. I force my image back into the mirror as I am becoming an apparition in the face of someone else's lack of recognition. I break the mirrors that do not reflect my image back to me, or reflect an image of someone I do not recognize.

The struggles I describe are not easy for any of us, students or faculty. I acknowledge the particular pressures faculty have, the specific incentives they have to participate in academia in ways that reinforce the institution. In fact, I think it is in the nature of the relationship between the individual and an institution that the member's participation necessarily fortifies the institution. However, this can be foregrounded as a problem, instead of implicitly validated. Professors can acknowledge the power they have over graduate students, instead of attempting to erase the construction and maintenance of that dynamic and inducing graduate students to collude in that charade. It is not my experience that queer faculty have to be gatekeepers, owing to the history of their generation, but that it is possible for them to be experienced double agents instead. I am thankful for the supportive queer faculty with whom I have been able to work, particularly given the unfavorable odds and the difficult terrain. I am keenly disappointed, however, by the specific undermining of queer graduate students by queer faculty, to which I have also been subjected. It is my desire for a queer-minded community that makes the loss of allies, particularly allies possessing more power within the community, feel so profound. I have witnessed and experienced queer faculty encouraging queer graduate students to closet themselves, pressuring them to modify their tone or their insights, undermining them out of jealousy, or promoting models of being queer that exclude self-identified queers, primarily bisexual women, from participating in the queer community.

The latter two dynamics seem related to the economics of scarcity. This illusory economy plays on the fear that there isn't enough room for work by all queer scholars, that there isn't enough room for all queer scholars. I want to destroy the underpinnings supporting that illusion, assert the consumer need for more air time, create a sense of expanding space. I don't want to just help fill the space of the category of queer studies; I want to be conscious of building that space. If part of the contract is square footage, I will negotiate not only for the largest space possible, but the least bounded. In the final analysis, I want to teach so much more than just individual survival in the space we have. I want to teach the art of exponential prospering, of communal healing.

I am well aware that the war will go on far longer than my lifetime. I stand at the center of the seven generations. It is the seven generations that came before me that allow me to be here today as the woman that people thought I was, as the woman I have decided I am. It is the seven generations that issue from me that I am always considering, the seven generations that I will affect as a teacher, that will carry on this battle. I keep the war in mind when I think about handing off the bow and quiver to the next runner, of giving her the quickest start, the warmest handoff that I can.

Notes

1. Susan Krieger, *Social Science and the Self: Personal Essays on an Art Form* (New Brunswick, NJ: Rutgers University Press, 1991), 244. Townsend Carr, personal communication. I'd like to express my heartfelt thanks to Townsend Carr, of the University of California at Riverside, for sharing her thoughts with me on issues of queer struggle. They are presented here in gist and spirit.

24

"Still Here": Ten Years Later . . .

doris davenport

I've been scarred and battered.
My hopes the wind done scattered.
Snow has friz me, sun has baked me.
    Looks like between 'em
    They done tried to make me
Stop laughin', stop lovin', stop livin'—
    But I don't care!
    I'm still here!

            —Langston Hughes[1]

Poet and professor, writer and teacher—for all of my adult life, I have had these main professional identities. Loving both, I was a writer long before I was a professor, and I thought the two would naturally complement each other. Yet I resigned from a tenure-track job as an assistant professor of English in December 1991. I left because I had an increasingly low tolerance for the pettiness, humiliation, and drudgery involved. Then again, I was forced to resign, or placed in a fight-or-flee situation; I chose the latter. I had also been given a grant to take a year off to write. A few days ago, my overall noncareer in academia, including having to revise this essay, made me bone weary, depressed, and semicatatonic. I decided to take a two-mile walk first, to clear my system.

To walk at all, here in the Southern Appalachian foothills, means to go up and down hills. So I went stiffly down my driveway, and at the bottom of one hill, at a stream and a neighbor's new garden, I felt some better. As I pulled up the next steep hill, past wild roses and honeysuckles, and spoke to two elderly neighbors, I was grinning. A few minutes later, as I thought about this essay, I had a few laughs too. Somebody hollered, "Hey, girl!" and I waved, and later I stopped

215

to tell Miz Gertrude who I was. She's asked, "How's your daddy?" thinking I was someone else. "I'm Ethel Mae's oldest daughter," I said. I needed that walk, to alleviate that depression, and to consciously remind me of who I am. And I came back to this essay, with my head somewhat cleared, more prepared to write about that last job I had, and my academic career.

There were other reasons for my leaving that last job, and the ones before it. First, I refuse to play a victim role, as expected for black wimmin who are also lesbians, especially just for being black and/or female. I refused to reinscribe the oppressor. In every position I've held, my assets (dedication to teaching, a sense of humor, commitment to students, and a knowledge and passionate love of multiethnic literatures) were turned into liabilities. I was constantly reduced to petty, bizarre skirmishes and to having only incidental positive effects (on a few students and new courses) as opposed to being granted the national and international scope I had envisioned for my teaching and my work. I'd hoped and planned for major impact, from teaching and writing to scholarly publications. Minimally, I'd hoped to be an asset to that department (and all the others) with new courses, curriculum changes, and relevant committee work. Instead, my physical and mental energy was drained as I dealt with the mundane on a daily basis, without receiving even nominal interest in or respect for my expertise or training. There was never, metaphorically speaking, anyone even slightly friendly to call out "Hey, girl!" as I went by. Or if someone had, it would have been intended as an insult. I felt battered. I was battered, and consumed by unreleased rage.

Even as I lived through these twilight zone experiences, I was frequently elated at the achievements of many of my peers, close friends, and acquaintances. Most of them had successful, tenured positions (in English, women's studies, or African studies); most were publishing, either with alternative presses or scholarly ones. And the lesbian feminists who chose to work outside academia were also successful, as writer-activists, publishers, or lecturers. But it seemed I lived, somehow, outside all these networks and realities. I couldn't understand why my life, my careers as writer-poet and professor, never seemed to take off as they should have. The irony was devastating, given my (modest) expectations of ten or more years ago.

My essay "Black Lesbians in Academia: Visible Invisibility" was published in 1982.[2] Now, more than ten years later, three major points from that essay are useful and illuminative. I wrote that I had been "operating off an unconscious incentive . . . a legacy from Black educators, of love, discipline, and high standards" (10). That legacy includes countless scholars and teachers, known and unknown, back to the earliest African griots on this continent. Specifically, I was referring to my own teachers, since the first grade. Because of them, I wanted to be a teacher in addition to being a writer. Because of them, I am a good teacher (sometimes even very good). In my teaching I encourage mental agility and expansiveness, flexibility, and infinite practice in the arts of communication (thinking, writing, verbal expressiveness). My pedagogy emphasizes active learning within a call-and-response mode, grounded in my background and heritage. Along with high expectations for my students, I try to maintain respect and a kind of love for them.

My being a lesbian feminist caused whiplash in some of my colleagues, but the students were my main concern. My goals are to encourage independent, original thinking and to enhance a tolerance and understanding of multiple viewpoints and lifestyles. Teaching, to me, includes incidents like one that occurred in an Introduction to African-American Literature course. A young blackmale asked, in a condemnatory tone, what I thought of James Baldwin's being gay. I laughed and say, "Why would I think *anything*, since I am a lesbian?" No one stampeded the chairperson's office, as I thought they would. I swear, I felt James Baldwin smiling at me.

In 1982, I wrote that I was in this profession because I "passionately love literature, although I know there is a great deal of unnecessary, humiliating absurdity involved in academia, period" (10). These days, I believe that academia is 95 percent absurdity, humiliation, and slaughtering of forests. (Daily memos would account for 50 percent; the rest is "publications.") Still, my passion for literature remains.

Most recently, that literature has been contemporary multiethnic wimmin writers of the USA mainly (and some males, too). It has been frustrating and depressing to teach this literature to mainly monocultural students who don't know, and frequently resist knowing, anything about alternative or parallel realities. But inevitably, there are students who find books like Cheryl Clarke's *Narratives*, Sheila Ortiz Taylor's *Faultline*, Leslie Marmon Silko's *Ceremony*, Sherley Anne Williams's *Dessa Rose*, Gloria Anzaldúa's *Making Face, Making Soul*, or Melanie Kaye/Kantrowitz's *My Jewish Face* to be exhilarating, illuminating, and inspiring. One white womon student ("blatantly het," as she put it) joined Naiad Press's mailing list, because of Ann Allen Shockley's *Say Jesus and Come to Me*. As a graduate student, I wrote, in a review of *Faultline*, that I hoped to someday see books like it taught in English departments. I did, at least, do that. As a reader and a literary critic, I enjoy these books. I mean, I have totally enjoyed the experiences provided in these, and similar, books. Then, there is the knowledge that I and many others like me—especially MELUS and NAES members—are doing similar work.[3]

Yet, too many of my students found those works alien, scary, and threatening. As I think about that now, I have to laugh at myself. I honestly did expect too much from that one class. They were, after all, in an introductory course, cross-listed with the English department and women's studies. For many of them, the course was simply a general education requirement, nothing more or less. Several of those students were graduating seniors and had no interest in the topic, and even less in a widened perspective. Most of them had never thought about sexism in their daily lives, and certainly not about the issues that these texts raised! If attendance was high, it was because many of them were entertained and amazed, daily, just to look at a black womon with dreds, with a Ph.D. (allegedly), who was also a lesbian. (I was constantly perceived as a circus act, even if I did nothing but hand out the syllabus.) I had set up a class for advanced students and thinkers, including teachers. Many tenured, veteran professors in women's studies and English departments have not dealt with their internalized misogyny and white-supremacist belief systems, or with their denials about the same. How, then, did I expect these students to get it? From this perspective, from these Georgia hills, I can laugh. But then it was quite painful and frustrating.

A third point that I mentioned ten years ago is all too lamentably obvious: "I guess we are a threat to the 'system' (since Blackwimmin are perceived as a threat to most everyone, period)" (11). Many Blackwimmin's experiences in the USA verify this fact. Both students and faculty have said that I "intimidate" or "threaten" them, in a tremulous tone more suitable for religious confessionals or in a belligerent tone that seems perfect for wrestling matches.[4] I have been reported to the chairperson on a vague, amorphous charge of "intimidation." (A charge with which the chair frequently agreed.) What I really think they mean is that the idea of a black (lesbian) womon as an authority figure, period, is too much strain on their nervous systems. Or rather, anyone but a whitemale is "intimidating" in that role. Ten years ago I also wrote that "I want to stay here long enough to make some radical, and positive changes . . . in the way Black lesbians are viewed and treated in academia, and the rest of the un-real world . . . in the way we are presented and perceived" (11). Well, I guess I stayed long enough to send people into denial and shock. I reckon they know what one black lesbian feminist educator looks like. But that is hardly what I intended. I seriously doubt that I positively altered anyone's perceptions.

Again, I have to laugh at myself, at my silly expectations and naïveté. In 1982, maybe because of my tendency to have multiple personalities, I thought there were lots of us; just *thousands* of African-American lesbian-feminist academics. Certainly, there were at least ten. (No doubt, many of my colleagues thought that too, and saw me as at least one hundred of those people—hence their fears and anxieties about our imminent takeover.) In the intervening years, my contact with African-American lesbian-feminist academics has been sporadic, at best, and long-distance. I don't remember that many gaysisters, period, at the places where I worked. You know why not?

There ain't that many. The joke is on me. No, this time, the people who say they just don't know or can't find any, just might be right. I'd hoped for a network, to share celebration, to support and nurture one another in our endeavors, to be visibly out and working together. A sisterhood interlocking with numerous others. Foolish expectation. There aren't that many Black Ph.D.'s in the humanities. Not that many African-American wimmin with Ph.D.'s who teach. There really aren't all that many tenure-track gay males or white lesbians either. Most of us, or of you, are too clearheaded to tolerate the sadistically prolonged, sententiously defended, ritualistically hermeneutic process of refined and torturous bullshit that is needed to get a Ph.D., especially in English.

So, the few black lesbians I encountered were either fighting their own battles, decimated by daily life, or closeted for self-protection. Anyway, educational institutions were designed primarily to underwrite this unreality called the status quo (worldwide white/male supremacy). Therefore, and in any case, life in the USA consists of layers and layers of unreality and smoke screens and denials, which keep people distracted from the fact that for the most part, their (our) lives are meaningless. Or rather, they would be meaningless, without those smoke screens, and daily delusions. (I am referring to the institution of heterosexual love; the empty materialism of many middle-class lifestyles; the fabricated wars of males against wimmin, Euro-Americans against people of color; petty sibling rivalries, and even the so-called traditionalists against some of us, in academia.) Few of us have the honesty or stamina required to admit that much of what we do is absurd, yet continue to do it anyway (with a sense of self-irony, or humor). Which is what I did, pursuing a Ph.D. Too many people have a vested interest in these smoke screens, and therefore see any suggested alternative perspective as a direct personal affront or attack.

In spite of all this, like most professors, I have had some impact on a few students. I was instrumental in helping a brilliant sistah finish her doctorate. An exceptionally astute young whitemale (quite resistant and ornery in a wimmin's studies class) now says I am his "mentor." A young white lesbian went from wanting to be a high school dropout to going to law school. There must be a few others, but nothing like my intended range, nothing like the impact my teachers had on generations of students, and nothing like the effect I should have had, given my training. Still, I insist that either as a writer or as a professor I must have reached more people than I know. If I really knew this (no doubt all teachers, from kindergarten through grad school, want to know this, too), I would feel less like Sisyphus, but people in hell want ice water too, my Grandma used to say.

On another level, maybe I and others like me have been catalysts for subtle changes, acting like laser surgery on cataracts. Maybe most of my students can now *see* that they can think, analyze, and be more active in all areas of the learning process, in school and beyond. No doubt, after their great sense of relief, several ex-colleagues of mine must have decided to hire a few other "tokens." After I left, they would have realized that nobody else could be nearly as bad (or as good). Yes. I'm sure that in my wake (like the one a big, fast-moving ship leaves on the ocean), lots of more moderate, more "acceptable," less threatening people of color and white wimmin have been hired. (In fact, in one place, I was on the committee that hired such a person.) Just like I am noticed by everybody when I go walking here (because we always notice everybody, nothing else to do), I believe that my presence, my ideas and principles have been noticed. Just thinking about that, I have to smile. The same applies to my writing and publishing career.

I came out as a published writer and lesbian feminist simultaneously, while I was in graduate school in Los Angeles. I will always be grateful to the wimmin and magazines (like *Azalea* and *Feminary* and *Sunbury*) who published my work, years ago. But still there is my essay in *This Bridge Called My Back*.[5] Inadvertently, that essay created lots of enemies. Several white wimmin especially objected to the essay's contents, and had to be reassured by their presumably safe negro girlfriends. There were some reading tours, as I recall, a few miles from my house, and I was not invited. (On the other hand, numerous black wimmin told me how much they needed to see something like my essay in print.) The very consistency of the denial about me in that book means that I am ever-present as an entity to be denied! The same thing applies to my other publications, from the three self-published books of poetry to book reviews. Maybe I should apologize: I thought I had lots of peers out there, folk who were ready and able to deal with some major truths; I was mistaken. About two years ago, I placed an ad in *Women's Review of Books* for my latest book of poetry. Two wimmin ordered the book.

Well no, I don't find this funny or amusing. Again, it is the reverse of my intentions, and counterproductive. I expected and hoped for an ongoing conversation with many wimmin, because of my publications. Sadly and ironically, that has not yet happened. I have published rarely and inconsistently, but rather widely, for an "academic." Those publications and my poetry performances do contribute (even if minimally) to the changes I hoped to bring about.

Change, to me, includes celebrating and sharing the richness in and of cultural diversity; the enjoyment of knowing numerous realities and cultures; the expansion and growth implicit in an open (or even unwilling) embrace of differences. But it's difficult to sustain a mood of celebration in absolute isolation and aloneness.

The world of academia (and at one point, the lesbian-feminist world, too) increasingly became a straitjacket. One in which I could barely breathe, much less think. My main metaphor was a sadistic marriage, one totally antithetical to my existence.

While writing "Black Lesbians in Academia" more than a decade ago, I only thought I was having a rough time, as I struggled through grad school madness, with the lesbian-feminist community (many accusing me of selling out, and why couldn't I just be a carpenter or something?) and with chronic alcoholism. But I was having a good time, compared to later battles.

In the past ten years, I have had five different teaching positions, in five different states in the USA. From temporary replacements for professors on leave to tenure-track, from the West to the South, the Midwest, and back to the South. Each time, I paid the moving expenses, and I paid in time lost from other areas of my life. Since 1984, I have been without the necessary context of a lesbian-feminist community. I have lost time from major writing projects. Having my works consistently rejected did not improve my morale either.[6] I published more as a graduate student than I have as a Ph.D., partly because I developed a case of writer's block at the thought of doing more esoteric writings for a singularly in-bred group of people which now included myself.

In my repeated moves, I have had the unbelievable (mis)fortune to wind up in locales where, as they say, those people need me. Meaning they deny the existence of feminists, or lesbians, or visibly ethnic professors. The intention was that I (and others like me) would single-handedly educate all of those folk about the major realities of the late twentieth century.[7]

Ironically, I thought that, post-Ph.D., my life would be more free, mainly because I am a dedicated educator. Some of my worse collegial wars were not only with a certain type of whitemale, but with black-males and whitefemales in academia. Because I am so out as who and what I am, I have been the target of numerous psychotic projections and reactions, from students and administrators alike. What has any of this to do with my being a Blacklesbian? Everything and nothing. Whereas I teach (and write) from a holistic perspective, bringing all of me to any situation, from one to five parts of me can be problematical for students and faculty. That is, if I merely say that I am from a working-class, Southern, rural environment; a lesbian feminist; the oldest of seven children; a poet; or even that I (really do) have a Ph.D., somebody is bound to freak out. Of course, as I list my definers, I am also inviting those folk to list theirs. (Perhaps that is the problem. Either they cannot or just don't want to.) It's not as simple as just being "it" because of being out as a lesbian.[8]

In each position, I was hired for some dubious, tangential, subjective reason that had nothing to do with my credentials or qualifications. The main criteria seemed to be an affirmative action agenda and whether or not the interviewers "liked" me. Often, the hiring committee didn't understand what my qualifications were. For example, I was a tempo-rary replacement for Michele Wallace for a semester, and I think the main criteria there were to be female, black, and available on short notice. Another position was at a junior college where we all taught composition only. In my last job, nobody knew why I was hired or what I was supposed to do. Literally. There was no job description; there were no courses on the books in multiethnic literature, and there was a severe budget crunch. (Plus, they already had two tenured blackwimmin on the faculty.) In other words, *I had no business at these places to begin with*. To me, they dealt with mediocrity; I only care about excellence. They (perhaps unknowingly) inculcated and endorsed reciprocal limitations in themselves and in the students. My concern is maximum expansion and transcendence.

Many people of color and white wimmin have had similar experi-ences. Even well-known, well-published, highly respected scholars (vis-ibly ethnic folk and white wimmin), people who are mainly heterosexual and/or otherwise "nonthreatening," have had difficulty maintaining a position, or getting tenure. The difference is in our perspectives, our responses, and our relative degree of (dis)comfort in the system. Because of the experiences of the last ten years, one thing is very clear: the problem really is academia.

When I quit that last position, I wrote a five-page, single-spaced letter of resignation and sent copies to colleagues and friends around the USA. In response, a friend told me about a tenured professor (a blackmale) with a student who calls him at home to shout "nigger" repeatedly. And there are always others: a Chinese-American womon denied tenure because her work (on Chinese wimmin) wasn't considered "scholarly"; ditto for an African-American womon at Emory; another one forced to leave a prestigious Ivy League wimmin's school because of racism; the blackmale at Harvard who resigned in protest against the sexism of his department; and others, embroiled in lengthy and costly litigation even as they continue to teach. My letter of resignation was redundant (I had said all that before), but I spoke for many of us in academia, a most exclusionary, reactionary world. That world, of course, has never intended to include us (members of the working class, wimmin, males of color, lesbians, gay males). And yet it must, and will, include us.

Although I quit my most recent academic job because of the ongoing pettiness of the monocultural, monolithic, myopic minority which controls the world of academe, I know our presence is important and necessary. And by "our" presence, I mean those of us who are politically and socially visibly ethnic,[9] those with more expansive lifestyles and perspectives, those with enough stamina, determination, humor, and commitment to remain in the profession. Although I have lived in isolation, alienation, depression, and demoralization, I know that I am not alone in teaching from a holistic, visionary perspective. However, given the way things are, this perspective will not be manifest until some time in the late twenty-first century. And I am so impatient.

I have not always done what I ought to, or what I wanted to, in all the ways I'd hoped. I have truly not been the success I'd expected to be in academia, but then again, I have not (yet) sold out either. All of this, and more, is why I took this essay's title from Langston Hughes's poem "Still Here." It most accurately sums up my major points in this essay and my career as a professor.

My first visit to Italy, in 1989, showed me a whole other reality, one confirmed by many African Americans: a life without daily white racism![10] An absence of the constant pettiness of white supremacy!

More preciously, a presence, in the students' knowledge of an attitude toward literature. They asked intelligent, interested questions about my poetry, and about other African-American writers as well. One young man asked about the prevalence of Yoruba belief systems in our literature; the average American college student (or teacher) can barely pronounce that word. The professors responded as if what I said was important—which, I might add, is what I have always expected to happen, how I'd always thought it should be. Or could be. Since then, I have wondered and fantasized.

What if wimmin—especially visibly ethnic wimmin—did not have to deal with the constant debilitation of racism and sexism in academia/ the USA? What could it be like to work in an atmosphere where respect and openness (not to mention an interest in our work, as opposed to a rather belligerent low-key hostility) were the norm, and given? What if our students saw learning as an end, rather than a means to an end (a high-paying job)? Although I am not so optimistic about the possibility of finding such a place in the USA, I know that such institutions must exist somewhere.

Before my latest resignation, I taught two classes on Zora Neale Hurston and Langston Hughes. Among other inspiring facts, Hughes had a good time in Paris—where I went in February 1992 to read poetry at a conference.[11] Zora Neale, metaphorically, traveled further as she "jumped at the sun." Which is basically all I've done all my life, just trying to get off the ground. Like Hurston (and Hughes), I have never been tragically colored, nor tragically female, Southern, or lesbian. If anything, I have been proudly comfortable with all that. And I am most amazingly and miraculously still here.

I have now been in Cornelia, Georgia, my beloved hometown, since March 1992. My extended sabbatical has been productive. Last summer, the North Carolina Arts Council awarded me a writer's grant. I recently finished a draft of my fourth book of poetry, an autobiographical work called "Soquee Street." I started work on that book with a grant from the Kentucky Foundation for Women. During the summer of 1993 I was a writer in residence at the Syvenna Foundation for Women. I have remained a sober alcoholic now for three years, and being here helps with that. Just being here is healing and regenerative; to watch a complete cycle of seasons while living in the book I am writing; to begin many days with a walk across the hill; to sleep in absolute silence and clear air, with crickets, trees rustling, and the moon's light. And here, I have begun to think about the institution of higher education more objectively, without the daily grind of teaching, grading papers, and petty skirmishes with my colleagues.

This euphoric environment could be altering my perceptions. My optimism of today might be because of that walk, and of being among people who more or less accept what I am and what I do. (This is a decidedly working-class, oral community where everybody knows I just "wrote a book,"and they all ask how it's going.) Still, I know that I honestly have teaching, as well as poetry, in my blood. More than ever, I believe that what I have to offer is necessary and timely. It's just a matter of my finding the right position, or an institution with the insight, creativity, and vision that will create a position for me. Meanwhile, I will continue to write, to do lectures and readings, and to think about a career as an exercise-aerobics instructor.

Notes

1. Langston Hughes, *Selected Poems* (New York: Vintage, 1959), 123.

2. doris davenport, "Black Lesbians in Academia: Visible Invisibility," in *Lesbian Studies, Present and Future*, ed. Margaret Cruikshank (New York: Feminist Press, 1982), 9–11.

3. MELUS is the Society for the Study of Multi-Ethnic Literature of the United States. NAES is the National Association of Ethnic Studies.

4. Each time this happens, I am somehow surprised, a little enraged, since I am never conscious of doing anything to provoke such a statement. Each time, I experience a feeling of total revulsion, as if I just fell into a big tub of live maggots or tiny albino spiders. To me, my teaching methods are not confrontational. My attitude is one of having found something (the literature and its contexts) wonderful, rare, and beautiful, and of wanting to share it with others. That folk constantly see that attitude as confrontational is further proof of a kind of sickness (of the mind and spirit).

5. doris davenport, "The Pathology of Racism: A Conversation with Third World Wimmin," in *This Bridge Called My Back: Writing by Radical Women of Color*, ed. Cherríe Moraga and Gloria Anzaldúa (New York: Kitchen Table Press, 1983), 85–90.

6. My dissertation, a cultural-stylistic study of four African-American poets (Clifton, Jordan, Lorde, and Williams) was several times on the verge of acceptance, but one press said the writers were "not well known" and hence, there would be no market for the book. An anonymous reader (a whitemale) said my poetry manuscript showed "no knowledge of what rhythm means."

7. That assumption is grounded in the "natural resources" approach to the realities of people of color and white wimmin. Especially all wimmin. It means that we/our energies are to be mined, tapped, drilled, used, and exploited, as diamonds, oil, and other natural resources are taken from the earth. It is a very dehumanizing

concept, cruel and vicious in its implementation. It never asks what we (the erstwhile natural resources) need or want. It assumes only that we should be happy to serve. In other words, these institutions might have "needed" me; I most emphatically did not, and do not, need them.

8. I have written about many of these experiences in two other essays. One, "Pedagogy of/in Ethnic Literature," was published in *MELUS* 16:2 (Spring 1989–90): 51–62. One of the major points I make—as numerous other feminist educators have elsewhere—is that teachers need to identify themselves and be more honest and accountable for their biases, limitations, and even text selection. In the other essay, "Dismantling White Supremacy" (in *Social Issues in the English Classroom*, ed. C. Mark Hurlbert and Samuel Totten, National Council of Teachers of English, 1992), my focus is mainly on the students, but I cover some of the same material as in the MELUS essay.

9. The old term here would be "minority," I suppose, or some other less appropriate term. To be "visibly ethnic" means to be one of us with hair, skin color, eyes, etc., that make us identifiable. The others (mainly called "white" in the USA) are "invisible ethnics."

10. I was invited to read from my book *eat thunder and drink rain*, which was translated into Italian by Professor Franco Meli for use in his American literature course at Instituto Universitario Di Lingue Moderne (IULM) in Milan. He chose it as "representative of contemporary African-American poetry." The book's Italian title is *Mangia il Tuono & Bevi la Pioggia: Poesie* (Milan: Cooperativa Libraria, IULM, 1988).

11. The conference was "Les Noirs Américains et l'Europe/African Americans and Europe," February 1992, at the Sorbonne Nouvelle.

25

Out as a Lesbian, Out as a Jew: And Nothing Untoward Happened?

Evelyn Torton Beck

What does it mean to be a women's studies program director and to be out as a lesbian and a Jew? How do these multiple identities affect my daily decision making as an administrator? What has been their impact on me as a scholar, teacher, activist?

These are questions that have pulled at me like an undercurrent for the past nine years that I have been serving as director of women's studies at the University of Maryland at College Park. In assessing the significance of these questions, in wondering why they persist even as the program flourishes, it is critical to remember that they are not abstractions in a hypothetical case study. These are real questions that I have lived with on a daily basis; they are embedded in the internal dialogue that informs every decision I have made.

When I first accepted the directorship, I assumed that in order to carry out the program's dual mission—radical-feminist transformation of the university and gaining credibility for women's studies—I would have to be closeted. In fact, going back into the closet was more accurate, since for years I had been out and active in my previous community and had actually developed and taught courses in lesbian studies at the University of Wisconsin-Madison. But now, for the supposed greater good of the program, I was willing to compromise—at least I thought I was.

To my surprise, I quickly found that going back in wasn't a meaningful gesture unless I was also willing to compromise my politics in curricular and academic matters. While I believed I was willing to be invisible as a lesbian administrator on campus, I had determined that I would never drop lesbian perspectives, themes, and issues from my classes or the women's studies curriculum. In fact, I would insist on

227

the inclusion of these and other invisible populations in the general curriculum as well. This insistence made both me and the program suspect, but I held firm. In fact, I had talked about this in my job interview because, while I thought I was willing to be closeted in the larger university arena, I had also decided that I would never take a position in a program that was homophobic. While no one objected to my general policy statements, we did not discuss my lesbian writings. I had the distinct impression that those who knew were protecting me. This felt very good and yet had serious repercussions with respect to my ability to assess the safety of the terrain for being out.

In my first year as director, as part of a strategy to strengthen the program and to give our efforts visibility, I worked hard to bring Audre Lorde to campus and was gratified when a thousand people from the campus and the community came to hear her. The next day the student newspaper blared headlines stating, "Lesbian Poet Comes to Campus, Sponsored by Women's Studies." I was terrified of an attack on the program, but nothing untoward happened. The next year we brought Adrienne Rich, and the same scenario played itself out again. The same crowds, the same headlines. Nothing further happened.

Also quite early in my first year, I was interviewed by a reporter representing a Jewish student newspaper, who asked me where I went for the Jewish high holidays. Self-conscious and caught off guard, I replied that I went to Bet Mishpoche because it had a "feminist service" (true enough, but I neglected to say it was a gay and lesbian synagogue). The earnest reporter did a bit of research, however, and in the article noted what Bet Mishpoche was. Again I was terrified, but again nothing untoward happened.

Nothing bad happened but I continued to feel fearful, not for myself (I was a full professor with tenure), but for the program. For me, this was a new and different arena of fear. When I first began coming out to people who had known me for years as a heterosexual woman, I remember feeling as if I were about to leap across a wide chasm— between the moment I said the words and when they responded—and I felt as if I might not make it across. But now I was a program director and the stakes were of a different magnitude. I was no longer just a private person or even just a professor. I had the responsibility to protect the program's credibility and to build it further, even while maintaining integrity—the program's and mine.

Then, still in my first year, an administrator from the Office of Human Relations organized a forum on homophobia—a first on campus—and asked me to participate. I hesitated and accepted. So someone knew something. But I didn't know how much or what they knew, or what was wanted of me. Was I expected to analyze the workings of homophobia in general, to speak about the need for creating a safe environment for "them," lesbian women and gay men, or was I expected to speak in my own voice? Did anyone even know I had a lesbian voice? When I asked, gingerly, how I was to speak, I was told to speak in whatever way made me most comfortable. But I had no idea what was meant by that, nor did I know what the unspoken rules of the university were. While the Human Relations office said it was instructed to hear complaints based on sexual preference, the university president had refused to include the latter in writing in the university's code.[1] I worried that those without job security and students would not be reliably protected. I worried about women's studies. I had no idea whether this administrator was "one of us" or simply an enlightened heterosexual, and I did not dare ask. In this exchange, I was speaking in code, and as a result, we unfortunately spoke right past each other.

Till the day of the forum I had no idea of how I was going to speak. It turned out that I was the only faculty member or high-level administrator on the program; the others were all students and academic staff. When I looked out at the crowd gathered in the auditorium and realized that most of those who had come were lesbians and gay men, I understood that whatever the outreach intent of the program had been, it would serve most significantly as a public affirmation of our lives, for ourselves. Under such circumstances, could I speak of "them" and not "us"? How could I not speak in my own voice? And nothing untoward happened, even when my presence at the symposium was reported in the student newspaper the next day.

In spite of the fact that, or perhaps because, nothing untoward happened, questions continued to haunt me. What exactly constituted coming out on campus? Teaching lesbian materials in classes? Bringing lesbian poets to campus? Participating in an educational forum? Attending a gay and lesbian synagogue? I have never offered a class in lesbian studies at this university, but I wonder to what extent this holding back really protects the program.[2] I still don't know with any degree of certainty who knows what, or what difference it makes, or to whom.

When I was hired, women's studies had only two core faculty, and I was fairly certain that they knew my work. Anyone who had read *Nice Jewish Girls: A Lesbian Anthology* had to know I was a lesbian, but had everyone on that large hiring committee of fifteen (including non–women's studies faculty and staff) read my work? I doubted it. And a lot of them had asked about my feminist Kafka work and *The Prism of Sex*, but no one mentioned *Nice Jewish Girls*.[3]

One can learn from this that the only way to be sure that anyone knows is to tell him or her directly, but I had determined to keep a low profile—a strategy that definitely has its limitations. In fact, this not knowing who knows turned out to be a tremendous burden that grew increasingly heavier, until in my sixth year as director I decided to come out to the extended women's studies steering committee. I had kept silent long enough for the supposed sake of the program. If by now, having doubled its size and gained a position of high academic credibility for feminist work, the program could not face squarely that it had a lesbian director, I was ready to step down. But nothing untoward happened. Does this mean that there is no homophobia on campus? in our classes? within the extended program? Not at all. Not even every single course that counts toward the women's studies certificate necessarily includes lesbian perspectives; we have not legislated inclusivity, though we strongly recommend it. And we do hear rumblings about some students and some faculty who stay away from women's studies because we focus "too much on lesbian themes," because there are "too many lesbians associated with the program." One newly appointed female department chair was warned by a woman administrator to stay away from me, no reason given. But whenever we have had complaints about lesbians, I have without hesitation defended the necessity of lesbian studies as part of the feminist agenda of women's studies. Recently I have come out in some classes. Often I use my own writings as texts. But I still don't know what all this adds up to in a big university. I still don't know who knows what. I have no idea if the program's development would have gone less well had I been less circumspect earlier.

Did staying in the closet to the degree I did make any difference? I doubt that I will ever be able to figure out how much of my strategy was fueled by political savvy and how much by internalized homophobia. Given the tenor of the times and the context of my university, would I do it differently if I had it to do over again? Truthfully, I doubt it. But clearly, however politically astute my choices may have been, some residue of discomfort with them remain.

In the beginning I worried less about being an out Jew on campus, although some colleagues who knew Maryland told me they were more surprised that the university would hire such an activist Jew (especially one working on anti-Semitism) than an out lesbian. But in the beginning, I didn't feel too vulnerable with respect to my Jewishness, except as a lesbian in the Jewish studies program to which I also belong, and where my being feminist was already a big deal. So I didn't burden Jewish studies with lesbian perspectives, though again, I wasn't at all sure who, if anyone, knew what.

But then we came to matters of money. Maryland is a large state university in which every department constantly has to fight for funding. I discovered almost immediately that I would have to fight not only to increase the women's studies program budget, but simply to keep the little we had from being cut. In this process, I discovered a few things about myself. I was outspoken, persistent, persuasive, and not afraid of authority figures. I believed passionately in the need for a strong women's studies program, and I marshalled moral arguments and evidence intended to remind the university of its own self-interest in the matter. I found ways of garnering allies and developed strategies for raising funds for the program from very diverse sources. What I had never been able to do for myself as an individual, I found I could easily do in fighting for the program. To some extent, this experience paralleled my only partly successful in-the-closet strategy as a lesbian program director. What I could not do for myself (stay in the closet, go begging for money) I was able to do for the program.

The implications of this willingness for me as a Jew only became clear the day a male Gentile administrator said to me, in tones that were at once admiring, slightly ironic, and somewhat chiding, that I was really good at getting money for my program. I don't know what these words meant to him, maybe nothing more than a passing observation. But I heard him as a Jew, and what should have made me proud made me ashamed and afraid. We all know about Jews and money.

In 1988, I was invited to San Diego State University at the time that Bonnie Zimmerman, their women's studies program director, also a lesbian and a Jew, was planning a big on-campus celebration of her new book *The Safe Sea of Women: Lesbian Fiction, 1969–1989.*[4] Within the past week I had made a difficult decision that had pained me deeply. The revised expanded version of *Nice Jewish Girls* had just been released, and while I was both pleased and proud of this edition, I had agonized about whether or not I should include its subtitle, *A Lesbian Anthology*, in the publicity that would be widely distributed on and off campus. We were in the middle of a drive for funds, and I decided that adding the subtitle would make the program too vulnerable; but omitting it, though expedient, felt demeaning. Neither decision felt good, but I stayed with the elision. When I told this story to Bonnie, she asked me whether I thought my discomfort at using the subtitle had anything to do with the resulting juxtaposition of *Jew* and *Lesbian*. The question hit me like a blow, and I knew instantly that she was right—that if my book had been about lesbian anything else (except maybe sexuality) it would have seemed more legitimate, less grotesque. Gay and lesbian studies have earned a degree of viability in the university, but Jewish lesbian studies? What legitimacy does that have? My 1988 essay "The Politics of Jewish Invisibility in Women's Studies" could easily be rewritten as the politics of that invisibility in lesbian studies and (more recently in the multicultural curriculum).[5] The much-touted *Lesbian Lists* does not include a single Jewish-identified name or category;[6] *Nice Jewish Girls* is not even listed as a significant lesbian text. The list of omissions remains long.

But I don't want to blame my decisions either on anti-Semitism or homophobia, although I think both are part of the larger context. And I don't think these stories reflect very well on me either. Yet I have a strong impulse to share them publicly, out of reasons that have nothing to do with confession or expiation. There are actually some who think I have been very brave through all this, drawing a fine line between giving up integrity and taking unnecessary risks. I don't know if I feel brave; I do know that I paid a price. I have the sense that there are lessons to be learned from what I've been through, though I am not sure yet exactly what they are. I do know that this story is not mine alone. I was surprised to understand that many lesbians who publish in lesbian studies and are visible as lesbians within the Modern Language Association or the National Women's Studies Association are not explicitly out on their campuses. Surprisingly few of our lesbian texts actually have the word "lesbian" even in their subtitles. I do not know what the shape of other lesbians' daily realities are, particularly those who are also program directors and have programs to protect. I do know that anti-Semitism and homophobia can fuse to create a powerful negative force, and that coming out as either a Jew or a lesbian is an endless, exhausting process in a universe that assumes Christian affiliation and heterosexuality unless otherwise notified. And there are no guidelines about whom to notify when, where, or how.

This is the place I always get stuck. Each time I have revised this essay I get to here and can go no further. This time I asked my life partner for help and right away she saw what the problem was.[7] She said that this was the only piece of mine she had ever read in which

I had not laid out a conceptual framework. Right away I knew she was right, but still I felt paralyzed and even a little weak. Knowing my history, it was clear to her that beneath this story was another story—one that inexorably pushed its way into the present. It is a story about elision and boundaries, about the tension between self-assertion and the need to protect others.

Elsewhere I have written about these events:[8] like the time, one of many I am certain, when I was given the task of buying butter for my family (a commodity forbidden to Jews) but at the price of hiding my identity as a Jew or risking the most dire, life-threatening consequences in the Austria of 1938–39; or when we were entering the United States in 1940 and I had to cover my face with a heavy, masklike powder to hide the measles for fear my family would be sent back across the ocean to certain death.

The job of a women's studies director resembles that of a mother: it is the director's task to nurture and protect. When that director is a lesbian and a Jew (a child survivor of the Holocaust at that), the charge to fulfill these twin responsibilities becomes particularly fraught. Far from seeing myself as a coward who compromised her integrity by trying to maintain some semblance of balance between caring for the self (by being out) and protecting the program (by remaining somewhat closeted), I now see myself as bravely going forth to get the butter I believe we deserve, knowing full well the dangers that lay in this task if I did not at least partially hide who I was.

The task of distinguishing the boundaries between the self and those in our care is not an easy one for those assigned to nurture, protect, and educate, nor is it for women's studies directors.[9] We are our individual selves, yet we can easily be mistaken for our programs, both by ourselves and especially by those who hold the final power over our well-being. If we are lesbian, the danger of that conflation can be especially damaging to our programs and hurtful to ourselves. If we are Jewish and lesbian, the burden of worry is doubled. Recognizing this, my sense of unease in spite of enormous gains becomes more meaningful.[10] How could I not worry that something untoward would happen? Though always building, how could I not be ever vigilant?

Notes

1. In 1992 the university chancellor of the Maryland system, with the support of the new president of the College Park campus, signed a mandate giving full protection based on sexual orientation.

2. The climate at our university has clearly changed since I began writing this piece. We have organized by forming the Lesbian/Gay Staff and Faculty Group, and two courses focusing on lesbian/gay material were offered through the English department. In the spring of 1994 the women's studies program will sponsor the first lesbian/gay studies course, tentatively titled Constructing the Field of Gay, Lesbian, and Bisexual Studies (to be taught by Katie King, a newly tenured women's studies faculty person); the following semester I plan to offer a course called Lesbian Lives. However, at that time I will no longer be director of the women's studies program.

3. Evelyn Torton Beck, "Kafka's Traffic in Women: Power, Gender and Sexuality," *The Literary Review* 26:4 (Summer 1983): 565–76; Beck, "Kafka's Triple Bind: Women, Jews and Sexuality," in Alan Udoff, ed., *Kafka's Contextuality* (Gordian Press and Baltimore Hebrew College, 1986), 343–88; Beck, "Gender, Judaism, Power: A Jewish-Feminist Approach to Kafka," in Richard Grey, ed., *Approaches to the Teaching of Kafka* (New York: Modern Language Association, 1994); Julia A. Sherman and Evelyn Torton Beck, eds., *The Prism of Sex: Essays in the Sociology of Knowledge* (Madison: University of Wisconsin Press, 1979); Evelyn Torton Beck, ed., *Nice Jewish Girls: A Lesbian Anthology* (Boston: Beacon Press, 1989).

4. Bonnie Zimmerman, *The Safe Sea of Women: Lesbian Fiction, 1969–1989* (Boston: Beacon Press, 1990).

5. Evelyn Torton Beck, "The Politics of Jewish Invisibility in Women's Studies," *NWSA Journal* 1:1 (Autumn 1988): 93–102. This article was also anthologized in Johnnella E. Butler and John C. Walker, eds., *Transforming the Curriculum: Ethnic Studies and Women's Studies* (Albany: SUNY Press, 1991), 187–97.

6. Dell Richards, *Lesbian Lists: A Look at Lesbian Culture, History and Personalities* (Boston: Alyson Publications, 1990).

7. My thanks go to my life partner, psychologist L. Lee Knefelkamp, whose insights are embedded in these last paragraphs and without whose gentle prodding they might never have been written.

8. See the introduction to *Nice Jewish Girls*, "Why Is This Book Different from All Other Books?" xv –xxxvii.

9. See Sarah Ruddick, *Maternal Thinking* (New York: Ballantine Books, 1989), for further discussion of the complexities and tensions inherent to the topic addressed by her book.

10. Under my directorship (1984–93), women's studies at the University of Maryland-College Park grew from three to seven core faculty; a graduate certificate program and an undergraduate major were approved and put into place.

26

The Ins and Outs of a Lesbian Academic

Mary Klages

I first came out, as a lesbian and as a lesbian academic, in 1976, when I was a senior in high school. Living in a conservative Republican suburb of a large Midwestern town, where "feminism" still meant radical bra burning, I knew that I couldn't talk to my friends, parents, teachers, or guidance counselors about my newfound sexuality. What I could do, however, was research; I wrote my term paper for a social studies class on lesbianism—much to the concern and dismay of my teachers, who insisted on having long talks with me about my motivations for writing that paper. To my relief they did not tell my parents, or the college which had already accepted me, about their concerns; so my first coming out remained our secret.

I went off to my Ivy League college eager to get away from home and the Midwest in order to explore this exciting identity of "lesbian" more fully. I won't go into the usual coming-out side of it—how I had my first lesbian sexual experiences, heartbreaks, traumas about coming out to roommates and friends, and their reactions, which ranged from absolutely horrified and overtly hostile to intrigued. What's important here is that, as with my initial high school articulation of identity, my lesbian identity was intimately related to, and part of, my academic identity. I took my first women's studies classes my freshman year, even though women's studies was a brand-new and rather suspect discipline at my college, and I began to define myself as a feminist scholar. When women's studies became a degree-granting program, I became one of its first majors, largely because I felt comfortable being out in my women's studies classes.

Being out in these women's studies classes wasn't easy, mind you. Virtually all of the women professors at my formerly all-male college in the late '70s were straight, as far as I knew, and more or less uncomfortable with discussing lesbianism in the classroom. I realize now that many of these professors felt threatened by their radical-feminist and lesbian students—not just personally, because they were uncomfortable with the idea of out lesbians, but academically, because so many of the works we students devoured and quoted from were unfamiliar to these women, who had learned their canonical disciplines in order to earn their degrees and positions in their male-dominated fields.

This was especially true because it was the era before "cultural diversity" became the buzzword it is now and before such concepts compelled consideration when planning a syllabus. "Woman" at that time was a universalized category, and few courses bothered to distinguish between "Woman" as white, straight, able-bodied, middle-class, Western/European, Protestant (etc.) and women whose experiences differed from that norm. Thus the consideration of lesbianism as a category of difference had to be forced into the discussions of many women's studies courses, and I often found myself being the spokesperson for "the" lesbian perspective. I think that my women professors felt threatened by this as well, as I forced them to deal with issues which seemed to them at the time more personal than academic. There were as yet no structures within the university system to validate and value academic studies that dealt with sexual preference.

Still, I was able to be out in my women's studies classes, and I did not dare to be out in my other courses. By the time I was a senior in college I had experienced a multitude of homophobic reactions to my lesbianism, both in and out of the classroom, ranging from disparagement and dismissal of my comments to threats and acts of physical violence, from both men and women students. This ever-present homophobia produced in me certain understandable psychological reactions, most of which can be found in studies of why so many gay people have histories of alcohol or drug problems, low self-esteem, and suicide attempts. It also made me extremely wary about how, and to whom, I would come out, either academically or personally.

Because of what I had learned about the dangers of being out, I was very careful not to mention my particular interest in lesbian studies when I applied to graduate schools in English my senior year. I did come out strongly as a feminist, as a women's studies major who intended to continue her pursuit of gender studies at the graduate level; but the word lesbian never appeared in my statement of purpose. Nor did I send any of my analyses of various dimensions of lesbianism as my writing sample; I chose instead to send off safe, straight papers that talked about dynamics of gender in various literary works, but didn't mention sexuality at all. I was convinced that announcing my lesbianism, or even hinting at it, would be sufficient to bar me from every graduate program in the United States; I had learned and internalized my homophobia quite thoroughly, even as I had based a lot of my academic life on my lesbian identity.

Much to my dismay, I soon discovered—after the deadline for graduate school applications had passed—that I had failed to share my reticence with the advisers who wrote my letters of recommendation. My thesis adviser sent me a copy of the letter she had written singing my praises to the sky. The letter had a full paragraph that talked about my lesbian scholarship and my outspoken contributions to class discussions, as well as about my lesbian-feminist activism in my community. Despite the fact that the letter also discussed the full range of my literary scholarship, and in no uncertain terms urged graduate programs to accept me, I was horrified. I was sure that the letter would prove the kiss of death to my application.

I now see that this incident marked the beginning of a pattern that would follow me through graduate school and the job market. My adviser, who was not (then) a lesbian, came out for me without asking or consulting me first—largely because she didn't realize that there was anything dangerous about coming out, and thus didn't think there was anything wrong with coming out for me without my knowledge or permission. She had seen only the positive side of my academic lesbianism: the scholarly studies, which had excited her with their insights, and the activism, which had earned her political approval as a feminist. I had not shared with her the threats, the homophobic comments, the terrors and traumas I had experienced as part and parcel of being out. She didn't think that coming out might be sufficient reason for graduate programs to reject me, regardless of my academic record; to her, my lesbianism was an academic credential.

As it turned out, she was right. As I later found out, my adviser's acknowledgment of my lesbian scholarship proved to be one of the deciding factors in my admission to the graduate program I most wanted to attend. Despite all my wary care, the secret had gotten out, and had gotten me in.

In graduate school, I continued the pattern I had begun as an undergraduate, of being out in feminist-oriented classes. This became easier throughout the 1980s, as considerations of race, class, sexual orientation, and other forms of "difference" increasingly had to be included in all analyses of gender dynamics. Lesbianism became more and more an acceptable, even sought-after, topic for academic exploration. This was due in part to the increasing numbers of out gay and lesbian academics who began to demarcate areas of gay and lesbian studies within their various disciplines, and eventually as an interdisciplinary field of study all its own. During the 1980s gay and lesbian studies followed something of the course that feminist studies had pioneered in the 1970s, being influenced as much, if not more, by activism outside the university as by scholarly pursuits within the university.

Because of the higher visibility and academic acceptability of gay/lesbian studies, during this period I was a lot braver about coming out in my nonfeminist classes, and I suffered many fewer negative responses. I still bore the scars of my earliest battles, however, and was cautious, though not silent, as a lesbian academic. While I would come out in seminar papers, I did not do so in conference papers or in other public forums in which I presented my research. When I chose my dissertation topic, I deliberately did not choose an overtly lesbian-oriented area of study, as I was still afraid that the label lesbian would be a hindrance in terms of getting things published, getting a job, and getting tenure.

This fear was confirmed by what I saw the few lesbian professors going through in trying to get tenure. One woman, whose work had earned national awards as groundbreaking in her discipline, was initially denied tenure by her department because some of the senior male members refused to have an out lesbian as a colleague. Her cause was eventually overturned by the president of the university, but only after an excruciatingly painful battle that included threats of lawsuits and student strikes in her support. Another professor remained completely closeted in terms of her scholarship, working only on safe gender issues without discussing sexuality; she vowed that she would start to write about gay and lesbian sexual issues after she got tenure, but not before. Though gay and lesbian studies was becoming more acceptable, the process was slow, and there were many martyrs to testify that being an out lesbian academic carried with it the strong possibility of homophobic responses.

With these cautionary models in mind, I prepared myself for the job market. The first time I went on the market I was very careful, as I had been in applying to graduate school, to make no mention of personal or professional lesbianism in my cover letter or my writing samples. I even went so far as to omit an actual publication from my vita because the title of the article contained the word "heterosexuality"—a sure clue, I thought, that the author was gay, because only gay people are careful to specify the "hetero" when discussing sexuality. I asked my dissertation director to look over my letters of recommendation to make sure that they didn't say anything, either overt or coded, about my lesbian scholarship or my lesbian identity.

The utility of this masking seemed confirmed when the more than sixty letters I sent out began to generate some response; I had several interviews at the MLA convention that year (1988). I dressed very carefully for my interviews, trying to find a correct balance between looking like a serious professional and looking as feminine as I am able to be; I wanted to be sure that my clothes didn't say more about me than I cared to mention. I did, of course, wear a skirt and makeup and earrings. This outfit seemed to have paid off in one interview, for a position which had been advertised as having a special focus on women writers. The interviewers were two very senior white men, both recognizable names in their fields, who began their questions after a quick glance at my vita by asking me about my work in "feminine studies."

Perhaps because being closeted had not paid off in a job offer the first time on the market, the next time I felt more reckless: I threw caution to the winds and put the publication with "heterosexuality" in the title back on my vita. I also applied for the one position that advertised for a candidate with a special interest in gay or lesbian literature.

Or so I thought. As it was a very small school, of no particular reputation, the interviewers' first question was, Why would a person with your credentials be interested in this job? I replied brightly that their ad had asked for a specialist in gay/lesbian literature, and that that had attracted me. The interviewers (two women and two men, if I remember correctly) turned pink, fingered their collars nervously, coughed dryly, and looked uncomfortable—and not at me. "Oh," one of the women finally said, "well, um, what we want is someone who can teach a lesbian novel in a women writer's course once every other semester, really." The interviewers went on to explain to me that their school was in a very small community, with not much demand for or interest in a whole course on, um, homosexual literature, and that their students tended to be very conservative. They themselves, of course, thought that such a course might be very interesting, but they doubted that there would be very many students who would take it, so it just wouldn't be feasible, would it? I knew I wouldn't hear from them again, and I didn't.

My best interview that year was with the English department of the University of Colorado at Boulder. (I can name names here because I got the job.) The interview went very well, with no particular mention of issues of sexuality, but no particular avoidance of them, either. I talked briefly about Gertrude Stein, and no one blinked an eye. I liked the interviewers' questions, and they apparently liked my answers, because they did ask me to fly out for an on-campus interview, and I was thrilled to go.

The interview went very well, I thought; the only peculiar moment was when a senior member of the department came up to me before my job talk and asked to speak to me privately. We went out in the hall, and I was asked, in hushed tones, if I would be interested in teaching a course in lesbian literature. Yes, I said firmly, I certainly would be. Later, when talking about this incident, I was pleased that lesbian literature seemed to be something the department would value, curious about the secrecy of the question, and puzzled about how this senior member knew to ask me. Had one mention of Gertrude Stein in the interview told more about me than I had suspected? The topic did not come up again during the rest of the day, and I didn't volunteer any hints about it, such as the fact that I would be coming with a female partner. Because she wouldn't need any help finding a job within the university, I didn't feel it necessary to include her existence as part of my salary and benefits discussion.

A friend of mine from graduate school had been hired in the English department at Boulder the year before, and I asked her about the senior member's question; she said she had mentioned to this senior member that I would be bringing a female partner with me to the job. I appreciated that the senior member had asked her question privately, as I was still not convinced that being out wouldn't adversely affect my chances at getting the job. While I was slightly annoyed with my friend for coming out for me without my permission, I figured that the damage would be minimal. Clearly the senior member felt that a lesbian literature course, and probably thus a lesbian professor, would be an asset to the department; the senior member would probably not mention our conversation to anyone else on the hiring committee.

Once again I was wrong. I did get the job, much to my delight, and my partner and I moved out to Boulder. My contract signed, I figured I had little to lose, and I discreetly told selected colleagues about my partner, as occasions arose—usually when I was invited to one of the numerous dinner parties given to introduce new faculty. I noticed that no one seemed surprised, which I attributed to the fact that Boulder is a pretty cool place, being one of the few cities in the US which had passed antidiscrimination laws protecting gays and lesbians in housing and employment. If anyone thought anything negative about my discreet coming out announcements, they at least knew it was terribly p.i. to say anything about it.

At one party, however, a department colleague was praising me for being so brave and being so out on the job market. I looked puzzled, and again wondered if discussing Gertrude Stein in the interview had revealed more than I intended. I asked my colleague how out I had been. What had tipped everyone off? The colleague looked puzzled and told me that everyone on the hiring committee had known. The senior member who had asked me about the lesbian literature course had written an enthusiastic memo recommending my hiring to the committee—a letter which explicitly said that one asset I would bring to the department was that I was an out lesbian. This letter was not only circulated among the members, it was read out loud at the meeting where the final hiring decision was made. Hadn't I know that?

Once again, someone had come out for me, in an important forum, without my knowledge or consent. And, perversely, once again that letter had had a positive effect, and may have made the difference in my being offered the job.

Sometimes I find this ironically funny. It's no good trying to be closeted, because the universe keeps making me be out in spite of myself. Sometimes I find this infuriating. How dare anyone presume to come out for me, to make a pronouncement that could have such negative repercussions on such centrally important aspects of my life? Most of the time, however, I find it a great relief. It's easier to be out, at least in my department, where everyone is either truly accepting or cool enough not to let it show. And I have nothing to hide or fear, as I did when I tried to veil both my lesbian identity and my lesbian scholarship; I'll get full departmental credit for having this article on my vita.

I am thrilled to have this job, in a department that is actively enthusiastic about lesbian and gay studies, and in which I have found full academic and social support. My story has a happy ending, the moral of which may be that my caution, my internalized homophobia, has been unnecessary and misguided.

But I have to end this piece with my worries, not my joys. I still find frustrating the lack of understanding, within the academic world, of the real-world problems of homosexuality. Those who have come out for me in the past have done so out of a spirit of helpfulness, but also out of ignorance of the possibility that such information could just as well be used against me as for me. I am also disturbed by the trend toward gay and lesbian (or queer) theories which construct gay identity as sets of ideas to be manipulated, rather than as concrete sets of practices embedded/embodied in complexly functioning human beings. I worry that the current popularity of gay and lesbian studies in the academy comes from the acceptability of these theoretical formulations, at the expense of concerns for real-world homophobia. Like feminist theories which became integrated into academic departments to the extent that they divorced themselves from direct political practice and concerned themselves with theoretical abstractions of gender, gay and lesbian studies within the academy seems to me to be in danger of losing its connection to the real world.

And, finally, I worry about one particularly pressing real-world problem: the growing trend, started right here in my own state of Colorado, toward legislation banning anti–gay discrimination laws. Such legislation effectively legalizes homophobia, and I wonder how successful any academic debates and publications can ever be in fighting the very concrete consequences of such sanctioned discrimination. As this kind of legislation appears on the ballots of more and more states, how will our efforts, as out lesbian and gay academics, affect the growing backlash against the "militant homosexual agenda"? These are questions that have more than theoretical ramifications, and to which we will have to find answers soon in order to save our own lives as well as those of our nonacademic brothers and sisters.

27

Queering the Profession,
or Just Professionalizing Queers?
Sarah Chinn

Profession: A public declaration; a business or profession that one publicly avows. . . . The declaration, promise or vow made by one entering a religious order; hence, the action of entering such an order. . . . The action of declaring, acknowledging or avowing an opinion, belief, intention, practice, etc. . . . The occupation which one professes to be skilled in and to follow. . . . In a wider sense: Any calling or occupation by which a person habitually earns his living.

—Oxford English Dictionary, 1971 ed.

Queer: Strange, odd, peculiar, eccentric, in appearance or character. Also, of questionable character, suspicious, dubious. . . . Not in a normal condition; out of sorts; giddy, faint. . . . Bad, worthless. . . . To spoil, put out of order. . . . differing in some odd way from what is usual or normal; mildly insane: touched. . . . absorbed or interested to an extreme or unreasonable degree: obsessed. . . . sexually deviate: homosexual.

—Oxford English Dictionary, 1971 ed.;
Webster's New Collegiate Dictionary, 1980 ed.

For we have to ask ourselves, here and now, do we want to join that procession [profession], or don't we? On what terms shall we join the pro[f]ession? Above all, where is it leading us, the pro[f]ession of educated men?

—Virginia Woolf, *Three Guineas*

As a lesbian academic I am committed to resisting being institutionalized.

When I was younger, "being institutionalized" was a polite way of saying someone was sent to the nuthouse, and we didn't really talk about that person anymore. Come to think of it, so was "being committed."

I want this essay to ask questions, not provide answers. We're in the middle of something, an efflorescence of queer-oriented academic work, that feels dizzying and risky, pleasurable and stimulating. But the advances of and inevitable backlashes against this work are not happening in a vacuum. Rather, they're unfolding in the context of academic institutions that lay down the ground rules within which such inquiry takes place—who gets listened to and who ignored; which work is legitimated, which discounted; what is valued, what is discarded. These negotiations are not innocent or unpredictable; they echo the calibrations of power, resistance, and absorption that vibrate throughout academia. As lesbians, gays, and bisexuals, educators must challenge the institutionalized racism and class bias of higher education, as well as cross borders that exist within our own communities. And yet we can't help but recognize the temptations and pleasures of belonging to any institution, the safety of the office, the paycheck, the name in print. For me at least, the minefield of queer studies is strewn with fragrant flowers as well as shattering mortars, and it's impossible to intuit which I'll step on at any given juncture. When we cross the minefield, do we leave it unchanged for those who follow behind us? Do we risk losing a limb, or dodge with our eyes closed, praying, or sprinkle more explosives behind us with the rationalization that the challenge of wading through bombs builds character? Do we drop the seeds for roses and hope they grow among the rubble, even as we leave them behind?

II

Letting the fashion industry influence your choice of clothes is a whopping mistake. . . . Your clothes should move you up socially and in business, not hold you back.
—John T. Molloy, *The Woman's Dress for Success Book*

[Men,] you can learn more from wearing a dress for a day than from wearing a suit for the rest of your life.
—Anonymous Queers, "Queers Read This"

At the March 1993 conference "Crossings Over: Queer Graduate Students and the Academy" at Columbia University, a young man stood up to comment on our discussion on being out as students and teachers. For him the basic problem was not how to speak his sexuality, but how to wear it. His passionate subjectivities—drag queen, gender bender, skirt-wearing sissy—were literally confined to the closet. In every classroom lurked the forbiddenness of his dreams of chiffon, silk, cotton, the sweet vulnerability of fabric rubbing against his thighs, the plain old funkiness of hairy legs against a swinging hem.

Professional men don't wear dresses.

III

I'm 26 years old, and I feel old-fashioned when I hear myself saying things like, "For a feminist, she really treats her students badly," as though a feminist ideological orientation should translate into day-to-day behavior. I've become aware that things don't necessarily work that way; power has a rich and tangled life of its own. I joke about it, hoping my listener will catch the trace of concern in my voice.

Throughout my time in queer studies I've recognized the centrality of learning from feminism, both academic and experiential. I've kept my ears and eyes open, trying to glean from teachers and colleagues the lessons that they can transmit from twenty-odd years of feminist scholarship and praxis to such a new and occasionally febrile field of inquiry. This is some of what I've seen: feminist professors fucking their students; feminists fucking their students over; lesbian administrators of women's studies programs sexually harassing their lesbian employees; Marxist feminists telling their students to choose between their children and their "real" work.

So much for prefigurative politics.

IV

To be a professional is to be public. Profession is a declaration of faith in front of the elect, a sign of conversion from the ways of common sin to the company of saints.

To be professional is to submerge our motivations, our desire, our (dare I say it in our post-postmodern, virtually real academic world?) agency to those of the institution. To recontextualize John Cotton: "In profession . . . [we] declareth not onely [our] good knowledge . . . but also [our] professed subjection to the [rules of the institution] with

[our] desire of walking therein." Is it any coincidence that Cotton advised against women professing in public, which would go against our natural modesty?

To be professional is to be legitimated (not altogether a bad thing); to deserve wider seats on airplanes, real glass instead of plastic; to be upscale.

To be professional is to be manipulated. As Paolo Freire has written,

> One of the methods of manipulation is to inoculate individuals with the bourgeois appetite for personal success. . . . Internalizing paternal authority through the rigid relationship structure empha-sized by the school . . . people tend, when they become professionals (because of the very fear of freedom instilled by these relationships) to repeat the rigid patterns in which they were miseducated. (Freire, 144, 153)

To be professional is to be paid for the work we do.

To be professional is to be a professional, not a worker; not to be amateurish; to be polished. ("Very professional, very good," said the man I recently counseled before his HIV antibody test. It's a compli-ment, but I'm an amateur. I do this work for love. There's no money in/for it.)

V

So here's a little personal history. I've already told you my age; I guess my age bracket makes me a "young professional." I'm a lesbian. I'm white. I grew up Jewish in an explicitly Christian country, England. I went to an all-girls school and we wore uniforms and one never ran in the hallways. I ran in the hallways, although I was an otherwise "good girl." I had a healthy disrespect for authority, which translated into attempting petty incursions against a given power structure while internalizing its primacy and taking its power over me for granted. Hence, I challenged authority while its exemplars got me hot and bothered. Life in uniform has a tendency to eroticize hierarchy, I've found.

I was raised to be a professional, and that's what I've turned out to be. The payoff is pretty good—long vacations, okay health benefits, free gym use for me and my "domestic partner," and I get to do the work I love. I have time to be an activist. I can afford to shop at the

Gap if that's my inclination (and given my class status and sexual orientation, chances are it is.)

But there are rules. Like every discursive system, the culture of professionalism attempts to make itself omnipresent and thus transparent, invisible. It maintains power through a delicate balance of approbation and punishment, through explicit rules and implicit etiquette; you know—"professional behavior" (no dresses, boys).

In his essay on gay studies and gay identity, Ed Cohen interrogates these rules and their very real application to his own job search: "One very supportive and well-meaning senior professor succinctly told me, 'You just can't use the word *gay* in your application.' (And I should say parenthetically that he also suggested very strongly that I cut my 'long' hair). . . . The experience of my own self-silencing—especially on a subject that it had taken me years to learn to speak and write about publicly—was acutely painful. Yet the payoff was clear" (Cohen 168). Cohen's payoff was one that seemed inevitable for a white male graduate student educated in an elite institution, carrying with him a "bouquet of academic awards" (167)—a job at Rutgers, name recognition in a growing academic discipline. This seems self-evident, and Cohen is willing to acknowledge it. Yet his honesty borders on a smugness that belies the rich array of choices he was offered and hardly mentions. What is the payoff for those job hunters without a prestigious Ph.D., for whom a shrinking job market could mean that the result of six or seven or more years of loans and temping and teaching wherever you can is, well, a dissertation that can't open too many doors, no matter what its title? Or those for whom the excision of the word "gay" on an application eviscerates the spirit and body of the work to which they have committed their academic career? For every compromise there are two questions, hovering like the emaciated, hollow-eyed children half hidden in the robe of the Ghost of Christmas Future: To whose benefit? At whose cost?

VI

Being queer is . . . not about the mainstream, profit-margins, patriotism, patriarchy, or being assimilated. It's not about executive directors, privilege and elitism. It's about being on the margins, defining ourselves; it's about gender-fuck and secrets, what's beneath the belt and deep inside the heart; it's about the night. Being queer is "grass roots" because we know that everyone of us, every body,

every cunt, every heart and ass and dick is a world of pleasure waiting
to be explored. Everyone of us is a world of infinite possibility.
                    —Anonymous Queers, "Queers Read This"

Reading "Queers Read This" on a hot and dizzying Lesbian and
Gay Pride Day a few years ago was an exhilarating experience. Here
were women and men rejecting the passivity of the discourse of rights
for an altogether different goal. As a child of the mid-1970s among
whose earliest memories are Watergate and the Brady Bunch, I found
language that spoke itself into being with anger and passion enticing,
seductive, even inspiring. Such an unvarnished call to solidarity, one
that celebrated the erotic and the cerebral, the active and the contem-
plative, appealed to my stifled political imagination.

The queer utopia promised by "Queers Read This," like many of
its predecessors, hasn't been realized yet. Nor, I think, did I expect it
to have been. For then, for now, the promise at least was enough.
Discord within the movement, the deaths of many of its leaders, and
the abandonment of its ranks by some for more comfortable places—
a seat at the table of power, or at least a place on the sofa in front of
the TV—have ground down the radical intentions of many activists.
After all, fighting a sexual revolution while wading through the disin-
tegrating bodies of our friends, lovers, comrades would make anyone
ready for a nice tenure-track position or at least a free E-mail account.

My fear is that whatever activist ethos the AIDS crisis summoned
up in the spiritually barren late 1980s has been little more than a
diversion from business as usual. That's not to say that progressive
social change has not been effected; the immensity of the backlash
against all elements of the left pays homage to our power, both actual
and chimerical. But that change is always on the cusp of getting swal-
lowed up by our voracious, much-vaunted service economy whose
motto is "a place for everything and everything in its place." Where
there is a place for queers to squeeze in and keep the academic machine
rolling, there will we reside. Cultural transformation will transmogrify
into domestic-partner benefits and nondiscrimination clauses. A few
radical dykes and fags will keep chugging along with a bit more visibility and grudging acknowledgment than before, but with the knowledge
that they must set and then exceed the boundaries of the acceptable
queer. Not that that's a bad position to be in; I welcome it for myself
even as I recognize that my radicalism occupies a paradoxical space
when it's attached to a Ph.D. and, more important, real power over
people's academic lives.

A friend in education studies, who read this essay before its completion, asked me, "What about teaching?" and that question holds a complexity and depth that belies its apparent simplicity. After all, as teachers we hope to effect some kind of transformation at least in our students, if not in the world. To be an openly lesbian teacher does challenge the expectations of students and employers alike; to teach queer material can shake up and expand the limits of a discipline; to be an out dyke student can reveal the strictures and biases of a classroom that excludes and silences queer voices as much out of a lack of imagination as out of unvarnished suppression.

But (and this is a but that feels very real to me) those possibilities do not germinate in a vacuum. The stakes of queer affiliation cannot be separated from those of institutional affiliation—how much room the institution allows to explore and teach lesbian and gay material, for example; whether there are more than a handful of out students in the entire college or university (I think here of states that have allowed their universities to effectively ban queer student organizations, or students who are simply too afraid for their lives to come out); how the resistance and homophobia of students and peers can make us bitter, resentful, and hateful and can blind us to the liberatory power that queer inquiry can embody. The recent debacle over lifting the ban on lesbians and gay men in the military is a horrifying example of how an institution can overwhelm and corrupt a political movement. As the US Air Force had just dropped bombs on Baghdad, killing dozens of civilians and soldiers for a months-old "reason," lesbians and gay men carried signs in the 1993 New York Lesbian and Gay Pride March reading, "We Support Our Gay Troops."

VII

> The invaluable forms of critique and dismantlement within the official tradition, the naming as what it is of a hegemonic, homoerotic/homophobic male canon of cultural mastery and coercive erotic double-binding, can be only part of the strategy of an antihomophobic project. . . . Most obviously, this would be necessary in order to support lesbian choices, talent, sensibilities, lives, and analyses.
> —Eve Kosofsky Sedgwick, *Epistemology of the Closet*

The possibility of remaining ourselves—angry, passionate, erotic, uncompromised—the possibility of transforming and healing a profession that seems calcified and fissured: we must not allow these things to feel or be unattainable. Our survival as lesbians depends on it.

Works Cited

Anonymous Queers. "Queers Read This." New York, 1990.

Cohen, Ed. "Are We (Not) What We Are Becoming? 'Gay' 'Identity,' 'Gay Studies,' and the Disciplining of Knowledge," in Joseph A. Boone and Michael Cadden, eds., *Engendering Men: The Question of Male Feminist Criticism*. New York: Routledge, 1990.

Cotton, John. *The Way of the Churches of Christ in New England*. London: Matthew Simmons, 1645.

Freire, Paolo. *Pedagogy of the Oppressed*. 1970. New York: Continuum, 1990.

Molloy, John T. *The Woman's Dress for Success Book*. New York: Warner Books, 1977.

Sedgwick, Eve Kosofsky. *Epistemology of the Closet*. Berkeley, CA: University of California Press, 1990.

Woolf, Virginia. *Three Guineas*. 1938. New York: Harcourt, 1966.

28

Life on the Fault Line:
Lesbian Resistance to the Anti-PC Debate

Toni A. H. McNaron

"Coincidence" no longer satisfies me as an explanation for oddly conjoined phenomena. Therefore, the current collision of a burgeoning of research and writing by and about lesbian history, culture, and theory with the virulent and often downright nasty attack on feminism and multiculturalism seems anything but accidental. Since its inception, the second wave of North American feminist activism and theorizing has been accused of being a "lesbian plot": first by misguided if committed heterosexual feminists; later by men and male-identified women worried about having to change fundamental ideas about how life is lived. While the current debate over political correctness (PC) has refrained from focusing on specific lesbian curricula and research, I do not believe that this deep-seated myth/fear has faded from such people's imaginations. Mary Daly has asserted that men often experience a woman's bonding with another woman as a withdrawal of attention from them. It is precisely this withdrawal of energy from their own preferred agenda that has so incensed academics spearheading the PC debate. Never mind that the arena has shifted from kitchen and bedroom to classrooms and refereed journals; the feelings are similar. These academics are angry at those of us no longer willing to limit our professional pursuits to the ideas and works of white male authors and scholars.

When I narrow my lens to consider the effect of the PC debate on future lesbian-feminist work in universities and colleges, I feel worried. In the past decade, a veritable flood of books and articles focusing on matters lesbian has appeared. *Signs* and *Feminist Studies,* two of the most prestigious journals in this country, along with *Hypatia,* a journal of feminist philosophy, plan special lesbian issues in the near future.

Lesbian-feminist scholars/theorists continue to uncover/discover/recover coded writers and events from our distant and not-so-distant past—a particular kind of intellectual archaeology that enriches our sense of history and strengthens our going forward into the next century assured that there always have been lesbian resisters.

Given all this good news, why am I worried? Primarily because this happy situation seems to me in large measure a consequence of the success of the broader feminist enterprise currently under vicious and well-funded attack by academics fighting to preserve an elitist, sexist, Greco-Roman heritage from perceived encroachments by women and minority writers.

I believe that curricular revision is a powerful strategy for continuing the production of lesbian knowledge. Courses on lesbian culture are taught in a number of women's studies programs, and such programs have in recent years stressed the importance of including lesbian material wherever relevant; it is also true that courses on lesbian literature or culture occasionally get taught within English or history departments, and up-and coming scholar-teachers in other fields, like anthropologist Kath Weston and sociologist Susan Johnson, are infusing courses with material about lesbians. But change at this level has been far less rapid or encompassing than some of us had hoped. And now faculty may well think twice before proposing courses on lesbian reality to curriculum committees peopled by colleagues emboldened by the media hype about "PC on campus" to vote against them.

And what about lesbian faculty and students—what is happening with their openness to self-identification in their classes or departments? The majority still fear coming out within the academy. Some of the reasons are old and familiar: endangering chances of promotion, most likely couched in some other terms; worrying about getting graduate fellowships when selection committees may be inhabited by homophobic faculty who remember linkages of one's name with certain conference paper titles or campus activities focusing on lesbian concerns. I know of graduate students who still ask their professors if there is some other way to sign up for a course whose title includes the word "lesbian," their eyes full of fear even as they evidence embarrassment at their political timidity. Since most of our campuses do not even have sexual orientation in their protected class statements, such vulnerable students and faculty have no legal protection upon which to rely. In the case of my own university, which has such a clause in its antidiscrimination statement, the atmosphere is not much better, because administrators are unwilling to bring policy into line with rhetoric for fear of antagonizing regents, parents, donors, legislators, and assorted others. Over a year ago, several of us introduced a policy extending benefits to domestic partners. We keep being told that the matter must wait until more pressing issues have been attended to. My most recent strategy was to place a motion before the campus senate striking sexual orientation from the protected class statement. I was unwilling to enable the president and his cabinet to claim they are addressing an urgent social concern, while remaining distinctly reluctant or oddly opaque about aligning campus practice with liberal rhetoric. However, my threat to cause public embarrassment led the president's office to pressure committees to vote on the proposal. At its spring 1993 meeting, the senate voted to refer to the Board of Regents a policy extending all benefits now enjoyed by heterosexual spouses to duly registered domestic partners.

Added to this familiar list of cautionary fears is the special vulnerability attendant upon being an open lesbian on campuses presently under attack from the academic right, that is, purveyors of the false argument about political correctness, a term behind which intellectual conservatives, antifeminists, and racists are hiding. Many of them list with pride their liberal credentials—lifetime membership in the ACLU, faithful contributions to the United Negro College Fund or other agencies devoted to helping minority students attend institutions of higher education, enlightened husbands who encourage their wives in careers or fathers who fund their daughters' years in law or medical school. But to resist curricular reform that opens up the canon to multicultural voices and to insist on retaining or reinscribing only the classics of Western civilization is to be part of a very old movement within higher education predicated on intellectual white supremacy—never mind if such faculty boast that some of their best friends are blacks and women.

This charged climate is exerting subtle pressure on lesbian scholars and teachers of this generation and the next to tone down, to pull in, to fade back a bit. I see this pressure succeeding in such linguistic ways as the current willingness to subsume programs which seek to examine the history and nature of lesbian sexuality under the less strident umbrella designation of "gender studies." Many's the time I have heard colleagues say with a wry smile, "Oh, you know what that means. So-and-so is really going to conduct lesbian research but knows the NEH is off funding programs that say they are focused on lesbianism." While I am willing on occasion to shape language to win monetary support, especially from institutional agencies, I nonetheless worry about the methods and outcomes of research that has had to advertise itself in less than honest terms.

At the very least, such strategic moves introduce a new level of coding seemingly necessary in some quarters if additional funding is to come to lesbian projects. I conceive of such ventures as existing along a fault line which offers its researchers little or no real safety, leaving them in the precarious position of being called on the carpet for being wolves in sheep's clothing. I want to live out my life as an academic lesbian feminist on firmer footing, wanting our own campus funding agencies and those outside to award us grants and support precisely because we are doing open lesbian work, not because we make ourselves presentable enough to fit into some narrow definition of worthiness.

We are poised at a dangerous if exciting moment in the generation of new knowledge in fields of lesbian research. It has not been that long since both faculty and students silenced or severely muted our lesbian intelligence. In my Shakespeare courses, I can track a journey from my insisting that his sonnets to the young man were merely paeans to platonic friendship, to my presentation of the sequence as a cogent example of Shakespeare's fear of intimacy with either the young man or the dark lady, of his distaste for heterosexuality to which he seems nonetheless addicted, and of his strong homoerotic impulses. On my campus this fall, rumor had it that the anti-PC people had recruited student plants who were going to begin infiltrating classes taught by feminists and multiculturalists. At my stage in the profession—I am a full professor with twenty-eight years of service and am completely out in my department—I can afford to ignore such unfortunate possibilities. After all, the FBI may still have the thin file in my name which it set up during the days of the anti–Vietnam War movement. In fact, I attribute my openness as a lesbian scholar-teacher with insulating me from any overt effort to undermine my work. By being out at the university, I effectively disarm the anti-PC critics who often depend upon veiled threats to intimidate younger or less protected members of university communities.

But my untenured colleagues and the lesbian graduate students just flexing their intellectual muscles must pay more attention to these ugly rumors. And I worry that they will need to shade their best insights and abbreviate their truest findings in the present atmosphere full of scare tactics from the academic right.

For lesbian research to achieve the maturity which it and its hungry readers deserve, institutions of higher learning must supply intellectual nurturance and protection in the form of rigorous academic freedom. Yet this need collides, not coincidentally, with the increasing pressure on administrators to discipline and monitor the voices of epistemological change on their campuses. A visible mass of such voices will be lesbian, and we must insist that our applications for grants, leaves, awards, research assistants, and the like be judged on their merits quite apart from what some of our colleagues may think about our work or our lives. Last year I chaired a committee that nominated candidates for outstanding teaching awards. One of our choices was an open lesbian scholar whose teaching has long been praised. When she was passed over, a heterosexual male dean and I sought an explanation from the chair of the final selection committee. We were told of statements made about our candidate which were clearly coded remarks about her ability to teach well despite her being a lesbian. Even the dean was offended at this cowardly tactic by faculty ascribing to the tenets of the anti-PC debate.

A healthy practice in my English department is for faculty and graduate students to organize ourselves into study groups structured along generic, periodic, or theoretical lines. One of the liveliest of these is the lesbian theory group. Like the other groups, we advertise meetings in the English department newsletter. Last spring, just as we were hearing that our campus would host a projected regional convention of anti-PCers, the lesbian theory group met to discuss Christina Rossetti's provocative poem "Goblin Market." To my astonishment, we were joined by a professor who is the regional leader of the conservative National Association of Scholars. His literacy training is in the nineteenth century, but he had read neither Rossetti nor the critical essays designated for discussion. He spent much of the hour sizing up the participants, most of whom were graduate students who had until that time felt safe to be in the group.

Several days after this unnerving session, the same professor stopped me in the hall and asked, "Are all the members of your group lesbians?" My instant impulse was to protect the younger scholars-in-the-making from the prying of a homophobe with the nerve to accuse me and my feminist colleagues of stifling debate and cutting off the free exchange of ideas. "Oh, no," I answered, "I'm sure not, though I don't ask that question myself, since we are there to discuss lesbian literary theory, not what it's like to live as a lesbian." I believe we lesbians on campuses must stock up on responses to such intrusive questions, since they often are so unexpected as to stun us into momentary silence just when we need a bright, pointed rejoinder. At the next group meeting, I did not hesitate to ask the graduate students their reactions to our visitor. They were nervous, puzzled, and uncomfortable, but they were also savvy. As one eloquently put it, "I felt like taking a bath when that gentleman left."

Extending the frontiers of knowing through vigorous investigation of matters historically silenced within our institutions of higher learning, whether done by lesbian scholars or our colleagues in feminist and multicultural studies, will alter the academic establishment. This alteration will undoubtedly make certain members therein uncomfortable; it may even offend some. Such consequences usually attend the creation of new knowledge. I recall the terrible reactions to sixteenth-century scientists who dared assert that the earth was not the center of the universe. Proponents of Copernician theory were drummed out of their universities or, in extreme cases, excommunicated, jailed, even killed. Those of us working to open curricula and research in this last decade of the twentieth century are part of another paradigmatic moment. While none of us will be so obviously punished, I am not convinced that we will be able to pursue our future work in optimal conditions. Virginia Woolf was convinced that many women writers' creativity was wasted or at least handicapped by anger and frustration over how their creations would be viewed by society. If lesbian-feminist research and teaching are to flourish, its practitioners must have conducive surroundings. The present animosity emanating from the likes of Christine Sommers and Dinesh D'Souza is antithetical to the open pursuit of intellectual theories and the expansion of curricular offerings. We must stand and resist wherever possible these onslaughts against our vital and long overdue work.

Such firmness calls for a variety of specific strategies. My own include the following: I am seeking colleagues who are out in other departments with whom to form alliances, so that when programmatic decisions are being made in the governance bodies of my college, I will have tangible support for lesbian-related matters. This means that I must extend similar support to them for policies and programs central to their work—a demand that will add to my already crowded schedule, but that is only fair if I expect their support. I have pledged to continue to speak honestly with students about what I see as false and repressive arguments against feminist and multicultural work, even if one of them turns out to be a plant of the anti-PC faculty or if others complain that I am politicizing the classroom.

Most important of all, I must refuse to recede into anyone's closet. This will entail saying the "l-word" at department meetings and in all the corridors of my professional life and asking the perennial question "What about the lesbians in this case?" It will mean continuing to help students see that Emily Dickinson's poetry is homoerotic, or that Shakespeare and Milton are drawn to and punitive of their own impulses toward gender likeness, or that a lesbian lens on literature will significantly enrich and clarify works and theories we have grown up with or are only just discovering. Most certainly, it will involve mentoring lesbian students and junior faculty rather more actively than I have in the past, because, as our future, they are the most vulnerable and precious of us all.

Notes

This essay was originally printed in the *Women's Review of Books* 9:5 (February 1992), in a special issue dealing with feminist reaction to the anti–political correctness debate then raging in the United States.

29

Gay and Lesbian Studies: Yet Another Unhappy Marriage?[1]

Jacquelyn N. Zita

The attempt to create an interdisciplinary area of queer studies, however it is named, has become a recent arena of academic struggle. Using the term queer studies seems to sidestep the contentious decisions of which categories to include and which should come first—lesbian, gay, bisexual, transgender, and so forth. Although meeting strenuous objection among older gay and lesbian academics, "queer" as a preferred term establishes a commonality of enterprise, an area of coherency overlapping lesbian, gay, bisexual, and transgender experience and scholarship. Queerness provides a positionality from which differences, such as class, race, gender, and sexual style, can be further theorized and reevaluated. As Lisa Duggan has written, queer theories place "the production and circulation of sexualities at the core of Western cultures, defining the emergence of the homosexual/heterosexual dyad as an issue that no cultural theory can afford to ignore" (23). From a pragmatic and institutional point of view, queerness must first be named as one side in a duality of oppression forged by heterosexual hegemony and its mandate of gender consonance. "Queer" like "woman" or "subaltern" is a pragmatically generic and diffuse category, outlining an area for legitimate academic condensation and contestation.

My concern, however, is with the nature of the marriage hidden behind the veil of queerness. I want to focus on a smaller but core subset of difficulties subsumed under queer studies, namely the dyadic conjunction of gay and lesbian studies. For the moment I will suspend analysis of bisexual and transgender studies and reflect on the union between the sexes required for the enterprise of gay and lesbian studies.[2] My concern is with the cosexual nature of gay and lesbian studies and

the translation of that cosexuality into a new heterosexual contract—
a marriage of minds, energies, and emotions to the academic project
of a new hybridized knowledge.[3]

Why should lesbian feminists accept this proposal? In 1984, Gayle
Rubin articulated the move from feminist theory to queer theory:
"lesbian feminist ideology has mostly analyzed the oppression of lesbians in terms of the oppression of women. However, lesbians are also
oppressed as queers and perverts, by the operation of sexual, not
gender, stratification" (308). According to this view feminist theory
has a tendency to subsume sexuality under gender, while the study of
sexuality requires its own discursive autonomy. Queer theorists argue
that sexuality is not fully comprehended in feminist analyses of gender
oppression and male domination. Accordingly, some lesbian academics
are encouraged by gay colleagues to leave the shelters of women's
studies and other departments and begin this new knowledge-seeking
project.

As a lesbian, I may understand the need for queer inquiry. As a
feminist, I understand the need to maintain feminist subjectivity and
autonomy in alliances with men. Not all lesbian academics want to
embrace the project of gay and lesbian studies, and not just for reasons
of closet securities. Yet there exists in myself—a white lesbian women's
studies tenured professor—a schizophrenic pull: the part of me which
often gets silenced in women's studies in the mixed company of heterosexual women is a more vibrant and playful queerness; the part of me
that gets silenced in the company of gay men is a more militant feminism. I can and often do speak out when the battles on either side seem
worthy of effort and urgency, but in both cases I feel self-monitored and
not entirely present, often challenged and at times confused.

Thus I often ask myself why I should venture away from a working
environment in women's studies with predominantly white, female
heterosexual colleagues who have done more work on homophobia
and other oppressions than many gay male academics have done on
sexism, or for that matter, race and class oppression. The stretch from
women's studies to gay and lesbian studies seems risky, the traps
multiple. Privileging the oppression of homosexuals may be necessary
to forge a new academic enterprise, but if this entails submerging the
differences between the sexes and erasing over two decades of feminist
work on gender, race, class, and heterosexuality, the effort may not
be worth it. The results could be fatal: the silencing of women and
unequal female sacrifice in yet another unhappy marriage. In what
follows I will elaborate on the danger zones for lesbians who fall for

gay men, even though the question for many may seem, as it were, purely academic.

The privileging of gay oppression. In the worst of heterosexual marriages, woman is incorporated under man, ensuring the loss of name and the loss of authority to name her realities. In gay and lesbian studies, the commonality of queerness, the crisis of urgency sirened by right-wing aggression on college campuses, and the perceived need for us to work together can result in the incorporation of lesbianism under gay-male centered paradigms and an erasure of difference between lesbians and gay men. This happens in blatant and in subtle, perhaps even unintentional ways, in the privileging of gay oppression.

An example of the latter can be seen in Joe Neisen's article "Heterosexism: Redefining Homophobia for the 1990s," in which he persuasively argues that the term "internalized homophobia" should be replaced with the phrase "shame due to heterosexism," thus shifting the location of blame away from the victim and onto the oppressing system. This is an important remapping of meaning and politics, but a problem emerges in attempts to translate this into operational measures. How would one separate shame due to sexism from shame due to heterosexism in the experiences of white lesbians? How would one separate shame due to racism, sexism, and heterosexism in the experiences of lesbians of color? Are the "shames" of internalized oppression color-coded or tagged by origin? In Neisen's essay, there is little pursuit of these difficulties.[4] The homogenizing term "shame due to heterosexism," while covering a gamut of self-destructive feelings and behaviors internalized and acted out by lesbians and gays, prioritizes the hegemony of one oppression, namely that of white middle-class men, as the paradigm of queer oppression. Terms such as "heterosexism," "homophobia," and "shame due to heterosexism" seem to hang in the air—genderless, raceless, and classless—defining a problem that relies on the denial of difference, the erasure of multiple oppressions, and the luxury of a singular cause.

Exclusionary intellectual practices. Over the last decade feminist writings on epistemology and science have argued that it makes a difference who says what when and to whom. Theories primarily built on the interests and values of white, heterosexual, economically and academically privileged men tend to distort and erase the experiences of those who are marginalized by these knowledge-seeking projects. Theoretical feminism has belabored the importance of articulating multiple perspectives and standpoints in the production of knowledge—an epistemic project far from completion but at least working towards inclusivity. Thus, it is disappointing when queer theorists unreflectively practice exclusion in their theory building, and even more disappointing when it is lesbian feminists who are among the marginalized.

This strategy of exclusion operates in Steven Epstein's argument that an "ethnicity model" best serves the philosophical and political interests of gays and lesbians and that this model synthesizes a moderate position in the seesaw debate between social constructionists and essentialists which pervades much of recent queer theory. While it is not my intention to review Epstein's ideas, I would like to draw attention to the essay's infrastructure and the theoretical containment of lesbian feminist ideas on essentialism and constructionism. First of all, there is simple omission. Very few feminist and lesbian-feminist theorists are mentioned in the article, as if the constructionism vs. essentialism debate were a conversation which is ongoing among and between gay male theoreticians, if not "owned" by Gagnon and Simon, Foucault, Plummer, and Boswell.[5] Secondly, the social constructionism vs. essentialism debate is recast by Epstein as a familiar philosophical conflict between nature vs. nurture or realism vs. nominalism, with constructionism's theoretical foundation grounded in symbolic interactionist theory, labeling theory, cultural anthropology, and the works of Michel Foucault. It is as if this ongoing dialogue, which is presented as the cutting-edge conversation on social constructionism, has only included Mary MacIntosh, the only woman usually mentioned in gay male introductions to these issues, and gay theoreticians, who seem to know nothing, care nothing, and have probably read nothing, of feminist social constructionist theory.[6] Feminists are quickly dismissed as naive essentialists, as fussy P.C. gangs, or as ghettoized theoreticians of a heterosexual problematic where men and women are forced to come to terms with gender.[7]

As Marylin Frye has recently argued in "Feminist Theory and Ontological Commitment," this pattern of omission, judgmental closure, and ghettoization of feminist and lesbian-feminist work on gender serves to obfuscate the heart of feminist social constructionist theory—namely an analysis of gender that examines the processes and mechanisms of socially constructed "men" and "women" as a central dynamic in women's oppressions in male supremacies. This is certainly not only a heterosexual issue; it is a matter of acknowledging the imbalance of power between women and men and a matter of reeducating men (and women) to this perspective. Gay men do not hold exclusionary status—they are still men. In his omissions, Epstein's representation of social constructionist theory overlooks two decades of feminist and lesbian-feminist political work on gender and sexuality, subsuming this under an ethnicity model which homogenizes queers and obscures women's heterosexualized labor in ethnic reproduction. For a theoretician interested in liberatory theory, this is quite simply unreflective supremacist misbehavior.

Camping up gender and gutting out feminism. While feminism has been accused of subsuming sexuality under gender, the reverse is evoked by many of the current paradigms in queer theory: gender is subsumed under an expansive notion of sexuality. One finds a preference in Anglo-American queer theory for analyses of gender based on performance theory, theatrical aesthetics, and interactionist and liminality models, engaged in the "politics" of "resistance to" or "creative reappropriation" of heterosexual hegemony.[8] These approaches tend to shrink gender to its local sites of performance and scene, assigning gender to the level of culture and the sexual symbolic, while gutting out a concept of gender as more than the individual and more than repetitiously performed. While I am personally drawn to the intellectual challenge of these new performance models, what is lost in their application is an understanding of gender as materialist and structural and as deeply embedded in nonsexual as well as sexual contexts which are rife with a long history of violent conflict and power struggles between the sexes, races, and classes.[9]

Unlike analyses of gender that reveal the materialist conditions of women's oppression, the abuse of white male privilege, the power politics of masculinity and femininity, race, and class, and the crisis of women's subjectivity and autonomy under the prerogatives of multiple hegemonies, current performance theories of gender seem to rely on what Kennedy and Davis have referred to as "queen aesthetics" and its insular sexualization of gender. According to Kennedy and Davis, "queen resistance" and "lesbian butch resistance," at least in their study of the Buffalo, New York, lesbian and gay communities, rely on entirely different resources. "Queens based their strategy of resistance on wit, verbal agility, and sense of theater and use these to create a common culture" (383). In lesbian butch artifice, according to Kennedy and Davis, there is usually nothing really humorous or explicitly theatrical: "the butch persona is centered on physically taking care of lesbians—butches and fems—and protecting and defending women's right to live independently from men and pursue erotic liaisons with women. . . . Butch effectiveness was based on concretely usurping male prerogatives in order to assert women's sexual autonomy and to defend a space in which women could love women" (383).

In contrast, "queen aesthetics" lends itself to a theorization of gender solely in terms of performance theory, often resulting in an insular sexualization of gender which reduces gender to an extended concept of sexual aesthetics, style, and individual expression, readily appropriated by postmodernist cultural queer theory and new queer liberalism. Within the history of women's oppression and lesbian repression, however, "gender" as an aesthetic gives way to a politics of nascent radical feminism, an awareness of the antagonistic social relations between the sexes and the density of historical and political contexts where gender performatives and encoded pleasures are located. The luxury of theorizing gender solely as a performance, an aesthetic, or an erotic script outside of these historical contexts is a function of social and theoretical privilege, where gender is radically deconstructed as an ontology-free artifice of sexual semiotics by the postmodern constructionists or as a history-free stylistic by whatever-turns-you-on pro-sex liberals. From the perspective of women's history, gender is more than an individual expression or a performative orientation toward fucking and flaunting, although it certainly may include these. Thinking in a more sophisticated way about gender may upset the guests at a contemporary "genderfuck" gala, but it is historically and more inclusively honest to the experiences of both sexes and all races and classes. Thinking more deeply about gender allows us to take seriously the possibility of historicized lesbian-feminist or protofeminist standpoints.

Gay genes and lesbian choices (or, who's more essentialist than thou?). While lesbian feminists have often been accused of being essentialist, ahistorical, and metaphysically frigid, there is a striking essentialist streak in the recent work of Le Vay and other gay male empiricists. Le Vay's work attempts to ground male homosexual orientation on a brain difference which he has discovered in dead gay brains. While this research is remarkably flawed,[10] it represents a tendency to locate a biological cause for sexual orientation in the inevitable proclivities of the body rather than in the intelligence of the human mind. Le Vay's work included no dead lesbian brains, nor has he obviously consulted the literature that springs from living lesbian brains on sexual orientation. Given Le Vay's theoretical persuasion, lesbian brains should have hypothalamic interstitial nuclei patterns like those of male heterosexuals (with a preference for women) as gay male brains have patterns like those of heterosexual females (with a preference for men). It would seem that sex brains are trapped in the wrong body again.

On the continuum of constraint vs. choice in sexual orientation, lesbian and obviously bisexual writing on sexual orientation, more frequently than gay male theory, is often couched in terms of choice rather than cause.[11] It is possible that this preference for choice over cause is a function of female resistance and agency in the context of women's oppression: for lesbians and queer-identified female bisexuals, it may feel like there are good reasons to exit the institution of female heterosexuality and its overdetermined abuse of female femininity. In contrast, the male penchant for biological determinism and its popular articulation as a civil rights strategy reflects unexamined aspects of male privilege and an investment in binary ontologies: for gay men it may feel like there should be no good reasons to leave the fold of heterosexual male privilege unless one cannot help it. At this binary switch point in the great hetero/homo division of bodies, there is no space for fluidity, choice, invention, and erotic ambiguity, just the mechanics of penile erection and only one of two object targets mediated by brain chemistries. The essentialism behind this research agenda is to discover what it is that makes a man gay. This immutable trait can then be treated like race and sex as an axis for civil rights protestation.

The essentialism which emerges in gay male empiricism and politics, unlike the penchant for postmodern constructionism in academic queer theory, sheds more light on what has become the lethal wound of lesbian feminism, namely, the unforgivable error of essentialism committed by lesbian feminists, lesbian separatists, and cultural feminists. A careful reading of this alleged essentialist canon, however, reveals that lesbian essentialism, where it is deployed, is not like that of Le Vay's camp.[12] Lesbian-feminist essentialism, so-called, is perhaps best understood in the context of women's oppression, as an effort to construct identifiable communities of lesbians to protect a space for woman-centered discourse, erotic and affectional expression, flirting and dancing, and political/cultural practices. It is a pragmatic essentialism (Fuss) or a way of forming identifiable communities (Hoagland), sometimes subject to misuse in racist and classist contexts, but nonetheless a call for women to separate internally, intellectually, libidinally, and externally from the domain of male hegemony and its long history of sexually colonizing and heterosexualizing the female sex (Frye, 1983). When the white queer critic charges lesbian feminists with essentialism, the real question is not who is more essentialist—gay men or lesbian feminists—but how gendered interests and politics implicitly inform the essentialisms and antiessentialisms of gay men and lesbian feminists, and when essentialism is no longer essentializing or no longer doing metaphysics with our bodies and desires.

The Achtenberg affair and the forced marriage. Since the 1993 March on Washington, new ultraconservative homophobia has become even more inclusive of lesbians, as can be seen in the public attacks on Roberta Actenberg, President Clinton's lesbian-identified administrative appointee and the first open homosexual confirmed by the US Senate for a high-level public office. Senator Jesse Helms has referred to Achtenberg as a "damn lesbian," and Jerry Falwell has created a new videotape, "The Achtenberg Affair," which focuses on the maverick kiss between a lesbian public official and her partner in the presence of their son at a Los Angeles Gay Pride march.[13] This attention marks a new epoch of lesbian hating, as lesbians move from relative invisibility into the higher ranks of government. The marketing of "The Achtenberg Affair" reveals that as lesbians enter more openly into the state apparatus, we are portrayed as a threat to the civil order, and as we do this, we are also homo/genized with gay men as the compliant female deviant of the gay agenda. In all of this, lesbian-feminist analyses of the state, electoral politics—of why not to form alliances with males and why there is a need for separatism—are erased by this media-made Falwellian marriage of the two sinning sexes serving under the flag of the L-word, now understood as "liberalism."

Pressure from the New Right, the AIDS crisis, and concerted efforts to pass new and more inclusive civil rights and other legislation in various states and at the national levels have converged in the demand that we must urgently work together as gays, lesbians, bisexuals, and transgender people for a common cause. In this time of crisis, exigency, and political pressure, female compassion and male seduction may be operative in ways that allow us as lesbians to forget our feminism. We are encouraged in the name of unity and historical urgency to work together—to assume a relentless drive toward status quo normalization or to assume a relentless engagement in the antics of in-your-face antinormalization.[14] In all of this panic, the issue for a lesbian feminist is with whom and for whom to stand, and why. As philosopher Sandra Harding has commented, the consequences for women who choose to work with men can be both epistemologically and ontologically dangerous: "Isn't it the worst kind of agenda to force women back into their traditional role of collaborators, their conventional position as men's helpmates? Many female feminists would rather be run over by a truck" (145).

Male approval and postfeminism. In many ways, gay and lesbian studies enters academia as the fledgling son with the Oedipalized wish to seek approval from the ruling fathers as a legitimate field of study with enough academic respectability to forge careers, names, and positions of prominence. However, the ruling fathers of the academy are by and large heterosexual or seriously closeted, so a strategy must be created that cuts through the virulent homophobia and ridicule directed toward the idea of gay and lesbian studies. Since the area in which academics feel most comfortable is theory, especially theory heavy with centuries of Eurocentric inloading, the polysyllabic turn toward theory becomes a way to seek institutional legitimacy and approval.[15]

The theoretical hauteur of queer theory occupies a niche with other bedfellows—the gender studies of postfeminism, poststructuralism, and postmodernism—produced during a period of rising capitalist backlash against feminism and women's studies. Like these other new areas of specialization, much of queer theory has hastily moved into esoterics and away from community politics. The result is a theory production for the chosen few (a new class of queer professionals), who can follow the appropriated curves and contours of Foucauldian, Lacanian, and Derridean (aca)robics in a conversation unrelated (if not unintelligible) to the political movements and communities that spawned the queer elite. This rapid ascent into the esoteric echelons of academic discourse seems not only related to a quick resolution of male Oedipal tension between disgraced gay sons and forgiving straight fathers, but also a quick cover of the ass—an overreactive if not homophobic attempt to sanitize and intellectualize over the cultural shame and embodied grit that grounds queer studies in the body and its heady sexual desire.

Feminist scholars who have not been heavily schooled in the privileged Eurocentric discourses appropriated by queer theory may find themselves marginalized from this drama between sons and fathers. However, it appears as if our role is not to participate, except occasionally as the snazzy superstar or as the exception. It seems as if our other role is secondary but crucial. While we as lesbian feminists may be simultaneously lampooned as devotees of the expressive politics, as naive essentialists, as humorless PC terrorists who lack style, and as typical women unable to do real theory, our role as gay wives and sweethearts of the new gay male academic is used to mollify the fears of the ruling fathers. At least the son returns, an educated, elite academic star in a sexless and intellectual marriage with the opposite sex. This problem is compounded if the marriage is interracial or too multicultural, since institutional approval encourages racial purification—a "white, straight-looking" couple. Why should we as lesbian-feminist academics participate in this drama? this conversation? this ritual of white male self-sanitation? Why should we learn yet another language of exclusion when there are countless other things to do, especially for lesbians?

Conclusion: Bitching Out

A lesbian and gay studies classroom, University of Minnesota, 1990: A white male student makes a point using the term "bitchy." An exasperated feminist student, a white female, reacts, drawing attention to the implications of sexism in the derogatory use of the term "bitch." This was discussed in class. Tension persisted.

I have been taken by surprise in writing this essay by my anger and bitterness. Many who know me and my commitment to lesbian, gay, bisexual, and transgender studies will also find this unusual, so I would like to turn to my optimism. I am not against committing some part of myself to the project of lesbian and gay studies.[16] Lesbian absence from this project will assuredly commit us to our further erasure from queer scholarship. At the very least out lesbian academics could hope for some help in opening academic closets and academic minds in queer studies. However, what is most frustrating for me, after thirteen years of my academic life in women's studies, is the backlog of unexamined sexism and the unawareness of other types of oppression often typical of gay men wanting to build the union of lesbian and gay studies. Certainly this is not true of all my male colleagues, including some male graduate and undergraduate students, many of whom have proven precious and conscious allies in this struggle. However, in contrast to the level of consciousness concerning sexism, racism, classism, and the like in women's studies (however roadblocked it may be), my decision to move partially forward into lesbian and gay studies requires personal and collective introspection with other lesbian aca-

demics. As one of my lesbian colleagues told me, there would be much
less of a conflict if we could create a lesbian studies program.

There is perhaps an alliance structure for lesbian and gay studies
which appeals to academics with both separatist and conjunctionist
leanings. It is important that both sexes have their separatist camps
politically and socially, and separate specialized courses on lesbian or
gay studies. However, what I find challenging and problematic are the
conjunctive courses in lesbian, gay, bisexual, and transgender studies
or queer studies.[17] Here it is important for those of us who are interested
to set our terms as lesbians and as feminists for our participation in
these endeavors and not resign ourselves to the secondary status of
traditional wifery in either practice, research, and scholarship or imagination and politics.

Regardless of the obstacles I have described in this essay, I see some
hope in the healthy tensions and contradictions of a lesbian and gay
intellectual endeavor: namely, the possibility of reopening a wider
discussion on gender, sexuality, class, race, and other differences in
the context of queer experience. As Eve Sedgwick has suggested, "it
seems inevitable to me that the work of defining the circumferential
boundaries, vis-à-vis lesbian experience and identity, of any gay male–
centered theoretical articulation can be done only from the point of
view of an alternative, femininocentric theoretical space, not from the
heart of the male-centered project itself" (39). Although Sedgwick in
her work acknowledges that she has not addressed this "scandalously
extended eclipse," the project still calls for careful articulation in its
communication and possible partnership with gay male theory.

Clearly, lesbian separatist literature was never meant to engage in
this project with men, but gay male scholars may blithely take this as
permission to ignore, ridicule, and superficially discard more than
two decades of lesbian-feminist work. At the same time, I find the
exaggeratedly negative stereotypes of heterosexual and gay men sometimes deployed in lesbian feminist and lesbian separatist writing in
need of a challenge from the cosexual interaction and self-reflective
dialogue engendered in lesbian and gay studies. This kind of honest
dialogue between women and men, uncluttered by the necessity to
reproduce heterosexual coercions and scripts, is something to hope
for in queer studies. Obviously, my reflections in this essay suggest
that such a state of interpersonal communication is yet to be achieved
and cannot be taken as a given. Communiqués from the heterosexual
front, from Angela Hamblin, Barbara Krasner, Amanda Utis-Kessler,
Naomi Wolf, and other women intimately involved in radical hetero-

sexual or liberatory het/bisexual practices, indicate that heterosexual relationships seem as historically unpromising or as treacherously difficult as they ever were. This does not bode well for the heterosocial project of lesbian and gay studies.

However, this new alliance between lesbians and gay men is forced into view because gay men need us. The emergence of lesbian and gay studies and queer studies coincides with the increasing momentum of the gay civil rights movement. This is no accident. These alliances require that gay men and lesbians march together, but there is no cultural mandate for gay men to "love and honor" the new brides of the civil rights and queer academic movements. The wedding of lesbians and gays to a common cause will require a move beyond the old rules of heterosexual marriage to new configurations of carefully limited and conscious alliances between lesbians and gay men and a new modeling of heterosocial or bisocial affectivities. It is here that I find some hope as I find hope in all "traitorous identities and practices" (Harding, Frye ["Some Reflections"]) which can emerge from the sites of social and historical privilege—in this case from white, economically and academically privileged gay men. Just as white lesbian feminists are making an effort to unlearn the habits and practices of racism and other oppressor behaviors, so I think a similar measure of hope and struggle may be possible with regard to gay men's sexism and their consciousness of oppressions.

Obviously this plea for constructive use of white male power and privilege reproduces the white context in which my entire essay has been situated. This is in part institutional in so far as lesbian and gay studies must work hard to diversify itself in class and race privileging institutions such as universities and colleges. Secondly, this is structural in so far as tenured faculty in a position to create an institutional space for lesbian and gay studies within the white male power structure of a university tend to be privileged by race and class. Creating such an interdisciplinary space is a task that only a few ranked faculty members seem willing to assume, and having sufficient institutional privilege becomes ironically a useful asset. Finally, my perspective is racialized by my own white identity and by the white tendency of privileging the individual while ignoring the efficacy of race identity in the construction of that privilege. White gay male regard for lesbian writing and scholarship would thus seem a detour from the strategies of individual-centered gay politics and academic careerism.

In contrast the writings of some gay men of color express a remarkable respect for and political bonding with lesbians of color within a politics of resistance forged by race identity and the survival metaphors of family. While lesbians of color have written less directly about their bonding with gay brothers of color and more about white lesbian separatism as a potential dislocation from deeper affinities in race and ethnicity, I take this to mean that gays and lesbians of color have a different cause to alliance, though not without some gender troubles, than that orchestrated by the white male call to arms in the name of a raceless and classless queerness. I have the feeling that gay writers of color, such as Donald Woods, Louis Alfaro, and Robert Reid Pharr, have seriously read and appreciated the works of their sisters. As a young African-American gay man said to me in an informal conversation at the OutWrite '93 Conference, "it's the race thing that brings us [African-American gays and lesbians] together, and we owe a lot to our sisters for breaking the ground."[18] Perhaps the search for "traitorious identities" among the privileged is better wrested by alliance building with cosexual "outsider" queer communities of resistance. My hope is that "queerness" can become a cyborgian and cross-cultural identity encompassing Digital Queens, academics, politicos, communities of great diversity—"a potent subjectivity synthesized from fusions of outsider identities" (Haraway 216) within and overlapping in many local communities of unmodified pluralism, continuously reworking the intelligence and feelings of differences into a politic of effective consequence and conscience.

In this new heterosocial modeling between lesbians and gay men, vigilant attention must be given to class privilege, money, resources, and their distribution and use. The rhetoric of diversity is not enough. Many lesbians know that the 1993 March on Washington could never have happened without the financial backing of gay men. Many lesbians know the difference between the Michigan Women's Music Festival and Gay Pride. Many lesbians know the difference between National Women's Studies conferences and national lesbian and gay academic conferences. Many lesbians know that we have flocked to the assistance of gay men with AIDS, a phenomenon which may never have had its gay male counterpart if thousands of lesbians were suddenly taken down by a similar epidemic. Many lesbians know that we have given much of our lives to feminist agendas and other political movements which were not necessarily organized around our own oppression as lesbians, and that a vast majority of middle-class white gay men have only organized around the suffering and oppression brought on by homophobia in their own personal lives. Many lesbians know the dynamics of double and sometimes multiple oppressions in their own lives, while many white middle-class gay men, who seemingly control the paradigms in the emerging field of queer theory, seem to theorize a singular oppression, one that keeps them from equal access to privileged white male entitlements. Many lesbians know that institutionalized marriages with men, even gay men, will require time, energy, a wellspring of patience, and a heterosocial pact of compassion which can drain resources and person hours from lesbian community and lesbian needs. Many lesbians cannot forget these differences, nor can we as lesbians afford to forget each other.

As Gayle Rubin has suggested in her axiomatic assertion, lesbians are oppressed as women and as queers. While this statement has served as a springboard for lesbian participation in queer studies, it is the "oppression of women" that is in danger of being overlooked by the rapid rise of male power in this new academic field. Many lesbians know that fighting heterosexism is minimally a two-front struggle: opposing the abuse of power emanating from heterosexual arrogance and fear, and opposing the abuse of power stemming from socialized male arrogance and privilege. Gay male bonding established through the codes of misogyny, the derogation of woman, and unexamined male privilege may not be the best shelter for lesbian activism or lesbian scholarship.

The truth of the matter is that almost all lesbians are oppressed as women and as queers; lesbians are also oppressed for not acting like women, and gay men for acting too much like women; gay men are oppressed as queers but also "as women"; gay men in turn oppress lesbians as women; and we all oppress ourselves as women and as queers. While we also oppress by race and class, the operative and redundant term here is "oppressed as women"—a misogyny which infiltrates every level of difference in queer oppressions and internalized homophobias. To construct a new field of queer studies without addressing misogyny, gender, male supremacy, race, and class as these are differently experienced by a wide diversity of female and male queers, is to seal the happy marriage of gay and lesbian studies with a Hallmark card and a Falwellian blessing. Should this happen, a new rebellion of bride resisters is in order, and you can bet we'll come bitching out of our britches.

Notes

I would like to thank the audience at the Midwestern Society for Women in Philosophy meeting, Cincinnati, Ohio, October 1–3, 1993, where I read this paper and received helpful comments, and also thank Linda Garber, Lisa Albrecht, Mary

Jo Kane, Pam Olano, Hilary Sandall, Amanda Utis-Kessler, and Karen Joy Clark for their careful readings and tough criticism.

1. My title indicates a generational standpoint on gay and lesbian studies by referring back to the 1970s when many radical women were articulating their difficulties and unhappiness with hetero-comradery and heterosex in progressive male-driven social movements. I urge the reader to remember these stories and to study carefully Marilyn Frye's remarkably durable essay from the early 1980s, "Lesbian Feminism and the Gay Rights Movement: Another View of Male Supremacy, Another Separatism" which re/minds me and incites me to create this sisterly writing for the gay '90s. I was disappointed to learn that Frye's early essay was not included in the newly inspired canonical anthology *The Lesbian and Gay Studies Reader* edited by Abelove, Barale, and Halperin. The editors chose to include Frye's "Some Reflections on Power and Separatism," an essay which provides more of a challenge to heterosexuals and lesbians than to gay males. In solidarity with Frye and new writings of discontent coming out of queer and AIDS crisis movement politics (Graff), I am inspired to re/in/cite a central question of difference along the axis of gender in the rush to canonize, academize, and seal the marriage of gay and lesbian studies.

2. Amanda Utis-Kessler has pointed out to me that once bisexual and transgender categories are added to this scene the project becomes even more deeply and inevitably cosexual. The extraction of gay and lesbian from queer studies problematizes the politics of gender differences in the constructed calculus of separate biological sexes and separately distinct mono-sexual object choices. The cosexual political alliance is made more contingent and problematic by this selective focus on lesbian and gay strains and tensions within queer studies (Utis-Kessler, personal communication).

3. For one lesbian-feminist interpretation of the "heterosexual contract," see Monique Wittig.

4. Neisen does mention Audre Lorde's definition of "heterosexism" in his review of the literature on homophobia, and he does recognize that lesbians and bisexual women suffer at least two oppressions—sexism and heterosexism—but these inclusions seem additive afterthoughts and not fully integrated into his analysis. There is no attempt to tease out operational measures or careful therapeutic methods for dealing specifically with the "internalized shames" of multiple oppressions experienced by a singular individual.

5. Epstein refers to the work of several women scholars—Barbara Ponse, Vivienne Cass, Mary MacIntosh—to support his own thinking. He buries Gayle Rubin in a footnote (n. 6, p. 49) to refer the reader to "the limitations of feminist theory . . . to the study of sex." He oddly equates lesbian feminists such as Adrienne Rich and "political lesbians" with murky essentialists, while the only significant feminist theorist who receives uncritical commendation is Nancy Chodorow, a non–lesbian identified feminist. These women constitute a small minority of the scholars among the mostly male and white thinkers Epstein uses to construct his theoretical edifice of gay and lesbian ethnicity.

6. A particularly egregious example of this is Edward Stein's anthology.

7. Marilyn Frye ("Feminist Theory") points out that the critique of alleged lesbian-

feminist essentialism is often hidden in attacks on radical feminism and cultural feminism which are further lumped together with the heterosexual feminisms of Chodorow, Dinnerstein, and Gilligan. See, for example, Echols, Alcoff, and Nicholson.

8. Women who write in this vein of queer theory are extremely popular among gay men. See, for example, Butler, "Imitation" and *Gender Trouble*, Rubin, Fuss, Sedgwick, Duggan, and Case. There are many lesbians, gay, bisexual, and queer-identified women who have allied themselves to the paradigms of queer theory and who participate in trashing lesbian feminism. I say this because I do not want to create the impression that my critique falls solely on the shoulders of white middle-class gay men. Nor do I wish to promote a monolithic category for all white middle-class gay men. My intent is to emphasize how the paradigms and infrastructure of queer theory production have created odd bedfellows in the currently momentous backlash against feminism.

9. I have addressed these issues in Zita ("Male Lesbians" and "*Paris is Burning* . . .").

10. See, for example, O'Connor.

11. See, for example, (Card "Lesbianism and Choice" and "Pluralist Lesbian Separatism"), Trebilcot ("Taking Responsibility") Van Gelder, and Kitzinger. Not all lesbians agree with this position, but such writing seems much more prevalent in lesbian than in gay male theorizing. See also Eridani for an insightful analysis of "females without preference."

12. Although there is no official lesbian-feminist or lesbian separatist canon, I have in mind the theoretical work of Allen, Anderson, Card ("Pluralist Lesbian Separatism"), Daly, Frye ("Some Reflections"), Hoagland, Lugones, Pierce and Ketchum, Potts, Rich, and Trebilcot ("Activism").

13. Helms as cited in *Newsweek,* June 21, 1993, 60; the videotape was advertised by Jerry Falwell on cable TV along with some other video titles in the same packet, including a new, second documentary titled "The Gay Agenda," "PC and JC," and "Hollywood, Homosexuals, and Hell." Falwell described "The Achtenberg Affair" as more shocking than the Rodney King tape.

14. Here I have in mind the tension between the Ozzie-and-Harriet strategy common among certain civil rights activists ("we are really just like everybody else") and the tactics of ACT UP and the Lesbian Avengers ("*épater le bourgeois*").

15. Obviously feminist academic theory, especially in the 1980s, has also transformed itself into heavy theory and Eurocentric-glossia. See Christian for a critique.

16. Word order is intentional.

17. To date I have been very much impressed with the balanced readings incorporated into *The Lesbian and Gay Studies Reader* edited by Abelove, Barale, and Halperin. (See, however, note 1.)

18. This conversation passed quickly among strangers in the Whittier Room after the session on "Construction of Homo-Identity" at the OutWrite '93 Conference, The 4th National Lesbian and Gay Writers Conference, Boston, October 9, 1993. I thank you for our brief encounter.

Works Cited

Abelove, Henry, Michèle Aina Barale, and David M. Halperin, eds. *The Lesbian and Gay Studies Reader*. New York: Routledge, 1993.

Alcoff, Linda. "Cultural Feminism versus Post-Structuralism: The Identity Crisis in Feminist Theory," *Signs* 13:3 (1988): 405–36.

Alfaro, Luis. "Pico Union," Unpublished performance manuscript presented at the OutWrite '93 Conference, The 4th National Lesbian and Gay Writers Conference, Boston, October 7, 1993.

Allen, Jeffner. *Lesbian Philosophies: Explorations*. Palo Alto, CA: Institute for Lesbian Studies, 1986.

Anderson, Jackie. "Separatism—In My Opinion." Unpublished manuscript, 1992.

Boswell, John. *Christianity, Social Tolerance, and Homosexuality*. Chicago: University of Chicago Press, 1980.

Butler, Judith. *Gender Trouble: Feminism and the Subversion of Identity*. New York: Routledge, 1990.

———. "Imitation and Gender Insubordination," in *Inside/Out: Lesbian Theories, Gay Theories*, ed. Diana Fuss. New York: Routledge, 1991. 13–31.

Card, Claudia. "Lesbianism and Choice," *Journal of Homosexuality* 23:3 (1992): 39–51.

———. "Pluralist Lesbian Separatism," in *Lesbian Philosophies and Cultures*, ed. Jeffner Allen. New York: SUNY Press, 1990. 125–41.

Case, Sue-Ellen. "Towards a Butch-Femme Aesthetic," *Discourse: Journal of Theoretical Studies in Media and Culture* 11:1 (1988–89): 55–73.

Christian, Barbara. "The Race for Theory" in *Making Face, Making Soul: Haciendo Caras*, ed. Gloria Anzaldúa, San Francisco: aunt lute, 1990. 335–45.

Daly, Mary. *Gyn/Ecology*. Boston: Beacon Press, 1979.

Duggan, Lisa. "Making It Perfectly Queer," *Socialist Review* 22:1 (1992): 11–31.

Echols, Alice. *Daring To Be Bad: Radical Feminism in America, 1967–1975*. Minneapolis: University of Minnesota Press, 1989.

Epstein, Steven. "Gay Politics, Ethnic Identity, and the Limits of Social Constructionism," *Socialist Review* 17 (1987): 9–54.

Eridani. "Is Sexual Orientation a Secondary Sex Characteristic?" in *Closer to Home: Bisexuality and Feminism*, ed. Elizabeth Reba Weise. Seattle, Washington: Seal Press, 1992. 173–81.

Foucault, Michel. *The History of Sexuality Vol. 1: An Introduction*. Trans. Robert Hurley. New York: Vintage, 1980.

Frye, Marilyn. "Feminist Theory and Ontological Commitment." Unpublished manuscript presented at Philosophy Department Colloquium, University of Minnesota, May 31, 1991.

———. "Some Reflections on Separatism and Power," in Frye, *The Politics of Reality*. Trumansburg, NY: Crossing Press, 1983. 95–109.

Fuss, Diana. *Essentially Speaking: Feminism, Nature, and Difference.* New York: Routledge, 1989.

Gagnon, John, and William Simon. *Sexual Conduct.* Chicago: Aldine Press, 1973.

Graff, E. J. "Not a Ladies' Auxiliary," *The Progressive* (October, 1993): 13–14.

Hamblin, Angela, "Is Feminist Heterosexuality Possible?" in *Sex and Love: New Thoughts on Old Contradictions,* ed. Sue Cartledge and Joanna Ryan. London: The New Woman's Press, 1983. 105–23.

Haraway, Donna. "A Manifesto for Cyborgs: Science, Technology, and Socialist Feminism in the 1980s," in *Feminism/Postmodernism,* ed. Linda J. Nicholson. New York: Routledge, 1990. 190–233.

Harding, Sandra. "Reinventing Ourselves as Other: More New Agents of History and Knowledge," in Harding, *Whose Science? Whose Knowledge? Thinking from Women's Lives,* New York: Cornell University Press, 1991. 268–95.

Hoagland, Sarah Lucia. *Lesbian Ethics: Toward New Value.* Palo Alto, CA: Institute of Lesbian Studies, 1988.

Kennedy, Elizabeth, and Madeline Davis. *Boots of Leather, Slippers of Gold: The History of a Lesbian Community.* New York: Routledge, 1993.

Kitzinger, Celia. "Sexuality: Cause, Choice, and Construction," *Lesbian and Gay Socialist* 15 (1988).

Krasner, Barbara. "Impossible Virgin or Why I Choose Not to be Heterosexual." Unpublished manuscript presented at the Midwestern Society for Women in Philosophy, April 9–11, St. Louis, Missouri. 1993.

Le Vay, Simon. "A Difference in Hypothalamic Structure between Heterosexual and Homosexual Men," *Science* 253 (1981): 1034–37.

Lugones, Maria. "Playfulness, 'World'-Traveling, and Loving Perception," *Hypatia* 2:2 (Summer 1987): 3–19.

MacIntosh, Mary. "The Homosexual Role," *Social Problems* 16:2 (1968): 182–92.

Neisen, Joseph H. "Heterosexism: Redefining Homophobia for the 1990s," *Journal of Gay and Lesbian Psychotherapy* 1:3 (1990): 21–35.

Nicholson, Linda, ed. *Feminism/Postmodernism.* New York: Routledge, 1990.

O'Connor, Peg. "Of Rats and Men (and Women)." Unpublished manuscript presented at the Inside and Out Conference, The Third National Graduate Student Conference on Queer Studies, University of Minnesota, April 15–17, 1993.

Pharr, Robert Reid. "Living as a Lesbian." Unpublished manuscript presented at the OutWrite '93 Conference, The 4th National Lesbian and Gay Writers Conference, Boston, October 9, 1993.

Pierce, Christine, and Sara Ann Ketchum. "Separatism and Sexual Relationships," in *Philosophy and Women,* ed. Sharon Hill and Marjorie Weinzweig. Belmont: Wadsworth, 1978.

Plummer, Kenneth, ed. *The Making of the Modern Homosexual.* London: Hutchinson, 1981.

Potts, Billie Luisi. "Owning Jewish Separatism and Lesbian Separatism," *The Lesbian Insider/Insighter/Inciter* 9 (December 1982): 3, 29–30.

Rich, Adrienne. "Notes for a Magazine: What Does Separatism Mean?" *Sinister Wisdom* 18 (Fall 1981): 83–91.

Rubin, Gayle. "Thinking Sex: Notes for a Radical Theory of the Politics of Sexuality," in *Pleasure and Danger: Exploring Female Sexuality,* ed. Carole S. Vance. New York: Routledge, 1984.

Sedgwick, Eve Kosofsky. *Epistemology of the Closet.* Berkeley: University of California Press, 1990.

Stein, Edward, ed. *Forms of Desire: Sexual Orientation and the Social Constructionist Controversy.* New York: Garland Publishing, 1990.

Trebilcot, Joyce. "Activism Broadly Defined," *off our backs* 16:5 (May 1986): 13.

———. "Taking Responsibility for Sexuality," in *Philosophy and Sex,* ed. R. Baker and F. Elliston. Buffalo, NY: Prometheus Press, 1984.

Utis-Kessler, Amanda. "Closer to Home: Bisexual Feminism and the Transformation of Hetero/Sexism," in *Closer to Home: Bisexuality and Feminism,* ed. Elizabeth Reba Weise. Seattle, Washington: Seal Press, 1992. 183–201.

Van Gelder, Lindsy. "The 'Born That Way' Trap," *Ms.* 1:6 (May/June 1991): 86–87.

Wittig, Monique. "On the Social Contract" (1989), in Wittig, *The Straight Mind and Other Essays.* Boston: Beacon Press, 1992. 33–45.

Wolf, Naomi. "Radical Heterosexuality . . . or how to love a man and save your feminist soul," *Ms.* (July/August 1992): 29–31.

Woods, Donald. "Sister Lesbos," in *In the Life: A Black Gay Anthology,* Joseph Beam, ed. Boston: Alyson, 1986. 104–5.

Zita, Jacquelyn N., "*Paris is Burning:* Black Looks, Queer Looks, and White Looks through a Feminist Eye," forthcoming in Zita, *Fleshing (Out) the Body: Reflections on Somatic Existence and Resistance.*

———. "Male Lesbians and the Postmodern Body," *Hypatia* 7:4 (1992): 106–27. Also forthcoming in *Adventures in Lesbian Philosophy,* ed. Claudia Card. Bloomington: Indiana University Press, 1994, and in Zita, *Fleshing (Out) the Body: Reflections on Somatic Existence and Resistance.*

Contributors

Kate Adams has taught English and interdisciplinary humanities courses at big state universities, small liberal arts colleges, and community colleges. She is a Ph.D. candidate in the American Civilization Program at the University of Texas, Austin. Her dissertation is titled "Paper Lesbians: Publishing Lesbian Identity in the United States, 1950–1990"; a portion has been published in Karla Jay and Joanne Glasgow, eds., *Lesbian Texts and Contexts* (New York University, 1990).

Michèle Aina Barale is an Assistant Professor at Amherst College in the Department of English and the Department of Women's and Gender Studies. Along with Henry Abelove and David Halperin, she is editor of *The Lesbian and Gay Studies Reader* (Routledge, 1993) and is currently completing a book entitled *Below the Belt: Essays in Queer Reading*.

Evelyn Torton Beck is Director of Women's Studies and Professor of Women's Studies and Jewish Studies at the University of Maryland-College Park. Among her books are *Nice Jewish Girls: A Lesbian Anthology* (Beacon, [1982] 1989), *The Prism of Sex* (University of Wisconsin, 1979), and *Kafka and the Yiddish Theater* (University of Wisconsin, 1971). She has written and lectured widely on issues of difference, especially the complex intersection of Jew-hating, misogyny, and homophobia.

Allison Berg is an Assistant Professor of English at St. Mary's College of Maryland, where she teaches African-American literature and composition. She has published articles in *Feminist Teacher* and *Women's Studies,* and is currently pursuing research in women's literacies and multicultural education.

Barbara Blinick has taught high school social studies for ten years and currently teaches at Lowell High School in San Francisco. She is the treasurer of the San Francisco chapter of the Bay Area Network of Gay and Lesbian Educators. From 1990 to 1992 she worked part-time for the San Francisco Unified School District's Support Services for Gay and Lesbian Youth.

Amy Blumenthal is an Associate Professor of English/ESL Coordinator at Oakton Community College, Des Plaines, IL. She has written and spoken about, and spends a lot of time practicing the art of, lesbian motherhood. In spite of this, she is now fully tenured.

Nancy Boutilier teaches English at San Francisco University High School. Her collection of poetry and fiction, *According to Her Contours* (Black Sparrow, 1992), was nominated for a Lambda Literary Award. Her writing has appeared in a variety of publications, including the *Bay Area Reporter, Deneuve,* and *GirlJock.*

Wendy Chapkis is the author of *Beauty Secrets: Women and the Politics of Appearance* (South End, 1986). She is currently completing a dissertation on the politics of commercial sex and soon will be selling herself on the academic market.

Sarah Chinn is a doctoral student in English at Columbia University. Her dissertation explores heresy as a trajectory in US women's writing, Anne Hutchinson to Gertrude Stein. In her spare time she foments revolution with the Lesbian Avengers.

doris davenport finally completed her Ph.D. at the University of Southern California in 1985, with the help of a few friends (like K. Newman, R. Yarborough, and M. Perloff). Instead of her relatives calling her "Miss Fool," they now say "Doctor Fool." She is presently working as a freelance writer, or unemployed, depending on your perspective. She recently received an Individual Artist Grant from the Georgia Council for the Arts. If you want to reach her with some good news, she will be somewhere in northeast Georgia.

Kim Emery is a softball player, a Lesbian Avenger, and a doctoral candidate in English at the University of Texas, Austin. Her dissertation, "Deep Subjects: Lesbian In(ter)-ventions in 20th-century U.S. Thought," is a history of ideas about lesbian identity. She has been an out teacher of many different courses, including Survey of American Literature, Rhetoric and Composition, Computer-Assisted Composition, and (most conveniently) Topics in Writing: Lesbian Literary Representation.

Maia Ettinger learned humor, resistance, and chutzpah from her mother and grandmother, survivors of the genocide in Poland. She and her lover, Leslie Caplan, are working on a thriller.

Estelle B. Freedman is Professor of History at Stanford University, where she teaches courses on the history of women, the history of sexuality, and feminist studies. She is the author of *Their Sisters' Keepers: Women's Prison Reform in America, 1830–1930* (University of Michigan, 1981) and coauthor of *Intimate Matters: A History of Sexuality in America* (Harper and Row, 1988). She coedited *The Lesbian Issue: Essays from Signs* (University of Chicago, 1985) and is currently writing a biography of the social reformer Miriam Van Waters.

Linda Garber is the author of *Lesbian Sources: A Bibliography of Periodical Articles, 1970–1990* (Garland, 1993). After completing her public secondary credential in language arts, she entered the doctoral program in Modern Thought and Literature at Stanford University, where she has taught a variety of courses in lesbian studies, women's studies, and/or literature. She is currently completing her dissertation, "Theorizing Lesbians: The Identity Poetics of Grahn, Parker, Rich, and Lorde."

María C. González, an Assistant Professor of English at the University of Houston, received her Ph.D. from the Ohio State University. Her areas of specialization include contemporary Mexican-American women novelists, Mexican-American literature, feminism and women writers, and nineteenth-century American literature.

Sharon P. Holland is an Assistant Professor of English at Stanford University. She recently completed a postdoctoral fellowship at the Center for Afro-American Studies at Wesleyan University and is working on a manuscript titled *Qualifying Margins: The Discourse of the Dead in Native and African-American Women's Fiction.*

AnnLouise Keating teaches multiethnic US literature, women's studies, and English at Eastern New Mexico University. She has published on black feminist theory, Paula Gunn Allen, Gloria Anzaldúa, Audre Lorde, contemporary Chicana writers, Ralph Waldo Emerson, and Herman Melville. She is completing a book-length study of Allen, Anzaldúa, and Lorde.

Sally L. Kitch is Director of the Center for Women's Studies and Professor of Women's Studies and Comparative Studies at the Ohio State University. Her research interests include feminist theory, women's literature and feminist literary criticism, and cultural theory. Her most recent book, *This Strange Society of Women: Reading the Lives and Letters of the Woman's Commonwealth* (Ohio State University, 1993) was awarded the 1991 Helen Hooven Santmyer Prize in Women's Studies by the Ohio State University Press.

Mary Klages is an Assistant Professor in the English Department at the University of Colorado at Boulder, where she teaches nineteenth-century American literature and is completing a book on Helen Keller and the cultural representation of disability.

Alisa Klinger is a doctoral student in English at the University of California, Berkeley. She is currently a Women's Studies Dissertation Scholar at the University of California, Santa Barbara, where she is completing her dissertation, "Narrative Uprisings: The Politics of Multicultural Lesbian Prose-Testimonials."

Jean Kowaleski is a graduate student in English at Indiana University, writing a dissertation on early nineteenth-century historical activity in Britain and America. She sorely misses the collaboration represented by "Breaking the Silence."

Caroline Le Guin teaches composition and literature at Blue Mountain Community College in Pendleton, Oregon.

Toni A. H. McNaron has been a Professor of English and Women's Studies at the University of Minnesota for thirty years. In addition to winning four awards for outstanding teaching, she has published three books and numerous articles. Her most recent publication is her memoir, *I Dwell in Possibility* (Feminist Press, 1992). Her research interests currently focus on Virginia Woolf's circle of women and on incest in literature and life.

Mary L. Mittler is the Assistant Vice President for Educational Services/Dean of Oakton Community College, Des Plaines, IL. A former English teacher at the College who moved into administration, she is now pursuing her doctoral degree in hopes of one day proving Thomas Wolfe wrong. In the meantime, among other things, she conducts training sessions in the construction and implementation of sexual harassment/sexual assault policies and procedures.

Cynthia D. Nieb is a doctoral student in American History at Cornell University and is currently working on her dissertation, " 'Class Racism': Lesbian Race Relations in the United States, 1965–1985."

Donna Keiko Ozawa is a third-generation Japanese American lesbian and native of San Francisco, now living in Berkeley. She is a guitarist and electric bassist and would like to form an Asian-American motown/r&b band called "Mochi and the Groovin' Rice Cakes." She is in the middle of her Saturn Return.

Polly Pagenhart is a doctoral student in American Studies and the Center for Advanced Feminist Studies at the University of Minnesota. She teaches in the Women's Studies Department and is involved in establishing an LGBT/Queer Studies center at the university. When she is not stirring up trouble in Minneapolis with the Lesbian Avengers or pining away for her homeland of Northern California, she finds time to work on her dissertation, which examines lesbian representation in contemporary mass media.

Ann Pellegrini holds degrees in Classics from Harvard and Oxford Universities. She is currently completing a Ph.D. in Cultural Studies where her dissertation considers 20th-century popular and "expert" discourses of the lesbian body. She has taught lesbian and gay studies at Harvard and MIT. And, all reports to the contrary, she still thinks Sappho is a right-on woman.

Janet Pollak is Associate Professor of Anthropology and Chair of the Department of Anthropology at William Paterson College in Wayne, NJ. She is faculty adviser to the WPC Coalition of Lesbian, Gays, and Friends and serves as an adult volunteer with Gay and Lesbian Youth-New Jersey. And yes, she has a cat.

Alison Regan is a doctoral student in English at the University of Texas, Austin. She is currently working on a dissertation on the history of writing instruction at American public universities.

Nancy Stoller became the first open lesbian to be granted tenure at the University of California at Santa Cruz, in 1987. She is now Associate Professor of Community Studies.

Anneliese Truame (formerly Anneliese Heyl) is pursuing her Master's degree in English Literature at the University of Washington, Seattle. She graduated from Stanford University with an A.B. degree in Feminist Studies and Anthropology in 1990, and received the Mellon Fellowship in the Humanities in 1991. She is a performance artist, a beginning archer, and a trouble-loving twin.

Ellen Weinauer is at work on a book titled *Property Writes: Ownership and Authorship in America, 1848–1870*. She teaches American, African-American, and Women's Literature at Carleton College in Northfield, Minnesota.

Eric A. Wolfe teaches at Indiana University, where he also co-coordinates the composition section of the Group Student Support Services program. He is currently completing his dissertation, "The Lure of the Voice: Subjectivity and Society in the Early United States."

Merle Woo is a widely published socialist feminist writer, and a lecturer in Women's Studies at San Francisco State University. She is a leader in the Freedom Socialist Party and Radical Women.

Jacquelyn N. Zita is an Associate Professor of Women's Studies at the University of Minnesota. She is managing editor of *Matrices: A Lesbian Feminist Research and Resource Network* and is currently completing a book of essays, *Fleshing "Out" the Body*. She aspires in her solitude to become a postmodernist lesbian avenger.